# PUBLIC DISORDER AND GLOBALIZATION

The current growth of incidents of public disorder around the world can be seen as symptomatic of major transformations in globalized society, government, and technology. But while disorder is routinely perceived as a disturbing phenomenon, it can also be a catalyst for positive transformation and regeneration. As social media is increasingly used as a platform for mobilization and organization, local disorder may spread outward through national borders, receiving international coverage and visibility as well as triggering a domino effect of global unrest.

Combining qualitative and quantitative research, this ground-breaking text analyzes oppositional notions of order and disorder in global, national, and local contexts and considers the role of the police, the justice system, and other authorities in developing a range of responsive strategies. The author develops a new comprehensive framework for engaging in comparative and historical analysis of public disorder by drawing upon international case studies of public unrest such as 2005 in Paris and 2011 in London; the events in Ferguson and Baltimore that seeded Black Lives Matter; the Occupy movements in Zuccotti Park, Gezi Park, and Hong Kong; and the terror attacks in Paris and Brussels.

This dynamic comparative study is informed by extensive international interviews and will be a required reading for students and scholars of criminology, sociology, political science, and urban studies.

**Sophie Body-Gendrot** is Emeritus Professor at Université Sorbonne-Paris IV, France, a researcher at CESDIP-CNRS-French Ministry of Justice, and co-editor of *The Routledge Handbook of European Criminology* (2013).

'The consequences of globalization and rapidly growing urbanization for shaping social movements are yet to be fully understood. In this elegant cross-cultural exploration of demonstrations, movements and risings, scholars will find a framework and a set of questions that will shape future research. This is a masterful and foundational work.'

**Peter K. Manning,** *Elmer V.H. and Eileen M. Brooks*
*Chair in Policing, School of Criminology and Criminal Justice,*
*Northeastern University, USA*

'In this moment of global crisis and conflict between people and the police, this book reminds us of the roots of the clashes and the difficult struggles of disenfranchised groups for security and dignity in the face of resistance from the state. *Public Disorder and Globalization* realizes the remarkable intellectual achievement of showing the contested moral and political spaces and meanings at the heart of these conflicts. We see inside police institutions in three global cities to understand the meaning of order and contested space to the state, and how police notions of disorder threaten state actors and political elites. We see how the state, through its police apparatus, reshapes the struggle for recognition and belonging of those on the outside into social and political threat that invites harsh responses to control both people and spaces. This is a wonderful book that uses thick case studies where the state speaks in its own voice to reveal the justifying ideology for its use of harsh social control to reinforce the power of the elites and frustrate the search for dignity of those left behind.'

**Jeffrey Fagan,** *Isidor and Seville Sulzbacher*
*Professor of Law, Columbia University, USA*

# PUBLIC DISORDER AND GLOBALIZATION

Sophie Body-Gendrot

Routledge
Taylor & Francis Group

LONDON AND NEW YORK

First published 2017
by Routledge
2 Park Square, Milton Park, Abingdon, Oxon OX14 4RN

and by Routledge
605 Third Avenue, New York, NY 10017

*Routledge is an imprint of the Taylor & Francis Group, an informa business*

© 2017 Sophie Body-Gendrot

*British Library Cataloguing in Publication Data*
A catalogue record for this book is available from the British Library

*Library of Congress Cataloging in Publication Data*
Names: Body-Gendrot, Sophie, author.
Title: Public disorder and globalization / Sophie Body-Gendrot.
Description: Abingdon, Oxon ; New York, NY : Routledge, 2017. |
    Includes bibliographical references and index.
Identifiers: LCCN 2016029580 | ISBN 9781138925427 (hbk) |
    ISBN 9781138925434 (pbk) | ISBN 9781315683751 (ebook)
Subjects: LCSH: Disorderly conduct. | Public spaces. | Political
    participation. | Social movements. | Protest movements. |
    Globalization—Social aspects.
Classification: LCC HV6486 .B63 2017 | DDC 363.32—dc23
LC record available at https://lccn.loc.gov/2016029580

ISBN: 978-1-138-92542-7 (hbk)
ISBN: 978-1-138-92543-4 (pbk)
ISBN: 978-1-315-68375-1 (ebk)

Typeset in Bembo
by Apex CoVantage, LLC

# CONTENTS

# FOREWORD

As one commentator has recently observed, we seem to be entering a new age of public disorder (Clover, 2016). Certainly in the eighteenth and the first half of the nineteenth centuries, collective violence, broadly understood, was a regular and important vehicle for expressing common grievances. To a degree for much of the period, the riot was superseded by other forms of protest, not least various forms of industrial bargaining, and in particular the strike. Very roughly speaking, it appears that the last half-century has seen the more or less gradual return of public disorder across much of western Europe, and more recently in the United States.

For much of its history, social science displayed, at most, a rather modest interest in riot and collective violence. Early psychologists – most notably Gustave Le Bon – were intrigued by the seemingly startling effects that membership of a crowd had on the behaviour of individuals (Le Bon, 1895/1947), and the Chicago School of sociology in the 1930s also took a keen interest in the dynamics of collective behaviour. In contrast to the generally negative view of crowds that infused Le Bon's work, the Chicago School's Robert Park and Herbert Blumer took a more optimistic approach, seeing the potential for positive social development and social evolution in such disorderly activity (Blumer, 1936; 1978). In many respects, however, it was the new breed of social historians, much influenced by the *Annales* school, whose work on the riots of the eighteenth and early nineteenth centuries has had the most lasting influence on social scientific inquiry in recent times (Hobsbawm, 1959; Rudé, 1964).

The revival of public disorder as a relatively regular occurrence in contemporary Western societies, and the revival of sustained social scientific interest in such events, has led to the development of a now considerable body of literature on urban violence, its causes, consequences, and control. Sophie Body-Gendrot has been one of the most important figures in this field with her studies of urban social control (Body-Gendrot, 2000), the policing of unrest (Body-Gendrot, 2004; 2010), and the impact of globalization on contemporary social order (Body-Gendrot, 2012). In her latest work, *Public Disorder and Globalization*, she brings these together to examine the challenges facing scholars seeking to understand the most recent developments confronting urban social order. It is hard to think of anyone better placed to attempt such work.

The opening chapters offer an analytical overview of some of the major theoretical approaches to understanding riot and collective violence, as well as an examination of some of the most recent cases. From Paris (2005), via London (2011), to Ferguson, Missouri (2014), Baltimore, Maryland (2015), and encompassing the Gezi Park protests in Istanbul (2013), and the various incarnations of the Occupy movement, this is an incredibly wide *tour d'horizon*. Attempting to find ways of understanding such complex events as outbreaks of mass urban violence, social scientists in recent times have offered a number of analytical models. Building on some of her earlier comparative work (Body-Gendrot & Savitch, 2012), the analysis in *Public Disorder and Globalization* further develops Body-Gendrot's fivefold approach to the dissection of riots. The elements that make up the analysis are identified as: *mobilization potential, triggering events, preparations, regime stability*, and *political/bureaucratic response*. *Mobilization potential* has two constituent parts: deprivation and integration/disintegration. *Triggering events* are, as they sound, broadly what are referred to as 'flashpoints' or similar – those matters that serve to focus and perhaps inflame existing grievances. *Preparations* as a concept refers to those matters that might help us understand how citizens become 'rioters' – those things which help explain the shift in self-identity and help to precipitate action.

In my view, it is the final two conceptual features of this approach that add most to the existing analytical models in this field. *Regime stability* focuses attention on the formal and informal bases on which states respond, politically and practically, to urban disorder, and *bureaucratic response* asks us to consider the importance of understanding how quickly and how effectively states are able to respond. The importance of these features is that they help shift social scientific attention away from its preoccupation with the 'causes' of public disorder and argue for the necessity of seeing riots 'in the round' (Newburn, 2016b). What, among a great many other features, we see in the abundant examples explored here are the variety of approaches the state adopts in response to perceived threats to the social order. There are a good number of commonalities, of course, but also some significant departures.

This leads us to another crucial aspect of *Public Disorder and Globalization* which is in line with Body-Gendrot's earlier scholarship, that it is a work of comparative analysis. The object here is not simply to use examples from around the globe to help build a general argument, though this is of course interesting and important but, rather, to use contrasting case studies so that we might genuinely come to understand how particular economic, political, and cultural contexts come profoundly to shape the matters at hand. Just as a growing body of work is illuminating the ways in which national histories and local political cultures come to shape patterns of punishment (Tonry, 2015), so too are scholars increasingly turning their attention to the ways in which such factors influence both the nature of, and the responses to, civil disorder. Indeed, and arguably just as importantly, national histories, local political cultures, and institutional practices also have much to offer the study of why riots don't happen (Body-Gendrot & Savitch, 2012; Newburn, 2016a).

The comparative study of policing is, in many respects, very much in its infancy. The field of public disorder arguably is one area where there is obvious scope for progress to be made in this regard. *Public Disorder and Globalization* necessarily focuses much of its attention on the policing of disorder. It involves a multi-layered analysis for the police, in their various forms. In addition to being the primary agency charged with controlling or preventing disorder, they are also regularly implicated in what is often thought of as the 'spark' or 'flashpoint' for disorder. In addition, what happens during significant outbreaks of disorder may have important consequences for both the politics and the practice of policing in particular contexts. How such matters play out in different contexts is potentially enormously instructive, as is regularly illustrated by Body-Gendrot's work.

There is one final aspect of *Public Disorder and Globalization* that it is important to draw attention to here. Unusually, but importantly, in its final sections it shifts attention away from the standard focus on riot and disorder and toward the recent attacks in Paris, Brussels, and beyond. In doing so, Body-Gendrot asks whether global terrorism might be considered to be an 'extreme case' of public disorder? There are many reasons for thinking such acts are of a different order from the bulk of the public disorder considered elsewhere in this book. As Body-Gendrot notes, the terrorist acts don't fit into the usual typologies; they cannot easily 'be compared with the public disorder caused by violent anti-police protesters'; and the response by supra-national, national, and local states 'are also singular and exceptional'. Indeed, in the end it seems clear that the differences are more significant than any similarities that might be found. Nevertheless, global terrorism and more traditional forms of disorder raise some similar questions about the nature of the relationship between nation states and marginalized populations, about the nature and use of urban public space, about the appropriate limits of state surveillance and intervention, and about the extent of the influence of new social media in the organization of varied forms of resistance.

As good social science should, *Public Disorder and Globalization* raises at least as many questions as it answers. A thoughtful and provocative treatise, as we have come to expect from Body-Gendrot, it draws together decades of learning about our understanding of public disorder and also begins the task of setting out elements of a new agenda for scholars in the coming years. Let's hope we are up to the task.

Tim Newburn,
London School of Economics

# ACKNOWLEDGEMENTS

I am deeply grateful to Jenny Fleming, who was very generous with her time in editing the manuscript for me and in providing critical remarks which were very helpful. I would also like to thank John Hagan. He invited me to write an essay on public disorder for his journal, *The Annual Review of Law and Social Sciences*, vol. 10, in 2014. I found the research so fascinating that it seemed to me that I could pursue that theme by looking both at public disorder and at globalization. (I had just completed a book on *Globalization, Fear and Insecurity* [Palgrave, 2012]). In a project that took two years, I benefited from the penetrating insights, help, and advice from colleagues and friends abroad – in particular Saskia Sassen, Malcolm Anderson, Betsy Stanko, John Linder, Bart Wissink, Peter Manning, Jeffrey Fagan, Enzo Mingione, Felicitas Hillman, Margit Mayer, and their colleagues. I wish I could name them all. Closer to home, I received intellectual insights from Jean-Marc Erbés and his friends, René Levy, Renée Zauberman, Jacques de Maillard, and younger colleagues at my research centre, Centre d'Etudes Sociologiques des Institutions Pénales (CESDIP-CNRS-Minister of Justice), at a time when I was discouraged by the terrorist attacks which dwarfed all my previous writing. They urged me to rewrite my chapters in a new light.

I also want to thank my research assistant, Thomas Klein, who spontaneously contacted me to offer support voluntarily and provided an invaluable help with intelligence, generosity, and reliability. I received his work from New York, Paris, or Tel-Aviv, as he blurred borders with his digital skills.

Finally, Routledge has been excellent. Tom Sutton, Hannah Catterall, and their colleagues have brought a lot of understanding and support when I was struggling with my complex and challenging topic.

At home, Alain Gendrot made all the difference with his continuous support, love, and laughter.

# 1

# INTRODUCTION

The concept of public disorder, a 'hot topic', is rarely defined. It is indiscriminately used by the media and by politicians when major social transformations take place. This labelling is anything but neutral. The term 'public disorder' yields a multitude of definitions and equally many disagreements about the authority of these definitions, often diverging over specificity. The term is to be interpreted against the backdrop of what Gallie (1956) called 'the essential contestedness' of concepts (i.e. the claim that debates about concepts can never reach closure). Such indeterminacy is at the core of this analysis. This research intends first to test the character of the dialectics of order and disorder and secondly to explore their recent disruption, revealing new patterns for understanding larger processes at work.

## The dialectics of disorder and order

Disorder is an important issue, incomprehensible without reference to the symmetrical notion of order. Order is a tacitly understood notion, a political matter that becomes problematic only when some 'disorder' becomes visible. If one cannot see the disorder, then it cannot have an effect. Its existence is conditioned on being visible via media coverage, political comments, or other sources. Both notions cannot be dissociated: order combats disorder and disorder gets its meaning by denouncing order; order is generated by disorder, which is continuously nurtured by instituted order (Chevallier, 1997: 5). In any society, order is seen as a fundamental value, allowing escape from initial chaos, founding social cohesion and elaborating norms. Order allows people to function efficiently via shared norms, social values, and customs and to reach public tranquillity. Conversely, disorder is routinely perceived as a disturbing and a destructive phenomenon, shaking collective norms and threatening the functioning of society in order to produce change or to simply release emotions. Disorder is a form of uncertainty which cannot be predicted or controlled – a fascinating issue for scholars. At the same time, disorder is not meant to last, and it calls for elements of treatment which generate new forms of order in the short and long term. It is likely that episodes of disorder represent the necessary steps in the adjustment of former situations to new ones. Chevallier (1997: 5) suggests that future order is inside the transitory disorder which acts as its envelope. Consequently, the opposition of order and disorder has to be bypassed, and the notion of intricacy is more appropriate. Order cannot be dissociated from disorder, and the former needs the latter for its regeneration, adjustment, and survival (Chevallier, 1997: 12). In the history of societies, there were always non-conformist collective behaviours, transgressions, denunciations of collective values, and norms and refusals to abide by accepted norms. Order has been contested by some as arbitrary and the product of a domination by the powers that be in various spheres. Retrospectively, this contest has been interpreted as a healthy signal for democracies. But in periods of significant change, power-holders and dominant classes perceive new types of contagious disorder as threats to the functioning of societies and to their own status and privileges. Elites mobilize all their resources to maintain the status quo, at a political and social cost which may be more or less onerous. Further, global cities need order, and it is an important factor for public authorities, investors, consumers, residents, and other city users. Consequently, states and cities cannot ignore demands for order. Do the police and justice institutions, called to intervene when 'order' is disrupted, manage to meet those demands? This study explores this issue.

In Paris in 2015, then in Brussels in 2016, then Nice, another type of disorder – terrorism – and deadly attacks – emerged more generally as a consequence of the struggles of Western states with radical Islam abroad. A new chapter had to be added to this work due to an awareness that we are no longer in a historical continuum and that major transformations are taking place. Here comes a new, more challenging perception of globalization. The bombers who operated in Europe were global actors – the product of global, national, and local dynamics – internationally connected, collectively organized, and motivated by a religious cause. They were willing to resort to extreme crimes and destruction in specific cities to get maximum visibility and publicize their claims and hatred of the West to the world. Do such actions belong to the repertoire of 'public space and globalization' or are we discussing an 'asymmetric war' in which states struggle with informal actors and reveal their limits, with no end in sight? I will return to this issue at the end of this study. The masterminds of the attacks, centred in the ISIS territory, amongst other places, exported their global views to Europe via radical channels of communication. Sophisticated skills and digital networks helped these groups command the vast array of small operators required to get locally organized actors to hit specific cities, with centralized centres of command and control supported by 'assemblages of fear built, trained, embedded, woven, wired, nurtured into the way the specific times, places and events work' (Pain and Smith, 2008: 3). This blurring of the global and the local is a perfect illustration of globalization, as described by Sassen (2001), defining a few global sites in cities as a requisite for the command, control, profit-maximizing, and planning of operations exerted in far-distant localities. Operating as multinationals, the terrorist leaders reveal national states' weakness and failures and the limits of their resources. Very few scholars have analyzed the social implications of public disorder and globalization in the context of risks for cities at various levels.

## Definitions

### Public disorder and public space

It all starts with a group of individuals eager to express their dissent for reasons that will be defined. Disorder results from their actions. Are they a social movement? It is too early to say.

As a conservative working definition, I suggest we refer to disorder as turbulent, erratic collective actions, seriously interrupting public tranquillity and disrespecting established order. Tilly (2003: 16) suggests that violent rituals, scattered attacks, opportunism, and coordinated destruction are part of the repertoire used in the many forms of public disorder. Adding *public* to *disorder* means that, firstly, the dynamics of disorder are empowered by – another interdisciplinary and elusive term – *public space*. Secondly, it means that public and private authorities will intervene to restore *public order*. Public disorder is supported by specific public spaces: streets, stadiums, squares – spaces with open access, trust, the domain of civil society, but also by private spaces with open access such as commercial malls, concert halls, public parks, and even privately owned ones like Zuccotti Park in New York City.

Public disorder has a long history in Europe. In France, the expression *public disorder* first appeared in 1377, referring to crowd agitation seriously interrupting public tranquillity. However, in the grander scope of history, public disorder refers to a spatial mythology founded in the Greek agora, the virtuous space of citizenship that allows the expression of differences, as suggested by Hannah Arendt (1958). While public space also evokes a space for debates in the sense Jurgen Habermas (1962) gave it, here the focus is on physical space open to random encounters, not only allowing freedom of expression – that is, to come and go and to assemble – but also, in a democracy, to express alternative cultures and dissent.

In the repertoire of collective action, the street is a construct built from practices, identities, and connections. In some cases, the voiceless and the weak use the street as a stage to express their anger and form or sustain coalitions. They stick posters, block flows of traffic, confront their opponents, and through intimidation and the disruption of public tranquillity, they gain visibility and publicize their position (Federici, 1791/2008). In European cities, this practice has been used for centuries, as is the case currently, even in the time of the internet. Barricades could easily block contorted streets, a phenomenon that Baron Haussman addressed in the middle of the nineteenth century. Public space is both the physical and symbolic site required by disorder and protests to be visible. Space remains an anchor, and it is my assumption that energies are continuously restored by the mobilization potential that space offers.

The popular genesis of mobilizations examined in this research appeals to a diverse set of constituencies, encompassing many young people concerned about social justice. Their hold of public space sometimes evolves into an occupation that disrupts public tranquillity. Their eviction by the police invariably causes, and sometimes boosts, disorder.

## Public disorder and globalization

The second term in the title of the book, *globalization*, provides the context for change and the innovation of this research. There are numerous understandings of the term *globalization*. The revolutionary impact of networks of information and communication that globalization has promoted has changed both the environment and the meaning of public disorder (Castells, 1996, 2009). The disorder locally produced in a city space impacts on a global stage. Networks link globally dispersed people, beyond national borders, and create visibility for their causes. Global societies, hyper-connected via smartphones, websites, GPS, or any other embedded application, provide another dimension to hyper-spatialized, quintessentially local events. Networks observe and interpret local disturbances, and they 'globalize' them. Anyone at any moment and from any place can connect to a world stage to inquire about an action taking place or to communicate that something unusual is happening and modify interactions taking place in the public space. How different is participating in a mobilization with handheld devices, clicking 'Like' in one second, effortlessly, rather than standing up in a specific space? Do social networks contribute to a new type of proximity/community, made of connected friends, followers, audiences linking and re-linking and mobilizing all over the world? How diversified is the leadership or, indeed, the organizing?

We should make one clarification at this point: We should not yield to the temptation of essentializing the social media. Its role needs to be examined in specific contexts of action or in regard to their *embeddedness* in the culture of a place, as the case studies selected in this research illustrate. According to Gerbaudo (2012: 2), 'this celebration of the emancipatory power of communication technologies (is) not much help in understanding *how* exactly the use of these media reshapes "the repertoire of communication" of contemporary movements and affects the experience of participants'. Gerbaudo asks whether tweeting and retweeting influence collective action, get people on the streets, and coordinate them on the ground. Or is this an illusion? A feeling while standing on the sidelines? It is my claim that all the disorder studied here is anchored in space. It is sometimes amplified by new technologies. The idea of world public space is erroneous. Technologies and processes allowing the internet to function are global but opaque. There is no world public space, only limited and temporary exchanges, interactions focused on specific issues and limited to those issues. As noted by Mathias (2016), our practices and our expectations, our civil and political representations remain localized. They acquire their meaning from our local experience; it is from a local perspective that people believe that they can make a difference.

## *Space over tweets*

The contexts in which physical or symbolic moves are made are fluid, indeterminate, and vulnerable to change. 'The solidarity provided by shared spaces that characterized former times is what is currently missing in the social space of contemporary societies. Sufferings are dispersed and scattered and so is dissent' (Bauman, 2000: 54). This means that social relations are characterized by uncertainty and dominated by weak ties. Consequently, when an event acquires visibility in the public space, it has an empowerment capacity. . . . It is my working assumption that

> movements appeal to the people more by their reclaim of streets and squares for public use and political organizing than by their tweets. People are fused via rituals of popular reunion and soft forms of leadership which exploit the interactive character of new technologies.
>
> *(Gerbaudo, 2012: 10–13)*

The study of the tortuous interaction between on-the-ground organizing and online communication from various contenders is one aspect of this research.

The first interpretation of public disorder and globalization is that for reasons to be defined, local actors feel the urge to express their dissent through disorder in the public space where they become locally visible. With the new technologies, they receive coverage all over the world. Due to their emotional resonance, these events become 'globalized'. Dispersed people relate to such events. Whether it takes place in Cairo, Tunis, Istanbul, Paris, London, Stockholm, Rome, New York, Hong Kong, Ferguson, or Baltimore, public disorder always comes as a surprise. Frequently mobilizations and organizations take place on symbolic sites like Taksim Square in Istanbul, Tahir Square in Cairo, Puerta del sol in Madrid, Place de la République in Paris, West Florissant in Ferguson, or Zuccotti Park in New York. Such specific urban sites are 'arenas in which conflicts and contradictions associated with historically and geographically specific accumulation strategies are expressed and fought out' and where alternatives are formulated (Brenner, Marcuse, Meyer, 2009: 176). Local confrontations between outraged protesters and the police in Clichy-sous-Bois, Tottenham, Ferguson, Baltimore, and Istanbul are nothing new, but during confrontations with the police, young participants equipped with Blackberries or other types of cell phones were given the opportunity to act, move, assemble, outreach, and organize in a way which is innovative. The use of digital devices boosts action: this is the first interpretation of 'public disorder and globalization'.

Secondly, via the widespread use of digital devices and the global capacities of social connections making communication ubiquitous, local protest and disorder starting in one place can generate other forms of unrest in another, by imitation and contagion. An event, a protest, a disorder such as the Arabic Spring may have social consequences miles away from their epicentre – this is the second understanding of 'public disorder and globalization'. The Occupy movements are an example of this interpretation.

Then related to that issue, the question is whether the forces of law and order, not always the best in communication skills, clear training, legal knowledge, and consistent guidance keep pace with the changing dynamics of disorder and protest and with the expectations of order maintenance by the public. This aspect of the research is supported by in-depth interviews with high-rank police commanders. It remains to be seen indeed whether law enforcers, either at the local, national, or international levels, are inventive enough in their methods and their use of high tech or low tech approaches to engage with hard-to-reach and resistant contenders.

It may also be that disorder comes from local police officers themselves when their responses, heavy-handed in approach, and bureaucratic chain of command become dysfunctional or when they are unable to protect peaceful protesters. For the police, striking the right balance between managing public space and the respect and legitimacy granted to the right to dissent and protest in a democracy is a heavy challenge. Law and order are in perpetual tension. The police are mandated to achieve the order defined by substantive law but without violating the due process rules of the game, limiting the means available to them (Skolnick, 2011). 'They appear as Hamlet-like figures juggling irreconcilable contradictory pressures' (Reiner, 2015: 317). The right to peaceful assembly is a qualified right. In Europe, it is guaranteed by article II of the European Commission on Human Rights (ECHR). It can be restricted in the interests of public safety, the prevention of disorder, and the protection of the rights of others. The authority to do so varies according to countries' legal arrangements and specific circumstances. The last interpretation focused on terrorism will be discussed in the final chapter.

## Methodology

Concentrating on interpretations of public disorder, this modest book is the product of two decades of comparative research focused not just on that theme but on urban violence, power conflicts, policing in inner cities, citizens' participation, globalization, fear and insecurity, and public policies. I draw on my previous work and attempt to provide new analyses but also retain a critical detachment from such issues. I am aware that I walk on risky ground, as this research is so new, and that, as an isolated researcher, I cannot reach definitive knowledge.

I conducted interviews with community leaders, public housing managers, and mayors in France, the United States, and Britain. I interviewed senior police officers in charge of intelligence and public order at the Paris Police Préfecture, at the Metropolitan Police service in London, and at the New York Police Department from 2014–16. While I received a most generous welcome from high-ranking officials at the NYPD and at the Met, it was most difficult to conduct interviews in Paris due to a different police culture looking at researchers with distrust, boredom, or annoyance[1]. Officials are unwilling to allow an outsider in who could question their explanations. For previous studies on the social control of cities (Body-Gendrot, 2000) and on policing in inner cities, I had talked to former judges and prosecutors in Paris and New York. For lack of funding, it was not possible to interview their counterparts in Istanbul, Hong Kong, Ferguson, and Baltimore. Via the Urban Age programme at the London School of Economics, I had conversations with aides to the London mayor on matters of security and ongoing discussions with my British colleagues. In Paris, my five-year involvement with the National Police Complaints Authority (a civilian review board) allowed me to conduct hearings and hear the inevitable conflicting accounts from the police and from angry residents, most of them from poor neighbourhoods. A member of a resource centre in Saint Denis, Paris, Profession Banlieue, for fifteen years, I have attended numerous meetings related to downtrodden neighbourhoods' problems with members of the local administration, police, tenant managers, mayors, and so forth involved in the neighbourhoods of Seine Saint Denis, the poorest geographic department in France.

The book benefits from numerous secondary sources, including the media providing excerpts from conversations with hard-to-reach actors of public disorder. The approach is unique and draws on a wide range of cross-disciplinary sources, surveys, monographs, and field work, and it links the criminology of exclusion to urban studies, sociology, and political science issues. France, Turkey, and Hong Kong are included in the comparisons, which is also innovative. Academic research, public discourses, media, and conversations with residents and colleagues in various world cities have helped me clarify my thoughts.

The study is qualitative, although wherever it is appropriate, quantitative data is used critically, particularly in the cases of opinion polls, supplemented by qualitative surveys. My approach is interdisciplinary: political science, sociology, racial and ethnic studies, urban geography, law, and criminology inform and complement various aspects of the research. There cannot be a unique theory or discipline to study the topic of public disorder and globalization.

Complexity requires an interdisciplinary approach. Each context is unique. The challenge is then to mix specifics and generalizations in order to find the appropriate questions and if successful the answers (if there is such a thing!). Each studied disorder takes place in a city, moulded by its essence, history, institutions, economy, culture, and social components. The account has to be taken in its context and frame of time.

My approach is interactive. Much material is provided by a rich scholarly tradition in interactive studies in the tradition of Goffman (1967) and della Porta and Reiter (1998). When a complex set of factors including, but not limited to, deprivation underlies public disorder, a perspective of interactive analysis is needed for understanding its impact.

This book is comparative. The tradition of comparative studies is strong, allowing the testing of hypotheses and reflecting from a distance on narrowly focused monographs. If most books are frequently national rather than international in scope, there is a reason. The difficult nature of the comparative exercise cannot be underestimated, such as comparing disorder under the same headings or categories for which the same terms are used (like police or protesters): terms differ in nature and scope when they take place in specific contexts. Such terms can be elusive on closer inspection. Categories obscure what lies beneath. Flexibility in the use of categories such as these should prevail, and one should resist the temptation of merely translating terms. At best, functional equivalences can be suggested, invalidated, or supported. The manner in which tensions are expressed and resolved, for instance, is uneven; how ordinary people interpret and make sense of such tensions and how their structures of feeling play out differ. Some of their perceptions are to be connected to everyday experiences of injustice and inequalities, defying generalizations. A term to term comparison is not just possible. Indicators concerning the feeling of insecurity one feels when order gets disrupted achieve their meaning only after the singular features of each context are understood. Taking the comparison differently and looking at the way the disorder problem is constructed and what responses are generated by this construction makes the comparison more relevant. It demonstrates that debates related to the production of disorder by global, national, or local forces are currently missing from research; they have been obscured by a refocusing on offenders, talk of 'hot spots' and buttressed control, a focus which externalizes the responsibility of global players and of governments and reintroduces a binary vision of 'us' and 'them'.

Keeping these obstacles in mind, I defend the cross-fertilization, the awareness of diversity, the clarification of concepts, and the theoretical challenges brought by comparative analysis (Body-Gendrot, 2012: 16).

## Outline of the book

To facilitate clarifications, differentiate case studies of public disorder from opinions and interpretations, and establish links with global, national, and local contextual logics, this book is organized in two parts.

I first focus on public disorder and globalization. Chapter 1 introduces the research and its rationale.

Chapter 2 outlines an understanding of public disorder. In the large cities or environments where they take place, the dynamics of public disorder suggest a wide range of interpretations. Variations among different types of local governance and political contexts impact on the coordination of violent actions, the types of behaviour chosen, and the unfolding course of events. Tilly (2003) argues that when a challenge to order occurs in a chaotic context, it allows for improvised looting, raids, or revenge actions. Despite what appears as similar patterns, there are major variations across sites regarding modes of operation, claims, and types of confrontation. Symbolic space and street empowerment make a difference as well as the history of places. What is brought by globalization to the observations of public disorder made by Tilly is illustrated by the violent rituals of the black bloc, symbolizing an extreme case of globalized actors.

Chapter 3 presents a selection of case studies illustrating new dimensions taken by disorder in a context of globalization or, conversely, the local dimension that they retain while receiving global coverage. I look at the concrete unfolding of social disturbances and riots in cities in recent decades. Following the prior interpretations of globalization discussed previously, I search for their possible local, global linkages. I introduce a typology distinguishing three categories of claims and situations. The case studies are all related with the police institution managing local public order. They set numerous questions and reveal the difficulty of fitting them into categories, since the context of each case is singular. The first type of public disorder is illustrated by two cases. After two youths' deaths in 2005, clashes or 'riots' from outraged youths in the Parisian region correlated with the police. Public disturbances, also called 'riots' in London in 2011, violent disorder, looting, and vandalism occurred after police shot a man dead in a minority neighbourhood. The second type of public disorder examines two cases associated with demonstrations protesting police officers' fatal use of firearms against minorities in American cities. At the end of such demonstrations, physical violence opposed militants and police forces. The third type is illustrated by three cases of Occupy 'movements' in which the police evacuating protesters contributed to public disorder in New York (2011), Istanbul (2013), and Hong Kong (2014). Chapter 4 provides a comparative analysis on the convergences and differences between those types of disorder.

Part II focuses on dynamics of order, on institutional forces' responses to disorder, on their preventative tools and their use of global communication. Studies on order maintenance yield numerous classifications on forms of control, styles of policing, and strategies. Three tendencies emerge: law is enforced by the police according to contexts, complex bargaining takes place before potential serious disorder, and intelligence services gather as much information as possible on suspected rebellious groups intent on causing disorder in public space (Della Porta & Reiter, 1998). The conception and management of order maintenance varies according to countries' traditions and forms of regime. Differences between police and military approaches are strongly emphasized in Europe.

Chapter 5 examines strategies of incapacitation by police forces. Police's use or non-use of force is part and parcel of public disorder. Police forces' responses are shaped and determined by the strength of the groups they confront, by the groups' goals and resources, and by the nature of potential disorder. Repertoires of disorder management reflect what the police have been trained to do and what is institutionally sanctioned. The weight of the social, spatial, and political environments interacts with the structures of involved groups and the modes of order maintenance. The police have to deal with those dimensions in their responses.

In the first part of the chapter, the case studies are re-examined from the viewpoints of law enforcers. Operations, intelligence, global modes of communication, techniques to disperse mob gatherings, and the use of sophisticated weaponry, for example, indicate that strategies of incapacitation are based on risk management methods and that they evolve with accumulated expertise. New York City illustrates the diversity of such methods when confronting the occupiers of Zuccotti Park. In Europe as in New York, police forces strive to maintain a physical distance with their opponents, avoiding close contact. In Ferguson, Missouri, in 2014, conversely, police forces made use of 'military weapons' to disperse crowds as they were in close contact with the peaceful demonstrators. Such an approach generated heated public debates about the right of the police to self-defence if they believe protesters are armed. Police responses in American cities reveal a large diversity of behaviours. The second part of the chapter reflects on the variation of reactions of police institutions in response to the new challenges that they confront. This section is based on interviews with top-ranking police officers.

Chapter 6 compares states', public authorities', and judges' responses to the cases studies explored previously. It ponders on the notion of state, which differs according to countries. In Europe, two theoretical models of authority, such as Beetham (1991) and Max Weber (1922), distinguish and define what is expected from the state. More generally, national cultures, institutions, and expectations influence police accountability or the lack of it. Yet, it may be that when it comes to the management of public disorder, a reconciliation between those various forms of expectations operates and the tools that are used by the states come to look rather similar, varying in degrees of enforcement.

States have a wide range of tools at their disposal from emergency laws and calls to army forces to police order maintenance. Laws, local ordinances, executive orders, curfews, judicial rulings, and repressive sanctions, including prison, are the tools of sovereignty contributing to maintaining public order. These tools vary according to national and subnational contexts.

Resistance to law enforcers is sanctioned more or less harshly by judges. Conversely, the courts' reluctance at indicting police officers seems universal. More broadly, how much do states, public authorities, and judges use communication to promote their action? How efficient are they at justifying what they do to put an end to disorder in the eyes of public opinion?

Chapter 7 was added after the terrorist attacks in Paris in November 2015, Brussels in March 2016, and Nice in July 2016. Should terrorism enter the category of public disorder? If I stick to my earlier definition of public disorder, in Paris, as in Brussels, turbulent, erratic collective actions took place in the public space, the streets, a stadium, a rock concert hall of Paris, an airport, a subway station in Brussels, and Promenade des Anglais along the seaside in Nice, challenging established order. Yet we are not in a continuum with the previous mobilizations studied here, and we see another story emerging. Innovative, determined, internationally mobile, connected, and organized actors of disorder operated collectively to cause hundreds of deaths and receive maximum visibility. Intelligence services, law enforcers, and state authorities were taken by surprise. They painfully gathered their resources to respond to such a challenge. The exceptional response taken by the French state, a state of emergency and the suspension of the rule of law, exhibits one of the tools it has to reassure the public. In some cases, the state can act very efficiently. Documented from interviews, the cases of policing Paris during the climate conference, which gathered 196 countries at the end of 2015, and then the European soccer championship illustrate the capacity of the French police to prevent disorder from happening in a context of global threats. However, just as the struggle of Americans in Iraq demonstrates, responding to the attacks of 9/11 by launching a war with no end in sight reveals a weakness more than a strength. Similarly, in Europe, the jeopardizing of liberties, the boosting of expenditures in matters of security, and erratic communication demonstrate a lack of vision in dealing with new enigmatic enemies more than a savoir faire. This observation applies at the city level as well. Cities are the recipients and the casualties of such an asymmetric war, and they may be the best actors to respond to such challenges.

Chapter 8, the conclusion, ponders on the study of public disorder and globalization. Globalization gives acceleration to the world and sets new hierarchies. The terrorist attacks of 2015 in Paris transformed the conceptual landscape. New patterns are emerging but conceptual tools are currently struggling to make sense of them. Are theories on urban space, on the right to the city, and on social disorganization to be revised? How helpful are interactive theories to study new forms of disorder? Is there an innovative perspective on disorder to be explored? Should studies on public disorder be correlated to macro-analyses of neo-capitalism and to the disorder that it generates? How useful is it to wish for a revolution that would put an end to it (Winlow et al., 2015)?

There is no straight answer to the correlation of public disorder, globalization, and change. For some scholars (Winlow et al., 2015), new types of public disorder such as the Indignant or Occupy movements are entirely powerless, but other scholars are more hopeful. Then what next? More research and more conceptual tools are needed to tackle new patterns emerging and possibly new ways of looking at the current dialectics of order and disorder.

## Note

1   Sociologist Dan Kaminski (2016) conducted an investigation among judges. He commented upon his conditions of interview. Some interviewees would show signs of disinterest, bother, and weariness caused by someone taking their time. The sociologist's questions would force those judges to examine issues that they thought were irrelevant in their daily experience and seemed useless, futile, and superfluous. Kaminski quotes Lenoir (1996), a sociologist who also interviewed judges and noticed the numerous phone calls needed to get an appointment, the elusive answers of secretaries acting as screens, cancelling the appointments at the last minute, and postponing them in the distant future. As a female researcher, I experienced all those difficulties when I attempted to interview French high-ranking police officials dealing with order maintenance. Most of them did not answer my letters asking for an interview, despite recommendations. By contrast, the high-ranking police officers' responses to my questions in London and in New York City indicated that the interviewees and interviewer shared an interest in the problems and issues at stake. The shared interest in the debate may not actually be missing from the French police. It may be that restrictions/limitations or just general protocol frowns on the whole collaborative relationship between scholars and practitioners.

# PART I

# 2

# UNFOLDING PUBLIC DISORDER
# AND GLOBALIZATION

The aim of this chapter is to provide a framework to allow a comparative analysis of public disorder, sometimes involving hyper-connected actors.

As noted, there are different interpretations of the significance of public disorder, of its objectives, and the responses given to specific instances of public disorder. For the purposes of my analysis, the assessment of these interpretations is as important as the detailed description of what happened. Three kinds of interpretation of social disorder should be distinguished: interpretation by the media, interpretation by governments and political groups, and interpretation by researchers. The interpretations are not always distinct categories, as one source may borrow from the other, creating overlap. For instance, the media's choice to call a great variety of social disruptions 'riots' is deliberate. The use of the term simplifies the coverage of some forms of public disorder. It instantly brings images and representations formed in the accumulation of contentious pasts that become increasingly appropriated by a wide public familiar with such images and representations. Yet for a researcher like Charles Tilly (2003: 18), the term riot 'embodies a political judgment rather than an analytical distinction. Authorities and observers label as "riots" the damage-doing gatherings of which they disapprove, but they use terms like demonstration, protest, resistance, or retaliation for essentially similar events of which they approve'. Researchers use 'riots' for its common and immediate understanding, but such use is not always appropriate. Participants never call themselves rioters. For many residents of Egypt, Tunisia, and Libya, the disorderly events that resulted in injury and physical damage were not an 'Arab Spring' but rather a cold winter; it was a description that made sense only to Western outsiders. The same observation applies to the use of the term 'war' in the case of terrorist attacks in New York and in Paris. There is no identified army of Jihadists, and they do not come from a specific state. As their attacks are unconventional and may never end, it is doubtful whether we can use the term *war*. Such an expression was used by head of state,

G. W. Bush, in the United States, in order to provide the rationale for formal permission to launch a military intervention in Iraq in the name of legitimate defence (see chapter 6).

Such an elusive object of study requires concepts like order and disorder to be continually contested—order by whom, for whom, and how (Young, 1990: 227)? In this chapter, I introduce theoretical research examining the causes of public disorder with structural, cultural, or multivariate models of analysis. Then, as suggested by Tilly (2003), I provide a frame for the understanding of violent collective actions taking place in public space, the types of behaviour chosen by those involved, and the profiles of violent groups. Violent rituals, opportunism, and scattered attacks are categories which are, as previous research has shown, part of the repertoire to which they resort. I bring in recent studies that focus on the incidence and patterns of violence. It appears that not all current forms of disorder are impacted by globalized modes of communication. For instance, hooligans' scuffles are usually local. They may reach international dimensions during international sporting events like the Euro in spring 2016 in France when Russian hooligans trained like military staff with efficient skills attacked British hooligans in Marseille, causing dozens of causalities and arrests. In other contexts, clashes between youths and the police are usually local and routine. They may take a global dimension due to specific circumstances making order a high stake in cities like Paris, London, Ferguson, or Baltimore. Among those eager to resort to interpersonal violence, old categories are visible such as anarchists, politicized radicals on the far Left and on the far Right, disenfranchised squatters, impoverished, marginalized youths that the French call *casseurs* (destructive protesters), or newer groups like the black bloc (discussed later), environmentalists, defenders of animals' rights, and so forth. In the last part of the chapter, I define the parameters of globalization to show how globally connected actors disturb local events and how difficult it is for local police forces to anticipate their moves and to halt them. The black bloc operating during global summits has always appeared as a daring group for forces in charge of order, with their violent rituals and scattered attack methods. They have also mastered the art of communication and of coordination via the social media, as do homegrown terrorists and their networks when they target cities (see chapter 7). Observing their operations, I suggest that new patterns are emerging.

## Theories

Theories of public disorder offer a basis for understanding the implications of particular contexts and dynamics.[1] They address causes (the relative deprivation theory, the broken windows hypothesis) or dynamics (the spark and tinder metaphor, the flashpoint model). I will offer my own hypothesis in chapter 3, introducing the case studies.

### *The relative deprivation theory*

How visible or obvious are the linkages between globalization, inequalities, and public disorder? In other words, does the current globalization phase promote and accommodate intolerable inequalities which, in turn, generate social tensions and expressions of dissent in the public space? Some kinds of public protest can partly be explained as the outcome of inequalities and the consequences of policies neglecting what takes place at the margins of society, which includes the poor, the young, low-income immigrants, and others.

In its conceptualization of public disorder, the relative deprivation theory refers to the accumulation of handicaps and difficulties in specific urban spaces where impoverished populations live. There, 'unemployment is massive and urbanism inhuman . . . children are school dropouts . . . too many youths have trouble finding work, even with diplomas' (Scarman, 1985: 38). Out of anger and frustration, people resort to violence in the public space they regard as their territory. Research by Davies (1969), Dollard et al. (1974), and Festinger (1968) interprets collective disruptions as responses to situations of frustration and discards the myth of the 'madding crowd' (Marx, 1970). Relative deprivation theory asserts that the withdrawal of public assistance from inner cities, shrinking welfare assistance, and a lack of jobs are structural contexts favouring collective exasperation (Singh et al., 2012).

But although there is a basis for deprivation theory, it is difficult to prove that, mechanically, disturbances are determined by aggravated poverty and frustration. The death of a youth in dubious circumstances or tough police intervention does not necessarily escalate disorder. Disorder may be triggered by unfulfilled expectations leading to frustrations and disruptive behaviour, for example, in free enterprise zones receiving public funding. Historically, it has been improvements in the living conditions of marginalized populations, rather than their deterioration, that have contributed to starting revolutions (Tocqueville, 1856/1952). The era of the mid- to late 1960s in the United States showed the highest levels of urban disorder, and this was a culminating point of policies of redistribution and improved opportunities for racial minorities. Nor does such a theory account for serious multisided communal conflicts taking place among populations divided by age, race, gender, origins, identities, and other attributes (Travers, 2013: 281–82). These considerations suggest that a complex network of factors, including but not limited to deprivation, is at the root of public disorder (Body-Gendrot and Savitch, 2011).

## The broken windows hypothesis

Another dimension of public disorder is related to the broken windows hypothesis formulated by Wilson and Kelling (1982). These authors suggest that if windows were not repaired on a street and if signs of social disorder accumulated, some residents would view this collective norm-breaking as an unbearable infraction and as a threat to their quality of life and that they would move out. Zero tolerance policing was thus advocated. Some scholars in the line of Durkheim went further, explaining that disorder awoke deep anxieties among insecure and vulnerable persons during periods of macro-mutations (Kalifa, 2013: 16). Elites, precarious categories, women, seniors, newcomers, and others could all feel a loss of bearings. In this context, the theoretical question set forth by Sampson (2009; also Sampson and Raudenbush, 2004) concerned the social meaning given to perceptions of public disorder.

Sampson posited that 'believing is seeing', suggesting that perceptions are socially mediated. Order would be a way of keeping the 'unknown' and the uncertain at bay, a notion that governing elites activate. As noted by Sennett (1970, 2009), the broken windows or graffiti in abandoned places are perhaps more important visual and physical measures of urban chaos for some people than a police officer's purely legal definition of disorder. According to the empirical work of Innes et al. (2004), the most commonly perceived top threats to safety are all disorderly events occurring in public space. In impoverished neighbourhoods, he adds, residents' responses show that, more than rape or murder, they notice graffiti.

The hypothesis of broken windows has been criticized, especially in the United States, where it echoed class and racial biases about policing (Manning, 2010: 150). Harcourt (2001) argued that lower-class lifestyles and street life are themselves disorderly in the eyes of middle classes and that the subtext of broken windows targets poor young blacks who may see merits in confrontations and in establishing an intimidating reputation to evoke fear and respect.

### The spark and tinder metaphor and the flashpoint model

Looking at successive clashes between the police and young blacks in England, John Benyon (2007) coined the tinder and spark metaphor, distinguishing between *tinder* – that is, contexts with structural handicaps – and immediate *precipitants* (sparks), which are related to police abuse or intervention.

Challenging Benyon's work, the 'flashpoint frame of public disorder' (Waddington et al., 1989) defined six interdependent levels of analysis for disorder. The flashpoint model is flexible enough to encompass a variety of types of disorder, while recognizing the uniqueness of each situation. The model's structural level of analysis refers to material inequalities, poor life chances, and political powerlessness. Its political/ideological level of analysis looks at responses offered by institutions such as police, courts, and the media to concerned groups' demands. The cultural level examines subcultural groups' shared conditions and experiences and their views on the merit of accommodation or of confrontation. The contextual level pays attention to the circulation of rumours, to the history of a place, to the media coverage of issues in these localities. The situational level analyzes the profile of the territory – who 'owns' public space, whether turf wars occur, what surveillance is carried out by the police. Finally, the interactional level focuses on the nature of encounters between the police and the public. In highly tense situations, a particular incident (the throwing of a brick, an arrest or police charge, the cutting of trees in a popular park, an increase in bus fare) may spark disorder. Particularly important are *intensifiers* which cause disorder to erupt in some communities but not in others (Waddington et al., 1989). In brief, the flashpoint model theorizes that the forms and outcomes of public disorder are influenced by contexts, political regimes, cultural values, norms, and circumstances.

The flashpoint model has been criticized as overly general and for its limited analytical utility. Due to their scale and complexity, some disorder cannot be explained by the model (Bagguley & Hussain, 2008; Waddington & Wright, 2008). But for Waddington (2013: 51–52), complementary levels of analysis before or after an important event must be incorporated in its study. The 'cumulative effect of prior incidents may create a sufficiently combustible environment for the critical exposure to occur'. (2012).

## The dynamics of agency

Theoretically, according to Tilly (2003: 16, 77), three processes explain why public disorder swells from small to large scale. The salience of violence increases when the participants are specialists in violence and resort to familiar scripts for coordinated destruction; when social and cultural polarization ('us' versus 'them') widens the space between contenders and when uncertainty about the outcome is marked. Tilly (2003: 16) suggests that the social processes behind public disorder – that is, the combinations and sequences of mechanisms generating their dynamics and producing similar effects in different circumstances – are better understood in examining types of collective violence rather than motives. He looks at combinations and settings of disorder, the people involved, and those that such participants address (other groups, authorities, various public). He examines the activation or suppression of existing boundaries, defining 'us' and 'them', and mechanisms that create new connections or sever old ones in the dynamics of disorder. Tilly's classification is useful to simplify the understanding of a complex reality.

## Violent rituals

Unlike other forms of disorder, violent rituals are characterized by a collective propensity to cause short-term damage and by a high degree of coordination among violent actors. Short-term damage encapsulates violent social activity taking place in local public space (arson, vandalism, stone-throwing). Spierenburg (2007: 17) offers a limited and clear definition of violence as 'intentional encroachment upon the physical integrity of the body'. Not all violent rituals resort to interpersonal violence, however; some of them just focus on material destruction.

According to Tilly (2003: 91,156), in order to reduce environmental uncertainty, violent rituals rely on public scripts, fixed stakes, and parameters sharply drawn around conflicts; clear distinctions are made between proper and improper participants and spectators.

Football hooliganism resorts to violent rituals. Tribal behaviours (dress codes, emblems, songs) and the extreme radicalization of supporters have been documented in this context (Dal Lago & De Biasi, 1994). A desire for peer recognition and visibility via allegedly aggressive feats may compensate for a lack of social status in society (Marsh, 1977). According to such assumptions, confrontational, lawless, and masculine behaviour are markers of identity, status, resistance, and exciting entertainment for football hooligans, all the more so if they occupy a structurally marginal position (also Elias & Dunning, 1986). The role of the media in turning those football hooligans into 'folk devils', in creating 'moral panics', and transforming violence into entertainment has been widely documented (Cohen, 1972, p. 28; Hall et al., 1978, p. 16). The media amplification of hooligans' behaviours thus reinforces the codes of the 'in group'. What happened in Marseille during the Euro soccer championship in June 2016 when thirty-five supporters were wounded by fighting English and Russian hooligans is a perfect illustration of the hooligans' will to become highly visible due to their feats of violence and of the 'disturbing fascination' they exerted on Broussard (2016), a journalist covering the event for *Le Monde* as well. 'The Russian hooligans have won, and they are probably very proud of it. Proud to see pictures of those English covered with blood in the streets of Marseille. Proud that the whole planet talked about them', he wrote. Then the journalist pursued his description of the hooligans' 'Warholian' world, a borderless world where anything becomes a challenge to their supremacy. He mentions the clans' use of cell phones and of social media, their paramilitary skills, and their extreme violence. He emphasizes their contradictions. They melt in the crowd of peaceful supporters to avoid being noticed by the police while going into a frenzy when seen (*rage de paraître*) by their rivals and the media.

New research focuses on factors boosting public disorder, such as heavy consumption of alcohol and, until a few decades ago, soft institutional responses to sports violence, attracting large audiences on television (Van Limbergen et al., 1989).

New criminological research, involving ethnography and social psychology, looks at the dynamics of disorder, at what actually happens when and where, and at what moves are made within the groups involved, from one field of contention to another. It shows how complex and fluid events shift and logics of context are transformed during the course of action.

### Incidence and patterns of violence

Recent studies such as those led by Collins (2008), Hochstetler (2001), and Weenink (2014, 2015) analyze deviant group behaviour. Starting with a study of how robbers collectively operate, Hochstetler (2001) emphasizes 'incremental signalling', small bodily or verbal cues indicating to each member whether they are ready for a confrontation in a specific situation. In such study of interactional dynamics during burglaries, Hochstetler examines how offenders construct opportunity, communicating expectations and negotiating shared meanings. He shows that decisions made in such groups are incremental, depending on context, and affected by the influence that some members exert on others. Those observations apply to the actors of disorder acting collectively.

Collins (2009: 568) has calculated

> on the basis of photographic evidence and available statistics, that virtually all of the violence in each conflict-engaging population – crowds in riots and

brawls, police, gangs, criminals – is carried out by a small proportion of participants, typically on the order of less than 15 per cent at maximum.

Due to tensions and fear, almost always, violence misses its goal.

> Violence is difficult, not easy; we have been led astray in thinking otherwise, both by media violence (which typically portrays fighters as good or bad, but nevertheless as brave and competent) and by our criminological theories (which assume that background conditions in an individual's biography are sufficient to account for violence). On the basis of micro-situational evidence, I say not so; the very situation of confrontation, when violence is threatening, generates tension/fear, and this creates a barrier to the effective use of violence against one's opponent.

In the next chapter, the case studies examined are unusual, but their global visibility cannot be denied and the task is to understand why.

If tensions and fear usually prevail among human beings, how do violent groups overcome their tension and fear and engage in action? Collins (2009: 570) asserts that they reinforce their collective identities in antagonistic situations, the us/them boundaries mentioned by Tilly (2003), and dominate the weak elements being attacked.

> Photos of hostile demonstrations and riots show two chief phases: either two sides are lined up in orderly masses, confronting one another, but without violence; or the crowd has broken up into small groups, which is when virtually all the violence happens. (I am ignoring here the occasional phase where a few individuals are in front of a crowd throwing rocks from a distance). This second phase may reveal a distinct numerical pattern: one individual has been isolated from supporters and is running away or has fallen to the ground, and is being attacked by small clusters of between three and six attackers (the upper number sometimes rising to eight).

> This pattern is found in police attacking demonstrators and demonstrators attacking police; in whites attacking blacks and vice versa and in many different ethnic combinations. The underlying dynamic is not merely racism or ethnic hostility, since one can find this in intra-ethnic violence, including labour violence and sports violence. Nor is it merely masculinity that produces this unequal violence; although most crowd violence is male on male.

This statement illustrates violence displayed by hooligans during the Euro championship by groups organized, specialized, using codes, defining their targets, acting rapidly with a perfect coordination. In the next chapter, this pattern will be illustrated by confrontations involving minority youths and the police. In groups of violent actors, there is mutual agreement on a target during action and a confident reliance on the group's past experiences to project its future action (Hochstetler, 2001: 750).

### Opportunism, scattered attacks, and coordinated destruction

Opportunism has also to be accounted for. When a challenge to order occurs in a chaotic context, it opens the door to improvised looting, raids, and revenge actions. And just as important as who is involved, where the disorder occurs reveals important variations on the coordination of violent action, the types of behaviour chosen, and the course of events.

Public disorder may occur in the course of organized social processes that are not themselves violent. To varying degrees, democratic regimes support citizens' rights to assemble, occupy public space, identify themselves collectively, and express claims. In Western countries, most police forces respect those rights. In Europe, older strata of salaried workers and threatened craftsmen, taxi, and truck drivers frequently take to the streets to express their grievances and create visible public disorder by halting traffic and pedestrians' fluid trajectories. Such actors know how to take advantage of global media coverage and gain the sympathy of public opinion. Frequently, in France, a demonstration will start peacefully in a carnival atmosphere. But when asked by the police to disperse, if collective effervescence and anger persist, then, opportunistically, disorder may escalate. What is of interest in this research is not the demonstration or the conflict per se, but the disorder occurring at the end of it, requiring authorities and police forces to intervene. A minority of dissident, opportunist, or anarchist demonstrators may then resort to scattered attacks, throwing rocks or breaking windows – 'the weapons of the weak' (Scott, 1985) – in encounters with law enforcement personnel. Such interactions pave the way for spirals that may then generate coordinated destruction. For instance, in specific regions of France like Brittany, unionized groups of farmers or fishermen may calmly walk to symbolic public sites like a regional Parliament or a television substation, vandalize them, break machines and/or valuable goods, and then walk back peacefully to their press conference.

Examining types of mobilized repertoires according to regions, O. Fillieule (1997: 221) remarked that violent groups are associated with cities like Nantes in Brittany. In 27 percent of their street actions, Nantes's farmers had occupied offices, and in 5 percent of them had launched commandos (ten times more frequently than the regional average rate). Whether these actions are planned ahead, thus violating previous agreements with police/gendarmes about itineraries and forms of action, or are a consequence of the organizer's weakness or even an opportunity taken to shift the course of a demonstration, the damages send a provocative and rebellious message to political authorities and to the public. However such costly public disorder is narrowly circumscribed to a place and to a labour category which suffers (like farmers or craftsmen); it is then (at least in France) not harshly sanctioned by courts.

## Third party involvement

Collective public disorder involves multiple actors, observers, and third parties. As noted in the following discussion of the black bloc (an intimidating group, dressed in black, wearing hoods, and highly visible in global summits), violent actors give the impression of acting as one because they are mutually aware of the physical co-presence of others in their group. My point is that interactional dynamics change both the perception of opportunities and the improvisation that can take place, due to the interpretation of fluid situations, shifting the centre of action.

Violent actors of disorder are frequently encouraged and even cheered by supportive spectators who may applaud when rocks and bolts are thrown at the police. These bystanders observe the scene, hesitate, and may eventually join the fray, as seen below in the testimonies from the 2005 disorders in Paris. Other observers may try to calm them down. But violence is a highly addictive passion for some individuals who need the adrenaline and emotional arousal that violence brings them (interview with M. H., a former violent actor). Frenzied attacks (Weenink, 2014) may be explained by the emotional release from tension and fear that takes place when the opponent appears weak and unable to resist. In this situation, a rapid shift occurs, according to Weenink, an emotional asymmetry felt by the dominating group and encouraging it to lead the dynamics of interaction. Collins (2009) gives the example of the Rodney King case when, after a long chase between him and the police on the road, generating high adrenalin on both sides, King surrendered and the release of emotions and accumulated adrenalin led four police officers to beat him up without restraint, encouraged by the cheers of other officers.

In general, socialization, fear, and inexperience prevent people from engaging in violent actions. In many Western countries, families, schools, and institutions teach young children to use verbal skills to deflect violence rather than resort to physical violence. Without training, people are often reluctant to physically engage in interpersonal violence to solve their conflicts. For Norbert Elias (1939/1994), the rise of the modern state and the emergence of professional police and justice have freed Western societies from practicing vendettas, mob lynchings, and deadly scuffles. This trend has led to a consolidaton of the modern state and to the pacification of morals (chapter 5). Although contested as too Anglocentric, the Eliasan thesis is still explanatory for the large decline in interpersonal violence, despite a resurgence of depacification in specific contexts.

## Global actors of public disorder

The second part of this chapter introduces globalization for an understanding of public disorder as outlined previously. The black bloc is used as an example.

## The black bloc's modes of operation

Studies of the black bloc (Dupuis-deri, 2003; McAdam, Tarrow, & Tilly, 2001) illustrate what global actors do when they engage in violent rituals, scattered attacks, and dynamics of confrontation. That the black bloc is a global actor is demonstrated by their organized and threatening presence in world summits, where they gather from diversified places of the world; by the global coverage they receive from the media; and in return, by their own 'explanatory' communication on the internet (Anonyme, 2002).

First, the black bloc is not one organization. Ephemeral groups made up of heterogeneous individuals get together at one point to lead a diversity of violent collective street actions, in particular during global summit demonstrations. What they have in common is their rituals: they dress in black; wear hoods, helmets, masks, shields, and other protective devices; carry batons, bricks, bolts, mortars, tear-gas canisters, cans of paint, or Molotov cocktails. As a group, they make the same gestures and chant the same slogans; they act like warriors. Thus, to the out groups, they give the impression of acting as one. But some of these individuals may choose to undress during the dynamics of disorder, to de-identify with the group and shift to another identity, which makes them harder to spot for police forces in charge of maintaining order. Such was the case in March 2016 in Brussels after the terrorist attacks when a peaceful demonstration in support of order was disturbed by what the media first called 'three hundred football hooligans', then neo-fascists, or far-Right groups. Later, in 2016 in Paris and in other large French cities like Nantes, Toulouse, and Rennes, strikes and continuous protests against a draft labour law led by radicalized unions were disturbed by what Paris Police Prefect described as 'activists from the ultra-radical line'. The head of one of the police unions warned that 'people should be aware of the violence of such destructive demonstrators (*casseurs*). . . . They throw bolts as large as fists, nail boxes with fire crackers snatched to them, agricultural bombs or mortars' (Pascual, 2016a: 7). Over three hundred policemen have been hurt in less than two months, according to official figures. Erratic bystanders prevent the police from stopping destructive activists, this police officer added, and they make order maintenance technically very complex.

What is sometimes called the 'tyranny of structurelessness' (Freeman, 2002: 54–62) refers to the fact that groups like the black bloc or the French 'casseurs' have no authoritarian pyramidal system of authority. It allows the ephemeral group to remain fluid and to adjust to circumstances. However complex, 'liquid' or 'soft' forms of leadership do exist, according to the social media specialist, Gerbaudo (2012: 13). Influential Facebook administrators and tweeting activists have played a crucial role in setting the scene for the movements gathering in the public space.

For the media, politicians, police, heads of organizations, the members of the black bloc or their like are perceived as enemies of order and of society motivated by a nihilistic rage and a force of destruction. Even opponents to the world summits' goals perceive the bloc as a threat. During the summit of Göteborg in 2001, Susan George, the vice-president of the reformist organization ATTAC (*Association pour une transaction des taxations financières pour l'aide aux citoyens* – association in favour of a tax on financial transactions to help citizens) pointed out that 'the violence from *anars* (anarchists) or destructive protesters (*casseurs*) is more anti-democratic than the institutions they supposedly confront'. Because of these protesters, the whole opposition to the summit is discredited (George & Wolf, 2002: 167). The same echo was given by the unions in France in 2016, showing their surprise at being violently attacked by the 'casseurs' who neither spared them nor the police nor peaceful demonstrators.

According to Dupuy-déri (2003), violent actors as such received their visibility in May 1968 in Paris as well as in other large cities around the world at that time. They confronted the police with batons, stones, bricks, and sometimes firearms. These 'folk devils' were always dressed in black, in contrast with those of Action Directe in France, the Baader Band in Germany, or the Red Brigades in Italy a few years later.

Then, in the 1980s in Berlin, the *autonomen* movement violently fought against squatters' evictions and resorted to arson and other direct actions to articulate their cause. World summits (Göteborg, Seattle, Davos, Genoa) provided opportunities to spread a confrontational counter-culture via various networks, attracting radical, anarchist, and violent groups from diverse parts of the world. Those groups knew how to take advantage of the global revolution of communication and technology. Locally, during those years, violent fights physically opposed radical Left actors, skinheads and neo-Nazi groups at specific times and in specific places. Not all the groups involved in the dynamics of contention claimed to belong to the black bloc. But as other politicized groups – such as national separatists, Maoists, and communists – and revolutionary, anarchistic, and radical groups resorted to similar violent rituals, scattered attacks, and destruction – window smashing, bank vandalism, attacks on the police or on perceived outsiders. In the use of those tactics, there were similarities: the small size of the groups resorting to incremental signalling allowed young men to shift rapidly from one type of action to another and from one place to the other. They entered fluid, informal power games, influenced by the group members' experience, or by a leader's charisma (Dupuy-déri, 2003: 43). As discussed previously, their domination over weaker elements was partly due to their in-group culture. They have the skills and the technical support to communicate on the internet what they do and why they do it. They frequently give the impression of being superior to their opponents in terms of organization, coordination, determination, and flexibility. The social media provides logics of aggregation for them, summoning dispersed individuals from a distance.

Despite these similarities, the form of these violent interactions are distinguished by their aims. The groups' forms of actions may look similar, but the content of their cause varies from anarchists searching for the abolition of any form of authority to the black bloc eager to demonstrate the superiority of violent direct action. Why would direct action be superior to negotiation? For the black bloc and their imitators, peaceful demonstrations accomplish nothing when they denounce the system as it is. In their communiqués to the media, black bloc members point out (with some relevance) that governing elites ignore peaceful demonstrations and that the media cover collective action only when violence occurs during public disorder (Anonyme, 2002). The Anonymous groups say the same, for all violent groups acting in local space: violence is a useful tool, since it attracts attention and makes actions visible. With just their bodies and without words, in a few hours, militants may appropriate space. In May 2016, in Rennes, a communist student union militant remarked that 'to make the situation unbearable, one must be ready to create an atmosphere of maximum tension with the state, in articulating mass demonstrations with some radical moves like economic sabotage or confrontation with forces of order if necessary'. The student added that he was not advocating the murder of policemen but explained that respect of law and pacifism do not change the balance of forces (Pascual, 2016a). Another militant observed that protesting and then going home is not enough. Direct action changes 'the way one relates to the city, to property and to politics. Violent groups' direct action allows them to mark their dissent, to participate in the old law tradition and in civil disobedience against an illegitimate authority' (Arendt, 1972; Dupuy-dery, 2003: 142). Such groups know how to communicate their message powerfully. Yet, without allies, it is my opinion that the black bloc and their likes are only mosquito bites for the powers that be.

Such extreme examples of public disorder, perpetrated by minuscule numbers of violent actors, illustrate the way in which global modes of communication increase rebellious actors' potential for nuisance and their capacity for renewing staple repertoires for action. At the end of this study, suicide bombers will provide another illustration of globalized actors' power of nuisance and disruption.

I now turn to a selected number of case studies of public disorder which have in common the physical concentration of participants in local public space at the same time. Arendt (1958: 199) insists on the political dimension of space which is not material in the modern sense but an appearance allowing individuals to be together in the manner of speech and of action. Public space has the capacity of filling gaps separating individuals, generating a common vision and the sense of a shared world. It may support civil disobedience.

## Note

1    This part on theories borrows from Body-Gendrot (2014). I acknowledge here permission to reproduce this excerpt given by *The Annual Review of Law and Social Sciences*, http://www.annualreview.org.

# 3

# ANALYZING CASES OF PUBLIC DISORDER

This chapter examines large-scale visible disturbances that recently occurred in the public spaces of Western cities. It examines their potential local and global linkages and points out a diversity of claims and situations, revealing both their specificities and their commonalities. The first set of case studies concerns France and England, where wide-scale clashes opposing police and youths respectively in 2005 and in 2011 were broadcast all over the world and received a planetary echo due to the media and the social media (which includes Facebook, Twitter, and Blackberry messenger). Unlike the global violent black bloc and their likes described in the previous chapter or the European terrorists analyzed later in chapter 7, the participants in these events were frequently local actors and not globally connected. It is intriguing to grasp then why their actions received a global echo.

After 2005, the specific social unrest which went on for three weeks all over France became indeed a landmark on the eve of major elections. The French terrorists who attacked Paris in January, then November 2015, all related to the *banlieue*s (depressed housing projects in the northern suburbs of Paris) or to a downtrodden Brussels neighbourhood, were analyzed by some commentators in the context of comments made after 2005. A similar observation applies for the 'riots' which happened in Greater London in 2011, just when the Olympic Games were about to attract large masses of people, including investors in that city a year later. For important events about to take place, representing major financial or political investments, national and city leaders cannot ignore disorders which may subsequently backlash. Concerns regarding security in global cities like Paris and London extend beyond the local spheres, and retrospectively, such events also become points of reference for further understanding of the meaning of public disorder. Why they acquire such a status is of great interest and marks the perceptions of the global tightly interwoven in local events. New patterns are thus seen as emerging, moving such issues beyond local and national spheres.

The second series of cases deals with public disorder, which accompanied protests against police's lethal shootings of minorities in American cities in 2014–15. In Ferguson and Baltimore, after a series of young black men were tragically killed by police officers, disorder spread beyond the streets of the local perimeters of the tragic incident. Protesters received a national and world audience with commentary circulating in cyberspace and with a profusion of editorials in the newspapers and TV shows. The protesters questioning the legitimacy of the American criminal justice system triggered a large public debate on racism, discrimination, and corruption. A new national organization, Black Lives Matter, then expanded, receiving attention from President Obama and candidates to future elections.

In the third series of cases, the disorder caused by space occupation in cities such as New York, Istanbul, and Hong Kong is analyzed not only because it received global coverage but because, as in the previous cases, it revealed the innovative skills of this new type of protesters, globally connected and using social networks both to mobilize their followers and public opinion and to respond to their opponents. Public disorder was also caused by the police forces managing public space with force and sometimes abuse. The police also used the social media to defend their views.

A method is applied similarly to all the cases for comparative purposes. It was previously tested in a research that I conducted with H.V. Savitch (2012: 505). The study compared 'riots' in Los Angeles (1992) and in Paris (2005). After examining contexts and the facts related to each incident, we used an interactive framework emphasizing the operation of multiple forces which, in the course of events, come together to produce a particular outcome (Goldstone, 1991; Skocpol, 1979). These forces may be independent of each other initially, but they interconnect as events unfold. Thus, in my view, in 2005 the heavy-handed police approach, the media coverage, the characteristics of local space, the cultural and religious dimensions intervening in the confrontation, in combination with other circumstances, created a highly combustible situation. Body-Gendrot and Savitch (2012) suggested that when collective violent disorder does occur, it is catalyzed through a labyrinth of relatively discreet, highly dispositional events which, at a defining moment, fold into one another. It is this combination of chance, context, and causation which guided the 2012 study.

In this study, I examined the components of urban rioting, and for each case, I looked at the mobilization potential, triggering events, and preparations for confrontations. (The political/bureaucratic responses will be examined in further chapters.) By *mobilization potential*, I referred to the relationships and attitudes that facilitate or inhibit the protesters' collective violence. I identified this potential as deprivation on one hand and, on the other, integration/disintegration. *Deprivation* occurs within logical and causative contexts. In Paris as in London, the protesters came from banlieues of Paris or from the dispersed inner cities of London. I refer here to economic hardship, the diminution of real and/or perceived chances for social mobility, and widening inequalities among the statuses of these areas relative to others. By *integration/malintegration*, I alluded to the kinds of organizations that potential demonstrators join or associate with.

I viewed *triggering events* or *flashpoints* (Waddington & Crichter, 1989) as publicized episodes that brought to a head or catalyzed cumulative grievances. Triggering events are usually filled with drama or tragedy of one kind of another. Finally, *preparations* refer to a process in which potential 'rioters' become mentally ready to engage in collective action/violence (Body-Gendrot & Savitch, 2012: 506–7). Such a method is applied to the three types of disorder selected, revealing how much each disorder is contextual, making generalizations hazardous. The first type of disorder focuses on Paris in 2005 and London in 2011.

## Public disorder in Greater Paris and London

## Greater Paris in 2005[1]

### The context

The dynamics of contention that unrolled in the Autumn of 2005 in France were not the first of their kind, but the intensity, contagion, locations, and scale of disruption which followed the horrifying deaths of two youths chased by the police in Clichy-sous-Bois were unusual and became imbued with symbolic global significance.

Such collective violence occurred in French neighbourhoods benefiting from specific public subsidies within what is called *politique de la ville* (a prototype for diversified forms of preferential treatment in selected problem neighbourhoods). This mode of territorial affirmative action was launched at the beginning of the 1980s after the return of the Left to power. The programme included 184 experimental zones in 1984. But four years later, under pressure from local mayors, this policy was extended to five hundred neighbourhoods in a context of economic changes and severe unemployment and marked by outbursts of collective violence (Body-Gendrot, 2000). After reaching 1300 in 1999, the number of subsidized neighbourhoods (referred to as 'sensitive urban zones' – ZUS – by French administration) came to 751. The majority of these neighbourhoods are located in Greater Paris. They are characterized by a large component of unemployed, large, immigrant families with social difficulties in extensive public housing. In 2014, they became known as priority zones. The maximum priority given by authorities to sites where the 2005 riots occurred was not due to their level of deprivation, but to their perceived risk of violence. Numerous riots occurred in free enterprise zones (Lagrange, 2009: 111). Usually located in the most deprived zones, the changes had generated a high level of unmet expectations that led to anger, especially among the youths.

My data for this research comes from conversations with involved participants, students who were then teenagers, residents, managers of large public housing units, local mayors, heads of community organizations, and senior police officers explaining what they observed during the unrest. Interviews displayed a wide diversity of attitudes and perceptions among the residents. Research on urban renewal programmes in metropolitan Paris reveals that only a minority of residents would want to leave their neighbourhood. The voice of the marginalized and angry youths or of disenfranchised and older residents, usually echoed in the media, do not then convey a wholly accurate picture.

When the incidents happened in 2005, France was in a pre-electoral context in which the minister of the interior was a likely candidate for the presidency. Via the media, the disturbances resonated with public emotions and tested the regime stability.

Without some unanticipated events, the disorders that erupted in Clichy-sous-Bois, a locality North of Paris, would have ended after three nights of confrontation, as was usually the case when youths clashed with the police during the 1980s and the 1990s in the banlieues. Instead, according to a leaked report from a police unit: 'Never have as many cities been hit simultaneously. Never has a movement lasted so long; it took twenty days for peace to return. Never was it so costly: over 250 million euros over one continuous event' (*Le Parisien*, Dec. 7, 2005).

## The facts

On Thursday October 27, 2005, in Clichy-sous-Bois, boys from public housing estates who had been playing soccer hurried home to break the day's fast during Ramadan. Three of them cut across a construction site, and an employee from a funeral home, fearing they might steal something, called the police. A patrol car arrived on the spot, followed by backup, a total of 14 police officers. Panicked, seventeen-year-old Zyed Benna, fifteen-year-old Bouna Traoré, and seventeen-year-old Muhittin Altun decided to climb over the wall of an electricity transformer station. One of the pursuing officers, after checking twice, returned to the police car and the squad headed back to the police station.

Bouna and Zyed were electrocuted by 20,000 volts. This incident was the first trigger for the uprisings. But that evening, a second trigger changed the young people's grief to indignation. Misinformed, Interior Minister Sarkozy suggested that if the boys had not attempted a break-in, they would not have run away from the police. In an instantaneous explosion of rage, dozens of young men walked through the streets of their neighbourhood, chanting 'Dead for nothing!', and hiding their faces with hooded sweatshirts.

On Sunday October 30, three nights after the disorder started, a third trigger re-ignited the dynamics. One tear-gas canister, like those used by the police, fell into the entrance of the Bilal mosque causing those inside – parents, family elders – to rush out, humiliated and upset. According to police data, seven nearby localities experienced urban violence that evening.

The situation was aggravated by a police decision on October 30 to assign eight hundred anti-riot police officers to the Stade Français in Saint Denis at the request of the Préfet of Seine Saint Denis. A soccer game involving Manchester United and the Lille Olympic Sporting Club was taking place the next day, and it was perceived as high risk by the police. The costly stadium is continuously given police priority. Local mayors' urgent calls requiring police backup because of the rioting in their localities were ignored. At least 250 cars were set alight that evening.

All Saints' Day on November 1 is a religious holiday in France. The four-day weekend prevented local mayors from mobilizing their human resources. Instead, they had to wait until Wednesday, November 2, for their employees to come back from their holiday. After six days, more cars had been torched and violent clashes and heavy damage to schools and public buildings had occurred not only in Greater Paris but also in provincial France.

The two youth casualties aside, no death was caused by the interaction of the contending parties. A French feature, burning cars and confronting the police, were the most frequent routinized actions in those events. Almost no looting occurred.

---

During the 21 nights of unrest, in 300 neighbourhoods of 200 cities, officially, 10,346 vehicles were burnt (4,207 in the Parisian region); 233 public buildings (sports centres, prayer rooms, post offices), 74 private buildings, 255 schools, 7 bus depots, 22 buses or railways, and 18 religious sites were vandalized or damaged; 4,770 persons were stopped (2,808 during the crisis); 4,402 were kept in custody; 763 people were incarcerated (including over 100 juveniles); 11,500 civil servants, including 4,500 police officers and gendarmes (60 units per night), were mobilized; and 271 officers were injured (Rivayrand, 2006). Damages were estimated to be over 200 million euros.

---

On November 9, 2005, a state of emergency was pronounced by decree. The political and institutional reactions were diverse. For French media (not the scholars), Islam was the culprit. A survey of newspapers during the events revealed that the term *Islam* appeared 718 times and *Islamist* 224 times, by comparison with *social inequalities* 182 times (Tiberj & Michon, 2013).

The 2005 incidents received worldwide coverage, and in that sense, globalization promoted their visibility. It was 'an immensely pathetic spectacle whose primary meaning has been that it happened. . . . It had no ideology and no purpose other than to make a statement of distress and anger', remarked Pfaff (2005), stressing the Muslim identity of the participants. Foreign emphasis was frequently put on 'race riots', and on minorities' social malintegration. The *New York Times* aligned the French disorders on those of the 1960s or of Los Angeles in the United States (Body-Gendrot, 2016). Such intense interpretative orientation also pointed at the absence of a systematic discussion of the ethnic characteristics of the neighbourhoods involved in the outbreaks.

### Mass mobilization potential

*Deprivation:* The département (county) experiencing most of the urban violence, Seine Saint Denis, has the highest unemployment rate in France. Clichy-sous-Bois (referred to by its shortened nomenclature as Clichy) is the poorest locality in the Department of Seine Saint Denis. In the neighbourhood from which the two electrocuted youths came, Chêne Pointu, immigrants account for 45 percent of the population (Kokoreff, 2008a: 166).

*Integration/Malintegration:* The topic of integration is all the more difficult to handle here, as there is no ethnic/racial categorization in France. Only the distinction French/non-national applies, ignoring the importance of French second or third generations of foreign origin in these banlieues. For Lagrange (2009), a number of localities with large families of African origin were the scene of riots. 'The concentration of large families correlates very significantly with the geography of the riots . . . and their level of segregation . . . there is clearly a marked tendency toward delinquency and school under-achievement' (2009: 113). The conflictual socialization of French boys from Africa led to a disastrous relationship with the police and judges (Lagrange, 2009: 120).

The localities where the sub-Saharan families settled were not riot zones in the 1980s and the 1990s. These young rioters have no stake in the existing political and social order, and due to their isolation, they have no spokespeople. There is no transmission of a culture of protest from the older ones to the youngest. Community organizations deliver service; they are not advocates for the have-nots. The political representation of these residents is non-existent (Body-Gendrot, 2016).

Did religion play a role? Did they mobilize as Muslims? Academics are divided. For Kepel (2015), 2005 marked a turning point, and after the Bilal mosque incident when a tear-gas canister was thrown, some youths thought that they would never be seen as 100 percent French, so they felt anger and turned to radical fundamentalism. But this interpretation is contested. A leaked official report from the intelligence service (Renseignements généraux) of the police firmly denied that religion played a role. The tone of the report intended to undermine Islamophobic reactions, especially from the extreme right after the reaction to the mosque incident:

> France experienced a form of unplanned insurrection with the emergence of a leaderless and program-less revolt in time and space. . . . No solidarity was observed between the public housing estates, youths identified with their neighbourhood and not with others. . . . No manipulation was detected and no support was given to the thesis of a general and organized uprising.
>
> *(General Direction of Renseignements généraux, 2005)*

For Roy (2005), 'there was nothing Arab or Islamic in the riots'.

Such statements rule out the character of an ethno-racial revolt, aligned on the American race riots or those in the 1980–90s in England.

### Triggering event

What many saw as the mishandling of the Clichy incident by the minister of the interior (Nicolas Sarkozy) occurred in a highly charged political atmosphere. Sarkozy had previously referred to the demonstrators as *racaille* (rabble or riff raff).

## Preparations

Several sets of actors were involved among the rioters. Roughly, three types of actors were interacting in the situations of disorder: on one hand, frustrated, angry teenagers (a small number per locality) and a small number of young adults collectively 'acted out' and engaged in what Coser (1956: 49) calls non-realistic conflicts – that is 'the release of aggressive tension' among interacting persons. All over the country, via the social networks, an entire younger generation identified with the tragic fate of the youths in Clichy 'dying for nothing'. Age was an important variable. The victims were young and, as in most riots, many of the participants were also young.

Older boys, young adults already on the labour market, and young fathers who wanted to express their claims and their rage after one more incident also participated. Others instrumentalized chaos to exert forms of local revenge or draw benefits in terms of image. According to Mohammed and Mucchielli (2006), the targets were chosen after deliberation, and the rebels did not act randomly. In-between, bystanders watched, hesitated to join in, or calmed down the youth. Then there were the police forces interacting with them and influencing sets of actions (see chapter 5).

## Times

No locality in France experienced more than four nights of riots (Cicceli et al., 2006: 3). What was unusual in 2005 was the contagion that spread from the north of Paris to three hundred neighbourhoods in France and the length of time that the unrest went on – approximately twenty-one days. There are several explanations for the increasing contagion over time. As noted, the local mayors' calls at first were not heard by the headquarters in Paris choosing to protect a high-risk game at the national stadium in Saint Denis rather than stop the rioters four nights after the beginning of the mobilization. They did not anticipate the media coverage either. The drama of extensive arsons across banlieues also attracted international television coverage. As soon as the numbers of cars ablaze were seen on prime time news, it was interpreted as a further stimulus to burn more cars the next time. The media acted as a magnifying glass for isolated incidents. Most adults in the affected localities did not support the offenders, but a lot of them said that they 'understood' these violent reactions.

## An interactive and comprehensive framework

My comprehensive and interactive framework emphasizes

> the operation of multiple forces which, in the course of fluid and undetermined situations, come together to produce a particular outcome. These forces may be independent of each other initially – i.e. the impact of the

media, the local actions of the police, the number of youths, the religious
dimension in a specific place -, but interact as events unfold.

(Body-Gendrot & Savitch, 2012: 505)

The dynamics of contention (such as crises) are a continuation of routine relations,
modified by the mobilization potential, precipitants, timing, and the structure of
opportunities (Body-Gendrot, 2014; Dobry, 1986). Here, the youths resorted to
their usual repertoire to express their grievances. The police forces anticipated that
after three nights, the disorders would recede, but no one had foreseen that a tear-
gas grenade launched at the entrance of a storefront mosque on a holy night for
Muslims would re-ignite collective anger and lead to more forms of destruction.
No one had thought that the toughness of prosecutors and real time summary processes would reduce the structure of opportunities for the protesters as rapidly. The
decrease in acts of violence followed closely that of arrests – the timing was correlated (Body-Gendrot, 2008). The political/bureaucratic responses revealing the
regime stability will be examined in chapter 6.

Disorder here called for a mobilization of resources from youths, the police, and
other intervening actors, who acted as they routinely did in previous and repetitive
clashes in the 1980s and the 1990s. But the duration and contagion of the events
and their timing (the pre-electoral context) allowed the media and local space to
introduce shifts within a routine order.

## The media

'Currently, everyone knows that an event publicly exists only after it is created
as such by the media' (Mauger, 2006: 46). The media reflected isolated incidents,
sending virtual invitations to join groups in action, broadcasting their repertoires,
rewarding negative heroes, and making sense out of their acts, but after a while
denouncing them for their excess. The media were assemblers of dispersed actions.
For philosopher Balibar, the broadcast repetitive images, the continuous use of the
same rhetoric were not without consequences in such an indeterminate and fragmented context, producing something, like a 'passive organization of revolt', with
the characteristics of a movement 'à distance' (Balibar, 2006: 95).

## Space

Space in neighbourhoods is frequently a source of contention between various
youths, residents, and the police. The role that residents hold and their experience
of social relations in space are constantly redefined and readjusted, according to the
positions that they hold. Public space is where youths, fleeing from overcrowded
apartments, spend most of their time – where they organize their traffics, appro-
priating 'turf' as their own. This is where youths draw their practices, identities,
and alliances (personal interviews of youths, currently students in 2006–14). Conversely, space is also where the police assert their dominance, where they distribute

status, where they fight the privatization of space by youths at the request of other residents and, in the case of disturbances, where they contain the rioters following authorities' orders.

In 2005, action took place within or near large social housing estates that are bounties for collective action. During those events, the spatial and the social interacted. Hundreds of different local and even parochial events happened, with each location unveiling its specific sets of causes and forms of collective violence. Disruptive actions seemed to be articulated with a real sense of opportunity and with a quest for public resources through collective violence (Jobard, 2014: 144).

Place matters, and in the areas which remained quiet, limited social control was exerted by local institutions, families, and community organizations. There, mediators like social educators, older brothers, or parents intervened and negotiated with youths in order to limit vandalism (personal interviews with public housing managers and educators by the author, 2006).

To a certain extent, the 2005 disorders in France were not like any other (Body-Gendrot, 2016). To Bertho (2014), they appeared as a healthy signal of *post*-political empowerment. Those youths acted as the 'primitive rebels' that Hobsbawn (1959) studied in the nineteenth century. For Lapeyronnie (2006: 435), a riot 'is a primitive political movement, devoid of ideology and rules, because the rioters are situated outside the system. They oppose their "we" to institutions that they reject and by which they feel disrespected'. In 2005, the 'rioters' did not compromise with conventional politics, but in disrupting order, their violent protest (against the death of the two boys, the daily harassment from the police, the 'gassing' of the mosque, the lack of equal treatment and disrespect, among other grievances) resonated with youth cultures.

## Greater London in 2011

### The context

In London, as in Paris, the trigger of the public disorder in 2011 was the fatal shooting by the police of a resident from a deprived, tension-filled neighbourhood, Tottenham, in North London. The most common feature among these incidents is the centrality of rioters' anger with the police (Newburn, 2016b). In London, several dimensions explain the contagion of the four-night disorder, involving 13,000 to 15,000 people, and the wide coverage across social networks and the media.

This analysis is based on discussions with British scholars and police officers, commission reports, and relevant literature.

### The facts

When travelling as a passenger in a Toyota, West Indian Mark Duggan was stopped late in the afternoon August 4, 2011 by an officer from the Metropolitan Police's Operation Trident and some of the specialized firearms unit. One of the officers fired two shots, killing the suspect (HAC, 2011; Metropolitan Police Service [MPS], 2012; Riots, Communities and Victims Panel, 2012). The family and 120 people from Broadwater Farm in Tottenham, a poor neighbourhood, marched peacefully on the local police station to protest Duggan's death, but their request to meet with a senior police officer was not met. This rebuke was followed by outbreaks fuelled by rumours and by unsubstantiated claims from the Independent Police Complaints Commission (IPCC, 2012). 'Tempers were further inflamed by both the very poor communication between the Metropolitan Police Service in London and Mark Duggan's family, and by the subsequent mishandling of the Saturday evening protest', Newburn remarked (2016b). No senior police officer handled the protest at the police station, and a young protester was not apparently treated properly. Two police vehicles were then set on fire, and rapidly the disorder reached other areas such as Shepherd's Bush (West London) and Enfield, Islington, Brixton (South London), and Croydon. Four hundred criminal offences were recorded, over 200 were arrested, and eventually 3,500 police officers were deployed (MPS, 2012).

On the first night, youths resorted to their usual repertoire: police cars were burnt, stores looted, and several buildings set on fire. On the following night, two officers were hit by a speeding car, and the rampage continued. The outbreaks reached Hackney, various other London neighbourhoods, and extended to Birmingham, Manchester, Salford, and Liverpool. Because the disorder kicked off in a different way on the third day (spreading to other parts of the country as well as across London), the police were able to 'protect' some locations in London (Oxford Street, Westfield shopping centres, for example). However, local high streets felt the full brunt of the disorder (e.g. Clapham Junction, Croydon, Ealing, Hackney). On the fourth night, about 700 people were arrested in London and 100 in the centre of Manchester. Three Pakistanis in Birmingham were run over and killed trying to defend their stores. Five people died during the unrest. In total, more than 5,000 crimes were committed: 1,860 incidents of arson and damage, 1,649 burglaries, 141 incidents of disorder, and 366 incidents of violence against a person (Riots, Communities and Victims Pannel, 2011: 11, 24). Over 4,000 were arrested (Ministry of Justice, 2012). Damages estimates exceeded £200 million and the cost of policing to £90 million. Independent communities and victims' panels pressured the state to deliver exceptional emergency funds to compensate the losses experienced by uninsured stores and homeowners.

### Mass mobilization potential

On the whole, 15,000 were estimated to have taken part in the disorders. The crowds involved were made of 'watchers, rioters, looters, bystanders, protesters, retaliators, thrill-seekers, opportunists and sellers. It was also pointed out that there was some movement between these categories – for example, a person who turned up simply to watch might opportunistically become a looter' (Morrel et al., 2011: para 3). Violent aggressors, allegedly 10 percent of them gang members, made use of the disruption and coordinated violence for personal benefits. Moving rapidly from one place to another, as a consequence of new technologies, they orchestrated looting with efficiency, intending to resell their stolen goods for a profit. Social media was used to warn youths to move away from areas that were well-protected by the police and go to others which were unguarded. Such efficiency and the loss of control of the street by the police, escalating the scale of the looting, distinguish this disorder from previous ones. 'Though it is important not to exaggerate the role of looting in the 2011 riots, it is undeniable that it was a very significant feature of what occurred' (Newburn, 2016b). What the participants had in common, it seems, was an unfocused hostility, a detachment from their communities that allowed them to act spontaneously, with hardly any guilt (also possibly boosted by the use of alcohol).

## Structures of opportunity

In a global city like London, the public disorder in 2011 caught the world's attention, especially on the eve of the Olympic Games with its extensive financial implications. Urban violence was vehemently denounced by the authorities. The situation offered an opportunity for political opposition and for the media to condemn the ruling classes' excesses, their greed, and their moral decay, after a phone-hacking scandal. A binary vision rejecting irresponsible youths, caught by the frenzy of consumption, and those behaving in the public interest of the country prevailed. This may explain why both Prime Ministers Thatcher after the incidents of Brixton in 1981 and Cameron in 2011 did not want to hear any sociological explanation regarding the linkages between inequalities, marginalization, and delinquent behaviours, but only the support for repression, better formulated by previous Prime Minister Tony Blair's sound bite, 'tough on crime, tough on the causes of crime'.

## Ferguson, Missouri (2014), and Baltimore, Maryland (2015)

### Ferguson

Race riots in the United States have an explosive, destructive, and amorphous character, which makes them different from those experienced in Europe, ruling out a useful comparison. However, the events that took place in Ferguson, Missouri, indicate that American cities or at least their suburbs may burn, after all, after two decades of relative acquiescence (Katz, 2012). They mark a new type of disorder involving the use of global connections to organize the mobilizations and also to sustain a worldwide interest.

Why did this city of 21,000, north of St Louis, experience ten nights of unrest over the fatal shooting by white police officer Darren Wilson in August 2014 of an eighteen-year-old African American, Michael Brown? Why did it receive so much attention in the United States and abroad, sparking public disturbances followed by a large debate on the deadly use of force by the police against racial minorities?

The official data registered by the FBI estimate that 409 civilians in the United States were killed by the police in 2012,[2] indicating that American police kill more than one person a day. In Ferguson, over the course of two weeks, US police killed twice as many people as police in Japan, a nation of 127 million, killed in the last six years (*The Economist*, Aug. 23, 2014). The president of the National Association for the Advancement of Colored People (NAACP), Cornell Brooks, denounced the likelihood of a young black male being twenty-one more times at risk of being killed by a policeman than a white male between fifteen and nineteen years old in 2010–12. 'When we know', he said, 'that one Black out of three went to jail and that each month, a Black says he or she was mistreated by the police, it indicates that we have a enormous problem with the police' (*Libération*, Nov. 27, 2014).

### The context

As in most cities of the Rust Belt, St Louis is plagued by entrenched poverty. Jobs and the white middle class have left the centre for affluent suburbs of a county fragmented in ninety municipalities. As recently as 1980, Ferguson was a largely white suburban enclave and 85 percent white. In the last thirty years, many poor black households moved north, to better suburban neighbourhoods in the St Louis County. According to the 2010 census, Ferguson's black population reached 67 percent, and the city's unemployment rose. Currently, 25 percent of Ferguson residents live below the poverty threshold ($23, 500 for a family of four) (Kneebone, 2014), especially in the public housing estates in the west part of the locality. The quality of the city's services (education, health, police) does not meet the residents' expectations.

The recent arrival of blacks in Ferguson has not allowed them to create powerful defence organizations or to become part of the power structure. White majorities have resisted such attempts, as they were able to get elected without the black vote. For Hazel Erby, the only black member of the seven-member county council, voting is critical. The city manager of Ferguson and the city council appoint the chief of police. For her, the arrogance of elected whites, such as that of the county prosecutor, Robert McCulloch, creates a sense of '"empowerment" among the police that may have contributed to the tragic events of August 9' (Pinckney, 2015: 6). The lack of residents' participation in the electoral process is indeed critical. In the municipal election before the incidents, only 6 percent of blacks voted. The turnout for whites was 17 percent (Smith, 2014). The tensions between poor racial minorities and the city's authorities comes partly from blacks' exclusion from economic and political arrangements.

The Department of Justice opened a civil rights investigation into the incidents, motivated by the protests and the disorder of August and November 2014. After six months of investigation, the federal report on the Ferguson Police Department, published on March 4, 2015, pointed at a highly toxic environment defined by distrust and resentment, maintained by years of animosity and fuelled by illegal and erroneous practices transforming the city into a tinderbox (US Dept of Justice Civil Rights Branch, 2015). Intentional discrimination was fed by biases and racial stereotypes. Policemen exerted force only against blacks and resorted to stops without reasonable suspicions and to arrests without likely cause, violating the Fourth Amendment (due process), the First Amendment (free speech), and the Fourteenth (civil rights). In 2011, police officers deployed a canine to bite an unarmed fourteen-year-old black boy waiting for his friends in an abandoned house. The dog bit him, causing him to fall to the floor. Police officers struck him while he was on the ground, one of them putting a boot on the side of his head. The boy recalled the officers laughing about the incident afterward (according to the US Dept of Justice Civil Rights Branch, 2015: 31–32).

The racial prejudice was so strongly ingrained that officials circulated racist jokes on the internet, the report pointed out. Blacks are pulled over, cited, and arrested in numbers far exceeding their population share. If they cannot pay their fine, they are sent to jail. In 2013, in Ferguson, 86 percent of stops, 92 percent of searches, 93 percent of arrests, and 100 percent of incidents with police dog bites involved black people – although police officers were far less likely to find contraband on black drivers (22 percent versus 34 percent whites) (US Dept of Justice Civil Rights Branch, 2015: 33). When in jail, the offender may lose his or her employment. No wonder then that, when police use violence against stigmatized minorities, especially when police kill minority youths with impunity, it sends a message to a community that their lives are not valued and the state does not represent them.

Another striking feature cited in the federal investigation report on the Ferguson police force comes from the municipality's revenue 'disproportionately' generated from traffic citations (DWB, driving while black) and other petty offences. Officer evaluations and promotions depended to an inordinate degree on 'productivity', meaning the number of citations issued. Black residents were seen as a source of revenue. Offenders were fined between $100 and $200. The police were no longer a public service but a cash machine for the city via the city court. Fines contributed 23 percent of the city revenue (from 10 percent in 2010). A woman who parked illegally received two citations and a $151 fine, plus fees. As she could not come to court when summoned, she was incarcerated for six days and, in the end, had to pay the court $550.

There were 490,000 outstanding arrest warrants in St Louis county, ten times more than in Dade County that includes Chicago (*The Economist*, Aug. 8, 2015: 31). However, Brendan Roediger, from the Saint Louis University School of Law and one of the groups of civil rights lawyers suing Ferguson, conceded that other cities in the county are even more prone to engage in such practices.

## The facts

On August 9, 2014, police officer Darren Wilson stopped black teenager Michael Brown and his friend for jaywalking in the neighbourhood of Canfield Green.

A confrontation followed, ending with the officer shooting twelve rounds, hitting Brown six times in the chest and forehead, after he had discovered that two young blacks were suspected of stealing cigarillos in a local market of West Ferguson and that Brown held cigarillos in his hand. Rumours circulated that Brown was shot in the back, or that he had said, 'Hands up, don't shoot'. Wilson said that he acted in self-defence and that Brown acted as a 'demon', grunting like an animal as he tried to grab the officer's gun. But 'it is hard to point to anything that the Ferguson police did that was not wrong', Gene O'Donnell at John Jay College of Criminal Justice observed. 'They left Mr Brown's body on the street for four hours. They withheld the name of the officer who shot him. According to a *Huffington Post-YouGov* poll carried out in the third week of November, 62 percent of African Americans believed Officer Wilson was at fault, but only 22 percent of whites took that position (Wines, 2014). The next day, protests began as well as public disorder, with businesses vandalized and a Quick Trip store arsoned. On August 11, schools were closed and police used tear gas on protesters. The following day, Reverend Al Sharpton, the head of the National Action Network, a defence organization for blacks, and other civic leaders met with political leaders in St Louis, before reaching Ferguson, where large protest movements moved through Ferguson and vigils were organized in local churches. The same day, President Obama offered his condolences to the family and the community. But soon after, the police, while not divulging the name of the officer who had shot Brown, released a video of the robbery of the cigarillos. The family condemned this release, calling it 'character assassination' following the 'execution-style murder' of their son (Veg et al., 2014). Preliminary autopsy results were released. During a week after the incident, protests spread, vigils were held near the apartment complexes on Canfield Green where Michael Brown died, stores were looted, windows broken, cars vandalized, and streets were blocked by the police, preventing residents from going home or going to work. On August 14, the Order Maintenance Highway Patrol was assigned to take charge in Ferguson, replacing the local police chief.

Rallies continued to take place in churches and protests on the streets. Molotov cocktails and tear gas were exchanged on both sides, police and protesters. On August 16, Governor Nixon declared a state of emergency, called the National Guard, and enacted night curfews. The next day, a petition signed by 20,000 people required the appointment of a special prosecutor to investigate the circumstances of Michael Brown's death. Schools closed for a week due to continuing disorder. A private autopsy revealed that Michael Brown had been shot six times, with the shot in the head proving fatal, but he was not shot in the back. Protesters blocked the roads and tried to overrun the police command centre. The National Guard was brought in, thirty-one arrests were made, two policemen were injured, two fires were ignited. As the funeral of Michael Brown was announced, the Republican governor, Jay Nixon, refused to replace the local prosecutor.

A county grand jury consisting of three black and nine white men started to hear evidence in the case *State of Missouri v. Darren Wilson* to elucidate whether the police officer had acted wrongly.[3] Attorney General Eric Holder arrived in

Ferguson on August 20, the day of Brown's funeral, to meet the family and community leaders. As the attorney general appointed by President Obama, he had launched federal investigations regarding violations of civil rights in twenty local police agencies. Clergy members in Ferguson had already started to alleviate the tensions by organizing meetings and prayers with the residents, calling for peaceful action and better organization. On August 21, the National Guard began withdrawing and West Florissant Avenue was reopened.

At the end of August, the police command post was closed. Governor Nixon rescinded the executive order declaring a state of emergency, and in October, the St Louis County Police were officially put in charge of handling street protests.

On November 23, numerous militants, including out-of-towners, moved to Ferguson in anticipation of the grand jury verdict. The next day, in a night press conference, the verdict of the grand jury not to indict Wilson was announced by local prosecutor McCulloch. He was later accused of manipulation and of not having been impartial, favouring the police's version. A petition with 70,000 signatures called for his recusation in this trial, but it did not go through.

Public disorder broke out after the verdict was given to the crowd; gunfire and glass breaking were heard, buildings burned, while heavily armed police forces resorted to techniques of incapacitation. Across the country, protests erupted in 170 cities, due to the global media coverage given the verdict and the amount of resentment felt by blacks concerning their treatment by the police. As Martin Luther King Jr. once remarked, 'riots are the voices of the unheard'. A poll from the *Washington Post* published on December 30, 2014, indicated that a majority of blacks did not believe they received the same treatment as whites from the criminal justice system. Six whites out of ten believed the opposite, all the more so among Republican white Americans.

On November 29, Officer Wilson resigned from the police force with no intention of remaining a police officer. In the months that followed, local protests continued in Ferguson. Then in March 2015, two police officers were shot and wounded by activists' bullets. A man was later arrested, pleading not guilty. After the two civil rights investigation reports were published by the Department of Justice, the police chief, the city manager, and the municipal judge resigned. The Ferguson events contributed to a national protest movement throughout the country.

Months after the incidents, the recovery in Ferguson has been uneven. The municipal elections slightly increased minority representation in the city council from one to three blacks out of seven members; the new interim city manager and the new municipal judge are black, but the white mayor has not resigned. 'Elections are thermometers, but social movements are thermostats', Martin Luther King Jr. remarked (Pinckney, 2015: 6); this means that the pressure must be kept in between the elections, especially after each fatal shooting by the police. On the streets of West Fergusson, near the apartment complexes on Canfield Green where Michael Brown died, a journalist reported that people felt just as estranged from the police as they did a year before, just as sceptical of the city's leaders, black or white.

Disenfranchised and dispossessed residents would not vote, expecting no result. Damage remained, as seen in the wealthier part of South Florissant, where businesses had been looted and vandalized. On the poorer West Florissant Avenue where the damage was worse, with some businesses burned to the ground, stores closed permanently. 'Some of the complexes have lost occupants, their residents fleeing to get away from the discord' (Smith, 2014). But a few others have opened, including Starbucks and a new community centre. The police force has only five black officers, including the interim police chief, Andre Anderson. Officers now wear body cameras, but not when protests and possible disorder are anticipated, as during the Ferguson Uprising Commemoration weekend on August 8–9, 2015. Crowds of insiders and outsiders gathered for a series of commemorations. But on Sunday evening, with still one hundred people on the streets, two groups shot at each other while looting was going on. A state of emergency was issued on August 10, 2015. An eighteen-year-old shot at police and was severely wounded in return.

## Mass mobilization potential

### A historical legacy

Collective violence triggered by police abuse has a long history in America. However, the sites and the timings for mobilizations are selective, and not any fatal police shooting gives way to protests and public disorder.

The most memorable time occurred during the 1960s when cities were aflame with burning buildings and demonstrators took to the streets. The civil strife began with 4 major upheavals in 1965, 21 in 1966, 83 in 1967, and more than 100 in 1968. During those years, collective violence brought about the deaths of 250 people. It left 12,000 injured, and approximately 83,000 people were arrested US Riot Commission, 1968.

In the 1990s, two major episodes of civil strife came to the forefront. Large scale disorder erupted in Los Angeles during 1992, and angry protests were seen again in 1999, after an African immigrant, Amadou Diallo, was shot by the New York street crime police in the Bronx. Those two incidents had a significant impact in the United States and abroad. The urban context contributed to mobilize the demonstrators, but both collective protests had the same trigger: acquittals of police officers charged with abuse of force by popular juries. In Los Angeles, the outrage came from the neglect shown by the jury members relative to the video that recorded Rodney King's beating. At last, minorities had proof of institutional racism and expected justice to redress the harm they felt. In New York, the repeated offences committed by the police department (the Louima case) and by the street crime unit in particular caused outrage. The police unit had mistaken street peddler Amadou Diallo for a criminal and the purse he took out to prove his ID for a gun. In both cases, the outrage came from an abuse of force and authority from policemen acting as 'Rambos' in a continuous context of violation of civil rights and brutality towards racial minorities, from the lack of supervision over rank-and-file policemen with no proper training, and from their acquittal. From then on, residents engaged in acts which tested authority (rock throwing, halting traffic). Those engaging in acts of defiance did not flee; they remained in the minority areas and exerted control over them. Then the attacks widened and became more lethal. The Los Angeles disorder left 58 dead (mostly among black participants) and led to 5,500 arrests and over $1 billion of damages in that city. Protests remained contained in New York City. Why is that so?

Both New York and Los Angeles are cities where the very rich live next to the very poor. Once the agreement on norms making living together possible is violated, such cities become tinderboxes. If unfairness characterizes the treatment delivered by institutions, why should people obey the law (Tyler, 1990)? Why would not they dissent, take to the streets, chanting 'No justice, no peace'? In his book *Injustice*, Barrington Moore (1978) asks, 'Why don't men revolt more often?' A number of factors explain the differences in the responses from Los Angeles and New York to the police officers' acquittals (Body-Gendrot, 2001). One of them has to do with the different styles of order maintenance, as will be seen in chapter 5.

## A new type of public disorder

Did global media and social networks contribute to make Ferguson an iconic leitmotiv of racist patterns displayed by some local police agencies in the United States? How new are the Ferguson incidents? Do they illustrate a new type of racial civil disorder?

As documented by Janowitz (1979: 263–65), the transformation of the patterns of collective racial violence in urban areas in the twentieth century fell into three different phases. First, the *communal racial riots* of 1910–50 were an ecologically based struggle at the boundaries of expanding black neighbourhoods. Black residents, overcrowded in constrained territories, expressed their outrage at a colour line segregating black neighbourhoods from white neighbourhoods in Northeast cities. But the public disorder was then caused by white majorities. For instance, the Chicago riot of 1919 was preceded by two years of bombings launched by small groups of whites encouraged by bystanders and rumours, targeting dwellings where African Americans were to live or actually lived. Deaths and injuries resulted from such racial confrontations: 'Frequently, the police were deficient in their duties and occasionally assisted white rioters' (Janowitz, 1979: 265).

Second, during the Second World War, *commodity riots* within black communities represented a form of collective behaviour against the agents and symbols of mainstream society. They reached a high point during the period of 1964–67. Blacks denounced absent ownership of property and retail establishments from which they were forbidden entry. Demonstrations were accompanied by looting. 'Deaths and casualties resulted primarily from the use of force against the black population by police and National Guard units', Janowitz (1979: 268) points out. Due to their decentralization, the capacity of local enforcement agencies varied greatly within those two phases. Capacity gradually improved during the first phase, but was frequently weak and irresponsible during the second one.

Then, a third period came into being at the end of the 1960s, an *essentially political racial violence,* 'a more selective, terroristic use of force with political overtones, again mainly directed against whites, with small organized groups of blacks' (Janowitz, 1979: 262). Many black leaders found that, by burning their neighbourhoods, they did not reach their goals. Instead, they opted for intimidation in resorting to violence, using it as a means to participate in the decision-making process. Empowerment, a learning experience, could be earned only via strikes, protests, intimidation, conflicts, and confrontations, even temporary. Without a learning process for seizing power, there was no collective capacity for teaching people how to decide for the best of their interests after solving their conflicts.

At the end of the second phase and at the beginning of the third phase of collective racial violence as analyzed by Janowitz (1979), a new process of global communication and innovation could be detected on the part of some black urban leaders, close to Black Power. They learned how to use their communication skills, in the media in particular, to denounce institutional racism and unfairness and spread their grievances as Third World domestic victims in America and beyond the American borders. They had understood that the media could give them visibility, sensationalize disturbances, overplay violence, and grant a lot of importance to emotions. As in the European cases studied here,

> Television images served to spread the contagion pattern throughout urban areas and the nation. Large audiences saw the details of riots, the manner in which people participated in them and especially the ferment associated with looting and obtaining commodities which was so much at the heart of riot behavior. Television presented detailed information about the tactics of participation and short-term gratification.
>
> *(Janowitz, 1979: 280)*

Demonstrators could see their actions on television, just as in 2005 in Paris, French youths saw themselves in the news via their cell phones and in 2011 London youths used Twitter or other social media.

Who were the protesters in Ferguson? They were a large number coming from various coalitions, but most of all they were 'young, black, queer, poor, working-class, "unchurched", or secular, and women' (Pinckney, 2015: 6). Some protesters were residents from Ferguson and the county; others were outsiders brought here by the social networks. All thought that what had happened was not right. Most young blacks were tired of being branded criminals at birth.

In Ferguson, in what appears as a fourth form of collective racial protest, thousands of demonstrators, supported by black national organization leaders such as Al Sharpton, Reverend Sekou (associated with the Fellowship of Reconciliation promoting a theology of resistance), or the former leader of the Rainbow Coalition, Jesse Jackson, urging calm, and by coalitions such as Don't Shoot, Black Lives

Matter, Organization for Black Struggle, and Tribe X grasped the opportunity that comes from the street. Groups were divided by goal and by geography. Peaceful protesters asked for justice, while radicalized groups denounced racial profiling, demanding the police's fatal shootings of frequently unarmed American blacks in numerous cities to stop. They chose the street as a political terrain or participated digitally, putting themselves on the line. A volunteer communications director observed:

> Numerous bystanders and activists streamed what they saw live from their smartphone. People around the world have been glued to live streams from Ferguson ever since the killing. . . . The glow of phones [is] everywhere. The revolution will not be televised, but it will be tweeted.
>
> *(Pinckney, 2015: 8)*

For their part, white local elites and the police expected the media to show what a lawless community black Ferguson was.

Public disorder in Ferguson displays a specific pattern. Blacks are a majority in this locality, where there is a strong mobilization potential due to frustrations and resentment against a notoriously abusive police and a neglectful white power apparatus. The structure of opportunity has been favourable to disenfranchised Blacks. President Obama denounced institutional discrimination. His successive black ministers of justice had been active in their fight against civil rights violations and made it known. Black leaders knew that they had some federal support and that the time was ripe to demand police reforms.

## Baltimore

### *The context*

Compared with the 26,000 residents of Ferguson, Baltimore is a dual segregated city of 621,000 inhabitants in the rich state of Maryland. The west part of the city is poor and deindustrialized; 88 percent of children in public schools come from welfare families and 88 percent of them are black (Le Bars, 2015). Baltimore is located in the northern region of the United States and its minority-majority population has a culture different from that of Southern Ferguson. In Baltimore, the African American community is represented in the institutions, with the mayor, Stephanie Rawling-Blake; the police chief, Anthony Batts; 4 percent of the police force; and the state of Maryland prosecutor, Marilyn Mosby, belonging to the black establishment.

Blacks have organized for decades, in part against a 'racist' police and in part against governmental neglect. Numerous experienced militants come from grassroots organizing. West Baltimore is plagued by problems of concentrated poverty, illiteracy, high unemployment, crime, and gangs, as portrayed in the television series *The Wire*. While by age twenty-two, 80 percent of the white residents of Baltimore have jobs, only 40 percent of blacks do (Le Bars, 2015). Out of 14,000 residents in this part of Baltimore, 450 are in penitentiaries, the highest rate in Baltimore. The homicide rate remains high, 34 per 100,000 in 2014, eight times higher than in New York (Shane, 2015). Tensions between marginalized youths and the police are continuous.

## The facts

On April 19, 2015, in Sandtown, a poor black neighbourhood in West Baltimore, Freddie Gray, a twenty-five-year-old black man, nicknamed 'Pepper', died following an arrest by six police officers near the Gilmore Homes public housing estates for possession of a switchblade. He came from a very poor background. His mother was illiterate, handicapped, and a former drug addict. She lived with her family on public subsidies allocated after it was proven that asbestos had poisoned Sandtown and that children concentrated seven times more lead in their blood than average. Freddie Gray was also a drug user and had spent time in jail for such addiction. The coroner's report determined that the police officers had caused a homicide: by not fastening a seat belt when Freddie Gray was in the police van and by tightening his legs, a usual police practice partly responsible for the brutal reputation carried by the Baltimore police, these policemen contributed to the severing of Gray's spinal cord. He was no longer breathing when he was taken out of the van and when policemen asked for medical help. The investigation also showed that Gray's knife was not a switchblade and that it was not unlawful in Maryland to carry a knife. Cell phone videos taken by bystanders showing him being dragged by police officers to their van rapidly circulated on the social network and regular media and were seen all over the world. The new technologies allowed a vast movement of protest against police violence to spread in West Baltimore and beyond. Baltimore residents were aware that 'the whole world was watching'. Spontaneous protests started, several including violent episodes.

As schools closed, it was observed, in the local press that 75–100 people who appeared to be high school students began throwing bricks and bottles at police near Mondawmin Mall, after police refused high school students access to their primary means of getting home. Violence spread, and later that day, two patrol cars were destroyed and fifteen officers were injured. One person was seriously harmed by arson.

Resorting to violent disorder was an opportunistic reaction for lack of other channels in the protesters' repertoire. Those actors were eager to be seen, to respond, and to express emotions. According to the national newspapers, as a consequence of six nights of disorder, at the call of social networks, violence, arson, and looting initiated by local young men disrupted the majority-black peaceful demonstrations. A total of 285 to 350 businesses, including a CVS pharmacy and stores in the Mondawmin Mall, were damaged or destroyed by fire, as well as a half-built senior housing project. Twenty-seven drugstores were looted and 144 cars were set on fire overnight, mostly in West Baltimore. At least 20 police officers were injured, and 250 people were arrested, according to the local news.

On April 24, a coalition of organizations including the American Civil Liberties Union, the NAACP, Leaders of a Beautiful Struggle, and other local organizations requested that Maryland Governor Larry Hogan act to address issues of police brutality.

Governor Hogan declared a state of emergency in the city limits of Baltimore and called the Maryland National Guard, about two thousand men and women, on the night of April 27, adding to the three thousand local police officers; the city was put under night curfew by the mayor. Maryland State Police activated five hundred officers for duty in Baltimore and requested an additional five thousand state police officers from other states.

Night curfews were lifted on May 6. The episode reminded old residents of the violent riots following the death of Martin Luther King Jr. in Baltimore in 1968. A flashpoint is enough to light a city on fire. In this case, the video of Freddie Gray being dragged to the police van and unable to walk did it.

### Mass mobilization potential

All the ingredients are found in Sandtown for disorder to turn violent. As mentioned previously, poverty and crime are high in this part of Baltimore, also a rich city. Residents are frustrated to see that not much is done to upgrade their neighbourhood. Drug addiction is widespread, and a tough policing approach leads to frequent and numerous arrests. 'Everybody knows that the Baltimore police are violent. That they are headed by an African American, that the mayor of the city is African American makes no difference. If not, tell me, how can one die in a police van?', a resident tells a reporter (*Le Monde*, Apr. 30, 2015: 2). Rumours circulated that gangs pushed school students to challenge the police. But church leaders; street mediators; as well as David Simon, the producer of the TV series *The Wire*; and stars from basketball and baseball also intervened to beg the youths to stay calm.

Similarities in the cases of Michael Brown in Ferguson and Freddie Gray in Baltimore explain why public disorder occurred after their deaths. When there are no alternative paths to pursue justice, riots are likely.

### The aftermath

The theme of police brutality had been articulated by black organizations like Black Lives Matter and ordinary citizens pursuing racial justice as a motivating cause for mobilization for a long time. Some of those organizations push specifically for the creation of national guidelines by the Justice Department for investigating officers when they use deadly force and for excluding local prosecutors who are too close to local police departments. Others require policemen to wear body cameras to avoid controversies. Via the media, angry younger militants from Black Lives Matter express their scepticism. As change is slow to happen and as more fatal shootings occurred after the Baltimore events, outrage led to demonstrations and civic disorder in a lot of American cities, covered by the media, nationally and internationally. In the first six months of 2015, according to an estimate from the *Washington Post*, American police officers had shot and killed 585 people, blacks representing 40 percent of those killed who were not armed (Paris, 2015). No feature of a racially divided society represents racial domination or instils the message of subjugation more forcefully than police. Therefore, riots are the last resort for those who find all other paths to justice blocked, Schneider observed (2014). One can add that the absence of a constructive conversation between the black population (including church leaders) and white decision makers in Ferguson or in West Baltimore also explains why federal levels of authority, including President Obama and the attorney general, had to intervene during the incidents, as will be seen in later chapters.

## The Occupy movements

The disorders emanating from the Occupy movements are of a different nature from those previously discussed, although, like them, they have taken place in specific public spaces acting as nodal points with symbolic significance. Participants have the 'privilege of presence'. Popular at first, they have lost the support of public opinion because disorder cannot last too long. Parents, educators, teachers, and religious and community leaders asserted that they understood the protesters' anger and frustration. After a while, however, they admitted that occupations disturbed residents' everyday life (blocking traffic and access to stores and banks, for instance, or accumulating litter in public space or attracting deviant and noisy individuals causing havoc) and more fundamentally, that they challenged order and common rules of social behaviour in a city. At first, such forms of protest drew massive acquiescence. Eighty percent of Spaniards in the summer of 2011 supported the indignants' protests in the public space (*The Economist*, Jul. 16, 2011: 32). A small booklet in France by Stephane Hessel (2010), titled *Time for Outrage*, became an instantaneous bestseller in numerous countries. The quest for justice is supported by a growing disenchantment for traditional representative democracy, and it explains why embryos of movements like Occupy are temporarily successful. Space occupation has been magnified by the differentiated use of the social media which gave it its global dimension. According to Gerbaudo (2012: 135), in the case of New York City, Facebook (1 billion global users, 42 percent of adults in the United States, in 2011) has been employed as a recruitment and training ground to

> facilitate the emotional condensation and common identification of a largely un-politicized middle-class youth. Twitter, in contrast, has been mainly used as a (rapid and concise) vehicle for 'live' internal coordination within the activist elite, besides its many largely 'external' uses, including as a means for citizen journalists to document police brutality.

The other cases are not as well documented regarding the use of the social media, but testimonies show that they were widely used in support of spatial occupation and against police brutality.

## Occupy Wall Street (OWS) (2011)

### The context

The 'Occupy movements' convey ambiguities. First, it is an abuse to call them 'movements' as the media do, because they were ephemeral. Referring to embryos of movement should be more accurate. They draw attention because a large number of discontented and dispossessed people gather in public spaces. Some of them, in creating disorder, force the public to pay attention, at least for a while.

### The facts

Officially, OWS began on September 17, 2011, and ended after a police evacuation in November. The idea of occupying Wall Street was launched a few months earlier, in Vancouver, by a magazine editor who suggested that her subscribers 'flood into lower Manhattan, set up tents, kitchens, peaceful barricades, and occupy Wall Street for a few months' (Greenberg, 2012; Schwartz, 2011). The role played by the social media was limited at first, and the start of the movement was chaotic. A call to protest on September 17 was launched from a hashtag, but only three hundred people turned up. Then dozens of individuals started to meet regularly in Tompkins Square Park in New York City, a park which had become famous in the 1990s after police fought a vigorous battle to reclaim the space from (to quote the police) 'squatters and anarchists' who had set up their living quarters there. The small group then moved to Zuccotti Park (renovated in 2006 and privately owned), two blocks away from Wall Street. It is called a park but it is actually a treeless concrete space that the sun does not reach due to the high buildings around it. Choosing a privately owned public space was a tactic. While the city can close its public parks at dusk, New York City zoning laws require the Zuccotti Park owner to keep it open night and day 'for passive recreation'. A sort of pattern then took place, and a decision-making body, the General Assembly, emerged in the public space in August. Vocal anarchists had a leading role in managing its set-up, according to Gerbaudo, a journalist and a participant to the OWS mobilization. Gerbaudo indicated it was not a spontaneous and leaderless gathering but a carefully orchestrated campaign by Adbusters and then by Anonymous, organizations remaining invisible and pulling the strings behind the stage, so that things could be properly done. They concentrated their efforts at first on communication and not on the organization of the event, which explains its relative chaos among the New York activists used to grassroots organizing.

> Social media only acquired importance during the phase of sustainment of the movement, being used to create a *sense of attraction* to the occupations,

and to invoke a sense of solidarity between 'physical occupiers' and 'internet occupiers', activists on the ground and people following the events from a distance.

(*Gerbaudo, 2012: 103*, emphasis original)

In the beginning, the organizers' attention was on Twitter, he says, ignoring Facebook. It was only in late September and early October, after two episodes of police repression and a threat of eviction, that Occupy started to attract attention on social media and eventually also in the mainstream media.

The face-to-face experience taking place in Zuccotti Park was unusual and attracted attention. The proposals made in the General Assembly were approved or rejected by the dozens of people present, through gestures and on the internet, day after day, in a revived form of participatory democracy. As early as September 22, 2011, the General Assembly adopted 'A Declaration of the Occupation': 'We write so that all people who feel wronged by the corporate forces of the world can know that we are your allies. . . . No true democracy is attainable when the process is determined by economic power' (Schwartz, 2011: 33).

The tactics developed by OWS activists were diverse. They led unpermitted marches, occupied illegally public and private squares, a bank, the subway system, and the Brooklyn Bridge, a high-traffic bridge. They attempted to close down Wall Street through mass direct action and sometimes took the police by surprise. At no point did they negotiate with the police.

On the morning of November 15, 2011, the mayor of New York, Michael Blomberg, justified the eviction of the camp at Zuccotti Park by the police for health and safety reasons. The absence of a symbolic public space to voice public grievances has been particularly apparent since 9/11, when the event was used by governing elites to restrict freedoms via various laws and restrictive measures. Law enforcers were given enlarged powers and created an asymmetry discouraging the expression of popular dissent (except for the Tea Party activists). In the case of Zuccotti Park, face-to-face interactions with bystanders were difficult, due to police barricades and presence. Participation in the occupation remained thus limited.

### Mass mobilization potential

Not until the movement made its spatial appearance, not until the protest camp attracted attention with the photos of activists sleeping in the park, did the 'We are the 99 percent' become an emotional rallying point and a cementing ethos. The succinct motto is associated with Vlad Teicheberg, a thirty-eight-year-old mathematician and former trader, who was part of the *Indignatos* movement in Madrid in the spring of 2011. He imported its lessons to New York City, and then launched an ongoing internet network to circulate the protest. (The site was also connected by Skype to Tahir Square in Cairo, also undergoing a public space occupation.) Yet, at first, the communication was cold and ineffectual, but after the occupation on September 17 and for a week, Gerbaudo remarks, the mention of Occupy on Twitter increased by 2,004 percent (Gerbaudo, 2012: 113, 116). In other words, events on the ground, space occupation, and police repression fed the Twitter interactions and support, and not the opposite. After the police pepper-sprayed three female partici-pants and were caught in the act, and after seven hundred marchers were stopped on October 1 on their way to the Brooklyn Bridge, these events reverberated on the social media. Gerbaudo points at both the poor communication skills of the police as well as at the activists' lack of competence for exploiting the emotional power of the social media.

What is striking, however, is how such disconnected occupiers, set in the small space of Zuccotti Park, managed to get the world connected for two months, and how their call against the 1 percent of the super-rich became heard by thousands and millions of people, in particular by those threatened to lose their jobs or homes. According to Sassen (2015), due to financial predation, 14 million American house-holds lost their homes after the 2008 mortgage crash; the better conditions of the economy did not benefit the middle classes, and salaries stagnated. This point will be evoked in the discussion that follows. Zuccotti was both a rallying space for activists and a mediated place, a source of identification for people following its activity through the social media. According to a poll published by the *New York Times* mid-October 2011,[4] 46 percent of Americans supported OWS (it allegedly had received $450,000 in donations).

The interest of such an embryo of a movement comes from its process – that is, its predilection for participatory democracy. 'The process is the message', someone wrote on a poster. An ongoing interaction went on between people differenti-ated by gender, race, age, and cultures, and mobilized by diverse motivations but focused on redistributive justice. People resented having to pay for the excesses of corporate greed which increased the governments' and citizens' debts and led eventually to large banks' insolvency (Greenberg, 2012). The occupiers of Zuccotti Park denounced having to undergo austere policies while the banking-industry regulations were not tightened; they demanded a ban on high-frequency trading and all the financial 'fraudsters' arrested (Schwartz, 2011: 32). Fear had turned into indignation.

## The aftermath

The elusive character of the mobilization partly explains its success. The huge mix of eclectic people gathered in one single space, night after night, demonstrates togetherness via face-to-face conversations and 'human microphones' (each one repeats sentence by sentence what the speaker says to the next person in one voice, a coded language of protest). Such process breaks individuals' solitude and isola-tion. The park allows all kinds of grievances to overlap and bridge into a consensus which builds community. However, as pointed out by Gerbaudo, it would be wrong to think that the mobilization was spontaneous. As many as twenty organizers man-aged the Twitter accounts. They were involved in the ground operations, in the General Assembly, and in the various commissions. They had access to the New

York Teachers' Union office space which was near Zuccotti Park, and they could centralize the coordination of actions, especially during police charges and after the occupiers had been evicted from the Park in November. While by then, there were 300,000 Twitter followers, these conversations were led and moderated by a handful of core organizers, 'otherwise it would be a mess', a social media expert observes (Gerbaudo, 2012: 129–32). The modes of expression of OWS and the responses it got in various parts of the world reveal its global character.

After its evacuation, which created public disorder at the initiative of the police imposing order, the movement disintegrated rapidly and no victory was achieved. But as remarked by Winlow et al. (2014: 168), if Occupy failed, following Beckett, it can be said that 'it failed better, in fact a good deal better . . . some genuine signs of progress can now be discerned'. I could add that it is not because there is no longer any occupation on Zuccotti Park that the movement does not linger in the imagination and emotions of thousands of occupiers on the ground and on the internet. OWS has become a landmark and a reference for future embryos of social movements.

## Gezi Park, Istanbul (2013)

### The context

Gezi Park is one of the few remaining green spaces on the European side of Istanbul. Under the mandate of the mayor, Kadir Topbas, the City of Istanbul visualized turning the nearby Taksim Square into a pedestrian zone and, within the park, building a replica of former Ottoman Military Barracks, destroyed in 1940, along with a shopping mall, luxury flats, and a mosque.

Hardly any consultation took place with the park users and residents before the urban transformation started. With the first signs of demolition looming, protests began in 2012. A petition was signed and an independent consulting board was summoned. It rejected the plan in January 2013 as 'not serving the public interest'. However, its decision was overturned on May 1, 2013, by a higher consulting board close to the national and local governing elites and business interests (Christie-Miller, 2013). A few dozen activists decided then to camp out in the park, in order to stop the bulldozers.

Environmental concerns were all the more exacerbated since, according to official data, as many as over two million seven hundred thousand trees had been cut north of Istanbul for the construction of an airport and its surrounding roads and for a third bridge on the Bosphorus River. The destruction of more trees in the park to build a commercial mall and luxury apartments was then just intolerable. Other concerns also motivated a diversity of participants to join the protest. They were angry about the opaque way in which decisions relating to the redevelopment of the park had been made – a process which critics described as characteristic of a government unwilling to respect civil liberties in public space, censoring the media, and more generally, supporting brutal police repression.

## The facts

In the specific political context of Turkey, the widespread public disorder which took place in Taksim Square at the heart of Istanbul in 2013 illustrates unconventional forms of protests around environmental issues. What started as a peaceful resistance to the decision of transforming a familiar park enjoyed by a large diversity of users into a redevelopment project turned into a nationwide confrontation between protesters and police forces, leading to wide-scale public disorder. As is frequently the case, the police, an essential actor in this dramaturgy, played a crucial role in the uprisings and the ensuing public disorder. The Gezi occupiers had started a conversation in 'a multiplicity of spaces such as social centres, graffiti walls, libraries, collective kitchens, music venues, conference venues, day care corners, bookfairs, barter tables, utopic streets and squares, and democratic forums, which provide room for experimentation, creativity, innovation and dissent' (Kaya, 2016, forthcoming) in the follow-up of other Occupy movements. Participants, old and newcomers, experienced direct democracy and interacted, respected, and influenced each other's views, whether they were atheists or religious practitioners, gays, Kemalists, Kurds, football fans from one team or another, elderly or young.

> What made Gezi Park Protests different from the other social movements was its capacity to reassemble the social, across ethnic, religious, class, cultural, and gendered identities on the basis of an ideology of change. Furthermore, Occupy Gezi movement was not televised, but tweeted, unlike the others.
>
> *(Kaya, 2016, forhtcoming)*

The global character of such contention came from the presence of onlookers communicating effectively what was going on to receptive audiences, via social media networks. As in Hong Kong, Ferguson, and other cases studied here, public outrage came both from participants and from the information broadcasted by media crews covering the local site of unrest. The extreme police repression of the public disorder created by sit-in protesters in the park fed a cycle of local and international protests. At the local level, the occupation of the park was highly visible in the city of Istanbul. On the internet, outrage at institutional unfairness, police excess, and brutality against what was perceived as a right to keep the park as it was for the public good was expressed on diverse channels and, even subsequently, by international decision-making bodies such as the United Nations, the European Union, and the Council of Europe, as well as national governments expressing their serious concerns. Atak and della Porta observed (2016), 'Even though the urban struggle against the renewal of Taksim Square and the demolition of the park next to it had been continuing for almost two years, unwarranted police violence became a flashpoint and backfired to a spectacular level'. The following account is based on Atak and della Porta's analysis, on diverse journalistic accounts and on conversations with Turkish scholars.

The observers for Amnesty International (2015) noted that on May 27, a coalition of non-governmental organizations (NGOs), professional bodies, and political groups hostile to the regeneration of the park gathered together, after the bulldozers arrived. A group of environmentalists staged a peaceful sit-in. On May 28, at dawn, the riot police fired tear-gas canisters on the occupiers, and two days later, they set their tents on fire. The crackdown was violent. The number of protesters then increased significantly. Footage on social media and news outlets showed the picture of a woman in red, her face pepper-sprayed by a policeman. The photos of water cannons used to disperse the protesters circulated around the world via international media coverage and the social media. Those pictures symbolized the brutal repression of Taksim Square's protests and its global character. It became an 'iconic leitmotiv' (Fisher, 2013). About one hundred protesters were injured in the initial clash with the police and two journalists had to be hospitalized. In the panic, concrete banisters in the park had collapsed.

Activists circulated online calls for support against police repression and the number of protesters increased. Due to social media and regular media coverage, on June 1, mobilizations spread to Ankara, Izmir, Eskisehir, and other cities in Turkey. Ten thousand people gathered in a major avenue of Istanbul (Istiklal Avenue), converging from the Asian and European sides of the city. Dozens of participants were arrested. On June 1, one protester was hit in the head by a tear canister fired by a policeman in Antakya. The following days, clashes continued as the police wanted to enter Gezi Park and were resisted by the occupiers. Police were reported to have attacked makeshift clinics in Ankara and Izmir. Interior Minister Muammer Güler said that in the first 6 days of the protest, 1,730 people were detained in 67 provinces, where 235 protests were held. Then, a protester shot in the head died. Dozens of people who had posted messages on Twitter were detained. The Turkish Medical Association reported that 4,355 people had been injured across 12 cities with a majority in large cities. On June 7, several officials brought their support to the participants. The president of Turkey asked the police for moderation and defended the right to protest. Yet Prime Minister Erdogan's rhetoric was to criminalize the demonstrators: 'they go hand-in-hand with terrorists and extremists', he said in a speech. Appealing to the religious conservatives, he also labelled them as 'drunkards' and 'alcoholics' (Oncü, 2014). He admitted that there might have been cases of excessive use of force by police.

On June 11, the peaceful occupation of the park involving diverse women from multiple generations was interrupted by the police using tear gas, plastic bullets, and water cannons. The governor justified the intervention on the grounds that banners of terrorist organizations had been placed on the statue in the centre of Taksim Square. Forty-five lawyers were detained for protesting the detention of their colleagues attempting to denounce police violence in Gezi Park at the Çaglayan Courthouse in Istanbul. Three days later, another protester shot in the head by a police officer with a live bullet during protests died in Ankara.

On June 15, many casualties resulted from a violent clearing of the park by the riot police and gendarmerie using tear gas, water cannons, and plastic bullets. The lobby of the nearby Divan Hotel, used as a makeshift clinic, was also attacked with water cannons and tear gas. According to media reports, 150,000 tear-gas cartridges were shot and 3,000 tonnes of water were thrown on participants by police cannons during those three weeks. A total of 7,478 people were injured across 12 cities, with a majority of them in Istanbul, Ankara, and Izmir. Amnesty International reported having received credible reports of demonstrators severely beaten and given a tough treatment when in official or unofficial police custody. Approximately 4,900 people were detained during various periods of time.

By the end of June 2013, the Turkish Medical Association (2013) had compiled data from 11,155 responses to an (online) questionnaire about the physical effects of anti-riot chemicals and less-lethal weapons used by the police during those disorders. A total of 8,038 people sustained injuries in 13 cities.

> 30 percent of those who were affected by tear gas were exposed to it within less than one metre distance, and 38 percent within one-to-five metre distance. In other words, 68 percent of the respondents were in physical contact with tear gas within a five-metre diameter. Moreover, 33 percent of the respondents were exposed to tear gas for more than five minutes when they were physically closest to it.
>
> *(Turkish Medical Association, 2013)*

On the whole, the zero tolerance police approach to public disorder in Turkey was the cause of eleven fatalities and over eight thousand casualties, according to the same source.

On June 22, the plans for the redevelopment of Gezi Park were suspended. Investigations for police brutality were launched by internal control bodies within the institution. Governor Hüseyin Avni Mutlu officially reopened the park on July 8, but for fear of occupation, riot police units remained stationed in close proximity to the park during the summer and autumn of that year. These officers used tear gas and water cannons several times to prevent any form of participation. Eighty-one journalists were forced out of their jobs as a result of their coverage of the Gezi Park protests, according to the Union of Turkish journalists.

## Mass mobilization potential

The Ministry of the Interior estimated that about 2.5 million people participated in the rallies, forums, and quiet protests subsequent to the May events of 2013 in seventy-nine of Turkey's eighty-one provinces. *The Atlantic* reported on June 2, 'The young and the old, the secular and the religious, the soccer hooligans and the blind, the anarchists and the communists, the nationalists, the Kurds, the gays, the feminists and the students' were involved in the protests. Half were estimated to be less than thirty years old and 70 percent had no political affiliation. When asked in a Bilgi University survey what their motivations were for participation, 92 percent replied that they protested against an authoritarian regime, 91 percent against police abuse of force and the violation of democratic rights, and 84 percent against the silence and lack of support of the media. The Occupy Gezi movement was also partly a social upheaval against the subtle Islamization of Turkish society and politics, according to participants (Kaya, 2016, forthcoming).

On June 4 and 5, a strike was launched by the trade unions in support of the protesters. According to the Human Rights Foundation estimates, on June 5 and 13, mass demonstrations gathered several thousand people again around the country. A silent protest and passive resistance were symbolized by a standing man who would not move for hours on June 17. (The author of this initiative, Erdem Gündüz, later received a prize for his creative dissent.) At least sixteen solitary protesters in Taksim Square were detained for eight hours.

Did public social disorder accompanying the protests justify such repression? According to one online source, petrol bombs were thrown at some police vehicles, vandalism was exerted on 200 private cars, 280 buildings, and buses across the country, but these data were not officially confirmed. Some looting was also reported.

### The aftermath

The social media and grassroots organizations were active in calling for protest support and in the reporting of the chain of events. They activated global protests all over the world. The global character of Taksim Square/Gezi Park events is supported by numerous examples. For instance, the $54,000 ad published on June 7 in the *New York Times* had been paid by over 2,600 subscribers in the United States and abroad. But then retaliation was exerted on some of them who lost their jobs (personal interview of a victim by the author, May 2016). A letter signed by artists and scholars was published in the *Times* in Britain in July 24, condemning the heavy crackdown on the Gezi Park protesters. In the two cases, Prime Minister Erdogan threatened to sue the papers. For foreign observers, the repressive approach of the Turkish power was perceived as the regime's sign of weakness. From a democratic point of view, it looked as such. But actually, just as the president of China was facing disorder in Hong Kong, Prime Minister Erdogan consolidated his powers subsequently and was reelected.

## Hong Kong (2014)

### The context

In 1997, according to an agreement negotiated with Britain before the return of Hong Kong to China, the Hong Kong Basic Law granted this autonomous territory of 7.2 million residents democratic institutions for fifty years.

After arduous discussions, Article 45 of the Joint Declaration stipulated that

> the chief executive of the Hong Kong Special Administrative Region shall be selected by election or through consultations held locally and be appointed

by the Central People's Government. . . . The method for selecting the chief executive shall be specified in the light of the actual situation in the Hong Kong Special Administrative Region and in accordance with the principle of gradual and orderly progress. The ultimate aim is that the chief executive be elected via universal suffrage, after candidates are agreed upon by a fully representative nominating committee, in agreement with democratic procedures.

*(Hong Kong basic law, chapter IV)*

This formulation was confirmed in December 2007, after the National People's Congress Law Committee of the Popular Republic of China officially ruled on the issue. Under the slogan, 'one country, two systems', the rule of law was seen as a fundamental pillar of Hong Kong's autonomy.

Would China adopt principles inherited from 152 years of British domination respecting the rule of law, independent courts, free press, equitable law enforcement, and civil freedoms? Several attempts were made by China to exert domination, but each time Hong Kong citizens showed their capacity of resistance.[5] Activists explained that they had been boosted by globalization and strongly influenced by protesters from Korea who they met during an anti–World Trade Organization (WTO) protest in 2005. Then in 2012, a pro-communist moral and political programme to be taught in Hong Kong public schools was vetoed again by Legco, after the Scholarism movement, founded by fifteen-year-old Joshua Wong via the internet, initiated opposition.

The first consultations to implement electoral reforms in view of the 2017 chief executive election started in 2013 and early 2014. A new organization, Occupy Central with Love and Peace, was launched by two academics from Hong Kong universities, Dr Benny Tai Yiu-ting and Chan Kin-man, and by Reverend Chu Yiu-ming to exert pro-democratic pressures on the electoral process. It organized three deliberative sessions as well as a referendum on the voting system. It then submitted its alternative proposal which was rejected by the Beijing power apparatus. Meanwhile, Chief Executive Leung sent a report to the Standing Committee asking whether an amendment was due to adjust the selection process.

## The facts

On August 31, 2014, the tenth session of the National People's Congress – the standing committee of the Popular Republic of China – decreed new rules for the election of the Hong Kong chief executive in 2017. A nominating committee, similar to the pro-Beijing 1,200 member current election committee, would screen out candidates. Only two or three of them would run for the election, after receiving the support of more than half of the nominating committee. After the popular election, the chief executive would have to be appointed by the Central People's Government. This process denied Hong Kong voters a right to genuinely choose their own candidate.

Beijing's August 31 decision generated a public response in Hong Kong, but the form it took was unexpected. On the night that this electoral reform was announced, hundreds of people gathered near the government's offices to protest and express their discontent at what they perceived as a betrayal of democratic principles. Unlike in New York, London, or Paris, there is no public space to be occupied in Hong Kong, and protest occupations have to take place on the streets. Occupy Central with Love and Peace (OCLP) announced that it would organize civil disobedience protests. University and high school students called by the Hong Kong Federation of Students and by Scholarism decided to boycott their classes and get involved in public rallies and sit-ins. A demonstration was organized outside the Central Government's offices by this latter group, eager to 'reclaim' a former place of assembly nearby. This square had indeed been 'confiscated' by law enforcers, with public entry barred since July 2014. On September 26, the convenor of Scholarism, Joshua Wong, after climbing over the fences, was arrested and held for forty hours by the police. Some seventy-eight protesters were arrested and detained as well. Occupy Central supported the demonstrators and immediately started the civil disobedience campaign and rally near the government offices. Protesters organized a blockade of three separate commercial downtown areas in Mongkok and Canton Road in the Kowloon area and across the bay, on Connaught road and Causeway Bay on Hong Kong island. The authorities were taken by surprise.

On September 28, as in other cases studied here, the local police overreacted to the students' three-day sit-in; they used tear gas, pepper spray, and batons, causing widespread anger among peaceful protesters. The televised police crackdown, seen by a wide audience on a Sunday, created a surge of public support by ordinary people for the core protester groups who were also connected via the social media. One hundred thousand 'firechat apps' were downloaded, allowing viewers to avoid China's censorship of the regular social media. The city's bar association condemned 'repeated, systematic, indiscriminate and excessive' use of tear gas, after forty-one people, including twelve police officers, were injured. On October 1, the fireworks celebrating the national holiday and the sixty-fifth anniversary of the founding of the Republic of China were cancelled. The Hong Kong riot police, perceived as too brutal by the chief executive, were sent back to their stations.

Tens of thousands of participants, armed with umbrellas, their rallying symbol and protection against rain, sun, and pepper spray, joined the original protesters. According to a poll, up to 20 percent of those surveyed responded that they had taken part in the protests (*Wall Street Journal*, Sept. 29, 2014).

For their part, Chinese leaders were caught in a dilemma. On the one hand, there was the danger of the contamination of dissent to Taiwan or to mainland China. Being closely watched via thousands of media channels, politically, China could not grant a more democratic system to Hong Kong. It would have sent a signal to insurgent territories such as Tibet or Xiangung that the iron fist was losing its grip. But, on the other hand, in resorting to vigorous repression, as China had in Tiananmen in 1989, there was the risk of harming Hong Kong as a stable financial and commercial centre. The spatial disruption had indeed started during the holiday, when wealthy Chinese customers who usually rushed to the city's luxury stores did not. Due to the students' occupation, the stores remained closed. On the other hand, as the images of police brutality were broadcast via the world media, China could not resort to harsh repression. Unlike his predecessor, Deng Xiaoping who, in the 1980s, had struck the deal with Ms Thatcher under which Hong Kong was returned to China (before launching the lethal repression in Tiananmen), Mr Xi Jinping expressed a strong distaste for negotiations and for political liberalization. Tightening controls over the media and on intellectuals, Jinping's approach was to let local governments deal with the hundreds of revolts occurring every year across mainland China and, in this case, Hong Kong – hence Chinese leaders' efforts to censor the media and the social media.

At the end of the holiday weekend, Leung accepted the principle of meeting students' spokesmen to discuss the evolution of the reform. His plan was to gain time and avoid students' intrusion in government buildings where retaliation would have been unavoidable. But then, in the densely populated area of Mongkok, hooded and masked thugs, allegedly affiliated with local triads as well as possibly paid peasants, brutalized students and journalists, provoking them and seeking their violent reactions that would have legitimized repression (*The Guardian*, Oct. 4, 2014). But the occupiers were determined to remain nonviolent. The three pro-democracy organizations (the high school and university students and the OCLP movement, all wearing yellow ribbons) decided instead to escalate their action in order to maintain the momentum. They converged on the Admiralty area, a symbolic site where the ministries are located.

On Monday, October 6, the chief executive threatened to use force to clear the streets in order to allow the city to get back to work. In response, the students brought more tents and prepared for a long street occupation. For them, only public opinion could give legitimacy to their action, and so far, they had its support. A poll carried out by Hong Kong Polytechnic University revealed that 59 percent of the 850 people surveyed since October 4 believed that the Hong Kong territory should reject the reform. Sixty percent of the respondents blamed the situation on the police and the thugs, and 29 percent on the chief executive, whose resignation was demanded by the students (*The Economist*, Oct. 11: 59). This poll, however, was not representative of the whole population.

At dawn, on October 12, when the occupation had thinned on the three occupied sites, the anti-riot police forces attempted to lift the barriers blocking the Central and Admiralty areas, the city's main business districts, in order to let masked thugs from the triads, some with knives, reach the peaceful students. They had the support of hundreds of other people, angry at seeing the city's orderliness and their own businesses disrupted by the occupations. Students were attacked and the metal fences pulled down. But at the end of the day, more people like construction workers, engineers, and even a few bankers contributed to help students build even more elaborate barriers made of bamboo, garbage cans, and other materials (Buckley & Forsythe, 2014). The ten-lane Queensway, alongside the Admiralty, was occupied again by thousands of students and supporters, then cleared by the police, chasing them with pepper spray. Two nights later, on October 14, violent clashes opposed police forces, thugs, and students again. A demonstrator received numerous blows in a police abuse of force, which shocked the public after it was recorded on video and sent to a popular TV channel. Rumours were spread by some political leaders that foreign outsiders manipulated the students in view of a confrontation with China. A meeting between Leung's representative, Carrie Lam, and five university students and leaders of the movement finally took place, but again, talks failed to bridge the gap between them.

On October 17, at dawn, the police tried to have the students evacuate the Mongkok site. Like a war of attrition, a few hours later, the streets were retaken by the students. Five weeks after the beginning of the movement, the occupied areas seemed to contract and expand as police and protesters tested each others' limits. The police chief asserted that it was a crime to post messages calling on people to attend the protests. One of the web users was arrested. An opinion poll carried by the Chinese University on the week of October 8–15 revealed that 92 percent of the 15–24-year-old youths supported (or partially supported) the movement, and that 38 percent of the Hong Kong population also did. On the Admiralty site, the number of colourful tents now reached 2,268 (de Changy, 2014).

Another poll of 513 people conducted a month later, on November 17, found, however, that more than four in five residents now wanted the demonstrations to end (Forsythe & Buckley, 2014). Obviously, time worked against the protesters and disorder could not go on indefinitely. Business and taxi drivers had gradually learned how to circumvent blocked roads and 'a new normal' had set in. A movement of opposition to the students had gathered 600,000 signatures. Some people were allegedly paid to participate in anti-Occupy riots (*South China Morning Post*, Oct. 5, 2014)

Towards the end of November, internal disputes divided the movement over how aggressive the confrontation with the local government should be. A radical minority group, calling itself Civic Passion, advocated more confrontational tactics. A few days before, two members of Civic Passion had been arrested after attempting to get into the legislative council building. Most of the occupiers, though, cautious not to alienate public opinion, defended non-violent civic disobedience. On November 28, the intervention of judges weighed on the balance of forces: a court injunction allowed the police to clear the Mongkok site. The police used pepper spray and batons. Fifty-eight wounded demonstrators were hospitalized, and over two dozen people were arrested for illegal assembly and obstruction to the police. On November 31, Joshua Wong started a hunger strike.

On December 2, only two protest areas, the Admiralty and Causeway Bay, were still occupied. To put an end to nearly three months of confrontations, the police resorted to aggressive raids, causing numerous casualties and raising indignation. The older members of Occupy Central, Benny Tai, Chan Kin-Man, and Chu Yiu-ming, before surrendering to justice, expressed their deepest sorrow for the students' blood and broken bones and said that they urged the students to retreat, put down deep roots in the community, and transform the movement. With their retreat, a source of management and financing of the occupation vanished (Buckley, 2014). On December 11, the last site, the Admiralty, was swiftly cleared; 209 demonstrators were arrested, including some lawyers, lawmakers, and student leaders. On the whole, according to the police commissioner, the protests resulted in 955 arrests. The students and their supporters vowed to be back and organize further protests. 'The Umbrella Movement is not ending, and this is just a small part of it' remarked one of the participants (Buckley & Wong, 2014).

## *Mass mobilization potential*

The young people's protest received a lot of support from ordinary people for a number of weeks. Many residents' anger did not just come from a violation of democratic processes by China but from a situation of extreme inequality in Hong Kong partly resulting from local policies benefiting the city's wealthy elites close to Beijing. In 2003, a Closer Economic Partnership Agreement signed with mainland China had allowed the Chinese to invest resources in Hong Kong's real estate and commercial properties (Lim, 2014). Mainland Chinese resources then poured into the territory. Chinese mainlanders rather than Hong Kong former graduate students currently occupy high-skilled positions. Local residents resent mainlanders driving up prices, which are comparatively high. Middle classes, including students, are thus unable to find affordable housing. As written by Joshua Wong in an editorial to the *New York Times* at the end of October 2014, 'my generation could be the first in Hong Kong to be worse off than our parents' (Wong Chi-Fung, 2014).

Besides such economic vulnerability, there are concerns about Hong Kong's identity: 'The current conflict has served . . . to bolster Hong Kong's identity, already strengthened in recent years by what many residents saw as intensifying attacks from China against its culture, political values and economic well-being' (Wong & Wong, 2014).

Many Hong Kong citizens do not feel Chinese, despite the fact that 90 percent of the residents are ethnically Chinese. However, they would have a lot to lose if Hong Kong were to become like just another mainland Chinese city 'where information is not freely shared and the rule of law is ignored' (Wong Chi-Fung, 2014). The huge presence of Mandarin-speaking tourists make the residents fear that their culture, their language, and their shared values will become diluted. Hong Kong's distinct identity comes from the dominance of Cantonese culture and language. According to a recent poll, 62 percent of the residents want to keep the pluralist and international identity of Hong Kong as it is and 29 percent that of historical and cultural China (Kessel, 2014). The brutality of police forces in their confrontations with the students has turned lots of bystanders into activists. People have been pushed to stand up, fight, and express their disapproval. Almost all Hong Kong families have experienced tragedies linked to communism. Banned in mainland China, memories of the Tiananmen Square massacre in 1989 are kept alive by candlelight vigils held in Victoria Park every June 4. In recent years and until 2016, a growing number of students participated in the commemorations.

The post-Tiananmen generation refuses the Hong Kong transformation, and the old generation has no solution to offer them. For students like Joshua Wong, the electoral reform is thus a form of generational confrontation. A new generation of well-educated Asian students from middle-class families, globally connected with the rest of the world, with skills for using social networks and the internet, form the basis of the movement. A Hong Kong associated professor of cultural studies, Chen Yun-Chung, calls them 'mutants', in the good sense. 'Their mentality is very different from the older generation. . . . They are not day-dreamers. They know they might not get what they want, but most of them are prepared to fight on' (Kessel, 2014). They opt for direct modes of non-violent action and forms of participatory democracy. They know how to use globalization on their behalf.

Nevertheless, their future may be bleak and, unlike the protesters of Occupy Wall Street, they are less antagonistic to financial elites than to their political leaders. The success of the street occupation is explained by several other factors: numbers, time, connections, and skills. Firstly, the number of participants exerting a watchful presence has been considerable, reaching tens of thousands in the several occupied sites. The quasi-colonial domination exerted by elites on the ordinary people explains why not just students, but young workers, many of them professionals, and ordinary employees came after work and mobilized together with young people. Altogether, they value the rule of law and civil freedoms and feel threatened by Chinese investments and domination. Secondly, time and the students' resilience worked for them. As observed by Joshua Wong, 'no matter what happens to the protest movement, we will reclaim the democracy that belongs to us, because time is on our side' (Wong Chi-Fung, 2014). Even if the ten weeks of mobilizations formally ended in December 2014, their spirit can persist via ties and bonds that have been established and the discovery of the new capacities of innovation and resistance of the protesters.

Thirdly, students have made the best use of their global connections, the social media, and the internet, despite an apparent absence of pyramidal organization. The whole world has kept an eye on them, and more communications have emanated from the pro-democratic camp than from the opposition. Despite China's censorship, news relative to the protests have leaked in mainland China. Fourthly, locally, students have displayed considerable skills at keeping the atmosphere peaceful and non-violent and at maintaining clean the areas that they occupied. The space was organized in 'stations' distributing water, food, umbrellas, anti-tear-gas masks, and first-aid kits given by anonymous donors. Art was successfully exhibited via posters, clothes, and mottos, for example.

Among the weaknesses of these types of demonstrations, after three months of an exhausting street occupation, that there would be divisions within the pro-democracy camp was predictable. Older members, like those of Civic Passion, wanted to escalate confrontations with authorities as the only way to win more concessions. The younger demonstrators defended non-violent approaches for fear of antagonizing public opinion and their generous backers. At strategic moments, though, the leaders of the three factions understood that it was in their common interest to converge and act as one.

The occupiers faced most powerful opponents. Wealthy elites opposed to change aspired to a return to order and supported the police. Elites dominate the Legco through functional constituencies, granting them political representation and economic resources coming from leases on real estate and commercial properties. The dominant status of seventy elite members was confirmed after they were invited to come to Beijing in August 2014 by the president of China, Mr Xi Jinping, ensuring they would support his stance on Hong Kong. The chief executive, CY Leung, close to Beijing, is himself a beneficiary of dubious elections (he was chosen by a pro-communist party in 2012, collecting 689 votes out of 1,200 votes). For corporations and wealthy individuals, granting universal suffrage to Hong Kong (which had never been done under British domination) would open the door to more freedoms and to 'irresistible demands for a welfare state, which would raise taxes . . . and sap Hong Kong's competitiveness' (Bush, 2014).

According to diverse editorials published in the *South China Morning Post*, the police acknowledged to have had support from up to two hundred members from two major triads. Businesses in densely populated areas of Hong Kong pay protection money to triads. Triads are said to have suffered a 40 percent decline in revenues due to occupations. Rumours – some coming from legislative council members – report that Leung himself hired three organizations of reckless 'thugs' to attack pro-democracy supporters (*The Straits Times*, Oct. 4, 2014). Mid-December, Police Commissioner Andy Tsang asserted that 955 individuals had been arrested and further arrests were to be expected. There were over 200 casualties. With the crackdowns, the legitimacy of the system so peculiar to Hong Kong (independent courts, mild law enforcement, free press) was damaged, in particular after the courts issued injunctions against occupations, opening the door to brutal but lawful repression.

China itself is a formidable foe, and as said before, it cannot lose face and accept compromises. With Xi Jinping's commitment to unbending authority, some observers remarked that the president's 'strongman style may have helped create the crisis in Hong Kong' (Wong & Buckley, 2014).

The resources of the movement are not negligible. When he was not even fifteen years old, Joshua Wong, the only son of Anglican middle-class parents, launched the Scholarism movement on the internet to prevent 'communist' propaganda in Hong Kong schools. This charismatic convenor's successful mobilization revealed the emergence of a new generation of young activists for whom 'social media is both an organizational tool and a means for publicizing each clash with riot police' (Lim, 2014). After September 26, 2014, hundreds of secondary school students boycotted their classes and occupied their own playgrounds. During the sit-in, Wong found a pathway to access the square where government buildings are located, hoping to convey collective demands to decision makers (e.g. the resignation of the chief executive and the cancellation of electoral reforms) and start a conversation. He was arrested; his room was searched and his laptop was confiscated by authorities.

Twenty-four-year-old Alex Chow led the Hong Kong Federation of Students (HKFS), a coalition of eight unions from local universities. He launched a students' general strike on September 22. With his ally, Lester Shum, from the HKFS, he defended a peaceful and non-violent approach within the pro-democracy camp. His first act of civil disobedience was to call a night sit-in in the Central area after a march on July 1, leading to the arrest of over five hundred participants. Fifty-year-old Benny Tai, a law professor, promoted the idea of civil disobedience in defence of democracy in an article published in January 2013 by the *Hong Kong Economic Journal* (*HKEI*). Convinced that peaceful protest marches would lead nowhere, with Chan Kin-man, a professor of sociology and Chu Yiu-ming, a Baptist clergyman and a veteran from Tiananmen, he created the movement Occupy Central with Love and Peace (OCLP). They organized a referendum in June 2014 on the proposed democratic reforms which, despite a massive cyber attack, gathered 800,000 participants (Changy & Pedroletti, 2014). The three men and their organization rallied the students' movement in September 2014, earlier than anticipated.

Sixty-six-year old Jimmy Lai, a tycoon from Next Media, is a long-time supporter of pro-democracy movements. As such, he was immediately the target of an anti-corruption investigation from the Legco; his email was checked and then leaked to the press. It was thus known that he had given large donations to politicians and activists. He was physically assaulted several times and, after the movement had ended, taken to court on various charges. Forty-six-year-old Edward Chin, a banker, created the OCLP's Finance and Banking Professionals Group, gathering eighty bankers. His goal was to demonstrate that the financial world was not opposed to the OCLP movement and its democratic goals. The group denounced the pervasive corruption and the nepotism associated with Chinese rule. Chin, who wrote a chronicle in the *HKEI* for eight years, had to stop for a while in August 2014, after pressures were exerted on the journal (Changy & Pedroletti, 2014). Other leaders such as Martin Lee, seen as the founder of the movement, and Cardinal Zen had been actively supporting the occupation.

In the end, the movement disintegrated as rapidly as it had emerged. However, the 2016 local elections confirmed some of the victories gained during the occupation. Political activists younger than 40 won seats to the Legco, defending Hong Kong independence after 2047. They are supported by 40 percent of youths. Joshua Wong created his own party, Demosisto, but was barred from lecturing in diverse Asian countries by China.

## The aftermath

The occupation in Hong Kong can be categorized in the new models of non-violent public disorder. What have these occupations achieved? In Hong Kong, the occupation movement has shown that China was not embarrassed by violating previous pro-democratic agreements. Via global media coverage, most Western democracies supported the activists' right to protest and claim for universal suffrage (*Washington Post*, Nov. 26, 2014). But the threat of heavy repression and the involvement of thugs and triads should not be minimized. The protesters were physically in danger. The activists broke new ground in challenging China, and they could do so, due to the support brought by the media coverage and to their organizational skills in monitoring the social media. They were also supported with both material and symbolic resources (the former Hong Kong Governor, the Chancellor of the University of Oxford, Chris Patten). There were rallies in support of the Hong Kong pro-democratic mobilizations in over sixty-four cities world-wide, including three thousand participants at one point in front of the Chinese Embassy in London. 183,000 signatures supporting the protests were sent to the White House (*The Guardian*, Oct. 1, 2014).

The next chapter will compare how those diverse types of global and local disorder unfolded and how efficient their mass mobilization and resources were before drawing temporary conclusions.

## Notes

1   A larger analysis is developed in Body-Gendrot (2016).
2   Less than 5 percent of the 18,000 police agencies replied to the FBI demand for this type of information. There is no national recording of such incidents. Data is therefore hazardous and open to speculation.
3   It took the jury three months to hear sixty witnesses, a highly unusual duration.
4   See http://www.huffingtonpost.com/2011/10/18/occupy-wall-sreet-hashtag_n_1017 299.html.
5   Just before the handover, there were indeed protest movements against Harbour reclamations, which resulted in the protection of the Harbour Ordinance in 1997. In 2003, after mass protests had taken place, a bill on sedition that would have made any form of protest unlawful in Hong Kong was vetoed by the Legislative Council (Legco). That year, there was again opposition to the demolition of Lee Tong Street. This opposition marked the beginning of Hong Kong's activism because many opponents met there and again in 2006 (Queen's Pier demolition). It started once more in 2009 when the Express Rail Link to China caused the demolition of Choi Yuen village.

# 4

# PUBLIC DISORDER AS AN
# ALTERNATIVE FOR CHANGE

How do current forms of public disorder converge or differ from each other, and how do they contrast with previous ones within respective countries? Logics of benign neglect, second-rate citizenship, the violation of civil rights, excessive abuse from elites, institutional racism, or mere political domination trigger the citizens' anger and outrage, some of them eager to resort to public disorder to make their emotions more visible, others preferring more peaceful modes of expression. Such behaviours indicate that alternative, horizontal modes of expression are currently taking place, accelerated and impacted by global forms of communication which allow bottom-up initiatives to rapidly spread among those eager to spatially participate in mobilizations or to bring them other forms of support.

My interest here is focused on disturbances giving globalization its confrontational dimension, without necessarily resorting to political claims. National and local decision-making systems and modes of order maintenance are challenged by groups resorting to direct action or powerfully communicating via the social media to denounce the excess of 'disjunctive' democracies (Holston, 2008), meaning that citizenship development is never cumulative, linear, and evenly distributed; it erodes in uneven ways. If democracies are not fully efficient in their short- or long-term responses, if public disorder lasts too long, governments' legitimacy can be jeopardized. Most of the time, the disorder is not anticipated (Paris, London). Sometimes peaceful demonstrations are appropriated by violent groups who then gain visibility from the media and whose words and actions circulate on the social networks (Ferguson, Baltimore). Sometimes, the authorities themselves disagree with the goals and methods of the protesters (Occupy movements) and the excess of repressive force generates disorder, often widely captured by amateur videos or other technologies. Although cross-national comparisons are filled with risks for obvious reasons, this chapter attempts to compare both commonalities and divergences in the three types of case studies previously examined and to test the impact of globalization on these recent mobilizations. It mobilized the comprehensive model of analysis previously described and used by Body-Gendrot and Savitch (2012).

## Public disturbances: Paris and London

### Commonalities then and now

In the 1980s, England and France were the only countries in Europe to experience repetitive disturbances in deprived urban areas. Such environments were marked by poverty and social exclusion, delinquency, illiteracy, unemployment, and the underground economy. Deprived areas are frequently symbolically and physically located at the margins of the wealthiest global cities in Europe, characterized by various types of large inequalities. However it does not imply that living conditions are a major cause of discontent for the residents. In London, for example, according to a Mori poll from 2010, only 13 percent of residents are either 'very' or 'fairly' dissatisfied with living in this city (Travers, 2011: 309–10). In metropolitan Paris, even in problem areas, only 20 to 25 percent of the residents would want to leave their neighourhoods (Kepel, 2013). In recent decades, due to macro-economic changes, the situation in the most deprived neighbourhoods has deteriorated and deprivation is felt in comparison with urban areas nearby. Moreover, racial tensions interfere with issues of social marginality. In France, due to continuous flows of immigration, many impoverished immigrants from developing countries keep set-tling in those neighbourhoods. The instability and destabilization of work and less performing institutions such as schools, unions, and parties turn a swathe of those populations into marginalized categories (Body-Gendrot, 2013a: 8). In England, at the end of the twentieth century, signs of looming social tensions appeared in multicultural cities as well. Widely reported incidents took place in large inner-city areas with relatively compact African-Caribbean and Asian populations. At the beginning of the 2000s, in English northern textile towns such as Oldham, Burn-ley, or Bradford, white youths clashed with the sons of Pakistani or Bangladeshi migrants (Body-Gendrot, 2012). In both countries, in the 1990s, clashes opposed ethnic groups or youths from public housing estates and police after incidents.

Commonalities can then be identified in recent events in the context of urban disturbances in England and in France.

Firstly, for authorities in the two cities, the challenges are frequently the same. On the one hand, residents of deprived areas want to visibly express their griev-ances. They require fair treatment from institutions and particularly from the police accused of racial profiling. On the other, the officers in charge of law and order are asked by their hierarchy to contain the most violent protesters without hurting them and to appease the wider number of outraged residents after someone is killed by the police. Police officers have to accept the freedom of expression, the right of assembly and protest, which are generally viewed as fundamental rights in a democ-racy. They are also asked protesters, to have the law respected, and to put an end to transgressions. The protection of order is continuously in tension with the rules of due process, making law and order conceptually incompatible (Reiner, 2015: 317).

Secondly, what forms of public disorder in 2005 in greater Paris and those of 2011 in greater London have in common – a new phenomenon – is that heterogeneous crowds with a large white component contribute significantly to public disorder. For the first time in decades, such disorder was not characterized as 'race riots' by political and media spheres. The youths, looking quite similar to the residents in the neighbourhoods where the incidents took place, chanted, insulted the police, expressed their anger and outrage, and vandalized public and private goods. They resorted to their usual repertoire of grievances, denouncing a lack of hope for the future, police harassment, the poor quality of schools, the lack of support and respect, and the absence of channels for grievances, for example. With the use of the social networks allowing youths to converge to the same sites, some of them took advantage of the chaos following the suspension of order and took advantage of the situation. A range of motivations drove heterogeneous youths from various racial and ethnic backgrounds to 'act out', to experience a 'happening', adding to the thrill of playing hide-and-seek with law enforcers on one hand and, on the other, the opportunity to commit arson, to vandalise, and to loot for petty profit.

Thirdly, the origins and the developments in 2005 in France and in 2011 in England appear alike. The police were the original trigger in a particular incident taking place in a highly charged context. They mishandled the treatment of the incident, did not express sympathy to the grieving families, and were reproached for acting routinely.

Fourthly, in both countries, the political responses displayed similarities. Both the prime minister in England and the minister of the interior in France demonized the 'rioters' (see chapter 5). In doing so, they received significant support from the public. In both situations, the police were taken by surprise. As for justice, as will be seen in chapter 6, in here and there, the prosecutors were asked to be tougher than usual. Summary processes translated into massive sentencing.

Fifthly, with their headquarters located at the core of their respective cities, the media could easily cover the incidents in real time. They became allies for the protesters, both in terms of opportunities or logistics before turning against them after the disorder receded.

Finally, the intensity of the riots and the resulting damages were unusual. Insurance payouts were large (although one of the outcomes of the riots was the startling number of people who were not insured).

### Divergences between Paris and London

A close examination of events reveals, however, that they are dissimilar regarding their duration, topographies, repertoires, use of social networks, cultural reactions, and police management of disorder.

Broadly, six features distinguish the Paris and London events.

Firstly, the duration of disruptive actions lasted three weeks in France in 2005, marking a difference with the three or four days of disorder in England.

Secondly, the sites of unrest were not alike: three hundred neighbourhoods in France were disrupted, compared with a limited number of neighbourhoods in some cities in the UK. Wealthy Paris is guarded like a medieval fortress, with two ring roads protecting the city from the poorer revolted youths from social housing projects, while the boundaries in London between affluent and more impoverished neighbourhoods are less sharply delineated. Mixed public housing estates are spread all over London, including at the core. Beleaguered youths could not march to Paris, and the railway stations at the periphery were under heavy police surveillance, as will be the case again during major events with potential disturbance.

Thirdly, looting in England was a way for young people, older than in France, to grasp something, anything, and to ignite a dull and frustrating daily life. Looting was a major feature in the London disorder. Little or no looting was reported in France where, frequently, the teenagers' goal was to confront the police and settle their score with institutions like schools which had excluded them earlier on. They also attacked vehicles, including police and bus vehicles, partly for fun, partly due to anger at the poor means of mobility characterizing these urban areas.

Fourthly, social networks played an active part in England. What was new was the use made first of Twitter, then of Blackberry's encrypted instant message service directing youths speedily to the empty streets with no police surveillance and giving the demonstrators the power to assemble, plan, and share. The Met Police seemed to be ill-equipped at that time to monitor those connections.

While fluidity and mobility also characterized the French events, with young bikers moving rapidly from one area to another, in 2005, cell phones rather than Twitter or Facebook were used mostly to coordinate local actions and check whether the youths' actions were visible enough, with a view to competing with other groups.

Fifthly, the cultural reactions were dissimilar. Extensive British television coverage was devoted to victims and to their emotions during the 2011 events. Calls for denunciation of offenders during unrest by authorities and methods helping citizens to do so via images caught by CCTVs were, then, enforced, while self-help and innovative collective actions intending to repair material damage were praised by the media. The British residents' spontaneous attitude of self-help, their expression of solidarity with victims, and the organization of collective actions are reminiscent of that of many New Yorkers rushing to Ground Zero to help after 9/11. Although it is reported that there is growing incivility in sections of British society, and increasing non-cooperation with the police, in hard times, surprisingly high levels of interpersonal trust and self-help distinguish British culture.

Like President Obama exhorting poor black households to take responsibility in their future, Prime Minister Cameron received a large echo in the media when he urged civil society to cooperate in the repair of their neighbourhoods after demonizing youths' behaviours. By contrast, a culture of 'excuse' prevailed in

France. The media point at youths whose lives are chaotic, parents overwhelmed, and education dysfunctional. Society is blamed for what is wrong, in a Durkheimian sense, and youths' personal responsibility is rarely pointed at as 'shaming the nation'. Juvenile court judges write editorials in major newspapers to support the culture of excuse. Nevertheless, among French majorities, this 'compassion' does not generate public mobilizations of solidarity with the residents from inner-city projects. Few residents from Paris travelled to poor localities to help the residents repair the material damage. Spontaneous action from civil society is filtered by the state bureaucracy.

Sixthly, in England, police forces received considerable criticism, including from the prime minister, who found the police tactics too timid. Cameron denounced the gangs. The Met Police blamed itself in its own report circulated on the internet for their lack of preparation. On the contrary, in France, the police were praised for their savoir faire in order maintenance, and no commission of investigation was launched to find out if errors had been committed in the handling of the incident by the police.

Regarding police reforms, in Britain as early as the 1980s, urban unrest had a positive effect on policing and on race relations; more anti-discrimination measures were implemented. A similar observation applies regarding the follow-up given to the Stephen Lawrence case (Rowe, 2007). In 2011, after the disturbances, new measures, such as the election of police chiefs, after being temporarily halted by the House of Lords, were implemented. The goal of the reform was to show that the institution was accountable to the public. By contrast, in France, historical centralization encourages the notion that the police are the 'strong arm of the state'. One can even speak, in some cases, of an over-investment of policy-makers in their attempt to secure sensitive areas marked by large public housing projects, leading to paramilitary modes of policing and a saturation of space by law enforcers. As the police were praised for their management of the 2005 disorder, there was no question of changing a 'winning team'.

## Public disorder and demonstrations: Ferguson and Baltimore

The Ferguson disorder, in suburban St Louis, occurred after almost twenty years, during which black urban areas 'did not burn'. Currently, in the United States, a majority of black households live in the suburbs. Their recent settling in Ferguson in the last fifteen years and their poverty did not allow them however to get organized to defend their rights and enjoy political representation proportional to their population. As seen before, the situation degenerated in Ferguson for lack of local leadership defending Black communities against institutional abuse. The situation is different in Baltimore, as shows the comparison of disorder following similar police abuse.

In Ferguson, then police chief, Thomas Jackson; the mayor, James Knowles III; and the county prosecutor, Robert McCulloch were all white men. This was not the case in Baltimore, and the large metropolis has a long savoir faire in the handling of civic strife. It explains partly why, after Freddie Gray was stopped by the local police for holding a knife and died after being held, the chief prosecutor rapidly announced that the six street policemen (half of them black) who had interacted with Freddie Gray would be charged with crimes and voluntary manslaughter. Local authorities took fast action against the policemen, while in Ferguson, the process was lengthy. First, the name of Darren Wilson was withheld; then the local police supported his claim that he had acted in self-defence and so did the local prosecutor instructing the popular jury. They did not try to appease the angry crowd.

In the two cities, after a few nights of disorder, Republican governors called the National Guard. In Baltimore, this added about two thousand men to the three thousand local police officers, and the city was put under night curfew. The early property damages were evaluated at $9 million. But after the message that 'black lives matter' was acknowledged by authorities, public disorder receded. In Sandtown and other West Baltimore neighbourhoods, lots of residents are involved in peace-keeping. By contrast, in Ferguson, disorder faded, started again several times before receding, and began again during the months following the events.

In both cities, advocate organizations played a large, often ambiguous role. They used their communication skills to spread the minorities' grievances as was done in the past. As in the European cases studied here,

> Television images served to spread the contagion pattern throughout urban areas and the nation. Large audiences saw the details of riots, the manner in which people participated in them and especially the ferment associated with looting and obtaining commodities which was so much at the heart of riot behaviour. Television presented detailed information about the tactics of participation and short-term gratification.
>
> (Janowitz, 1979: 280)

Such an impact via communication skills was immediate in Ferguson, in Baltimore, and in other American cities in 2014 and 2015, where the media and social networks' pressures asked for responses. It galvanized demonstrators who could see their actions on the communication channels. This kind of coverage starting contagious behaviours reminds that in 2005, when French youths saw themselves in the news via their cell phones and were eager to cause more spectacular damage than others. This phenomenon can also be compared to 2011 in London, where young people used Twitter or Blackberries, emulating each other efficiently.

In Ferguson, as in Baltimore, disruptive actors also used the social media to mobilize and organize crowds. The television coverage that they received may have boosted their impetus. But at various levels, the authorities' strong response was able to put an end to embryonic collective violence.

Numerous criteria would be useful to evaluate the impact of communication on other forms of demonstrations elsewhere. It should be done in further research.

At this point, it does seem that the demonstrators' and the police's communication skills had a strong impact on the events. Both mayors, in Ferguson and in Baltimore, saw their reputation tarnished after the disturbances.

## The Occupy mobilizations

### Commonalities

All the Occupy movements studied here started as peaceful oppositions to a decision. In Taksim's Gezi Park, they opposed the partial privatization of the park, its redevelopment, and the increasing authoritarian discourse of the prime minister, based on Islamic references. In Hong Kong, the undemocratic election process decided by China pushed pro-democratic activists in the streets. In New York City, it was the financial domination exerted by Wall Street and the growth of inequalities which, among others, became a rallying cause on the ground and on the internet. Hardly any consultation with civil society linked elites and constituents about such decisions or processes. Authorities were taken by surprise when public disorder took place and, overreacting, inadvertently boosted other forms of disorder.

Participation in these various expressions of opposition was massive at first. In Hong Kong, the numbers of participants reached tens of thousands at times, not just students but also young workers, many of them professionals, and ordinary employees coming after work and mobilizing together. Other participants joined in the social media.

In the Taksim's Gezi Park protest case, it is estimated that about 2.5 million people participated in rallies, forums, and quiet protests, subsequent to the events over the next three weeks, in various parts of Turkey. In New York, 'Compared to both Egypt and Spain and to the turnout to the different US protests, day-to-day participation in Zuccotti Park was around one tenth or less. It never went over the ten of thousands' (Gerbaudo, 2012: 126). But with the potential of one billion subscribers to Facebook, the extended participation on the internet was huge. It explains why around 950 cities experienced various forms of occupation in 2011: in 82 countries, 950 mobilizations expressed indignation, and in December, OWS counted 300,000 followers.

### Space

The occupied sites allowed all kinds of grievances to overlap and converge into a cementing ethos due to the support provided by space. 'Consensus builds community. . . . It becomes an architecture of consciousness', someone remarked in Zuccotti park. A park in Istanbul, another park in New York, three urban sites in Hong Kong, those were symbolic nodal points gathering a wide diversity of voices. Democratic space gives the occupiers visibility. People feel that they exercise a right to peacefully assemble, occupy a symbolic space, create a process to address problems. Occupying and staying on a site which belongs to all is a form of resistance in a world of mobility, with tents planted as a flag indicating the ownership of a place (Ogien & Laugier, 2014), except that there is no will of conquest here, just democratic assertions confronting powerful opponents.

Space is reinterpreted as a strategic site in a drama led by various interacting actors. There is ongoing cooperation between the symbolism carried by space, the significant presence of anonymous young occupiers, and the coverage given to their actions on the media and social media. The resources provided by digital activism are paralleled by the importance of street-level activism.

> Once a movement is out on the streets, there is more room for ordinary participants to shape its action, as the influential individuals and groups are physically submerged in 'a much bigger crowd'. Activists involved in the tiny but vocal anarchist community in New York definitely had a leading room in managing the setup of General Assemblies.
>
> *(Gerbaudo, 2012: 142–43)*

## Digital activism

A new generation of well-educated people, mostly from middle-class families, directly connected with the rest of the world, with skills for using social networks and the internet, formed the basis of the movement in Hong Kong, partly in Taksim's Gezi Park, and gave it visibility in New York. By skilfully using the social media, what these actors revealed is that they were well aware of efficient tactics, of the risks they were taking, and of strategies to cope with them.

They were not day-dreamers. They knew that they might not get what they wanted, but most of them were prepared to fight on. They opted for direct modes of non-violent action and forms of participatory democracy.

## Innovation

The actors involved also showed a lot of imagination and innovation in their modes of expression. For example, in Taksim's Gezi Park, the passive, non-violent resistance was symbolized by a standing man, Erdem Gündüz, who would not move for hours. The choices made sometimes looked like those of the occupiers in Zuccotti Park, with an impressive self-organization in the park, a library with a few thousands of books, a field hospital, and food distribution, for example. The communicative tools were efficient. All these movements inspired and responded to each other.

In local Hong Kong, students and their followers also displayed considerable skills at keeping the atmosphere peaceful and non-violent and at keeping the areas that they occupied clean. The rules were strict; cleanliness expected and the respect for each person's freedom were shown in the time limit allocated to public speeches. The space were organized in 'stations', distributing water, food, umbrellas, anti-tear-gas masks, and first-aid kits given by anonymous donors. Art was successfully exhibited via posters, clothes, and mottos. Zuccotti Park occupiers were very imaginative, as shown in multiple videos on the internet. From a very 'catchy' motto, 'We are the 99 percent', they started the models for modes of horizontal expression, the assemblies, and the self-help organization.

## Police and public responses

What all these movements confronted, however, was an overreaction of police forces. Protesters were repressed brutally by police forces in the three Occupy cases studied here. Unwarranted police violence became a *flashpoint* and *backfired* to a spectacular level. The televised crackdown on non-violent protesters raised feelings of outrage and contributed to public disorder and mass rallies.

In Taksim's Gezi Park, the brutality of the police repression made it a case apart. Hundreds of protesters were injured by the police, and journalists and lawyers had to be hospitalized. At least eight deaths were numbered.

In Hong Kong, the brutality of police forces in their confrontations with the students turned lots of bystanders into activists. People were thus motivated to stand up, fight, and express their disapproval. In mid-December 2014, 955 individuals had been arrested. There were over 200 casualties. The evacuation of Zuccotti Park by the New York police will be documented in the next chapter.

Historically, wealthy 'revanchist' elites are usually opposed to change from below, and they aspire to order (Kalifa, 2012). Activism is bad for business. As seen in Hong Kong, numerous luxury shops closed during the long weekend marking the beginning of the students' occupation. Political and financial, mostly conservative, elites stigmatized the protesters, and on the whole, they expressed fears regarding the contamination, 'the pandemic unrest' that this form of direct participatory democracy could establish. At first, public opinion showed support for the occupiers and their cause, but gradually they disapproved of the disorder, largely due to its duration that was disrupting daily life activities.

Yet the occupiers had powerful supporters, including among the financial, intellectual, and political elites. In New York City, prominent political characters, such as US Vice-President Joe Biden, US Congress Representative Nancy Pelosi, and Wolfgang Schäuble, the German finance minister, took these protests seriously. Even the former president of the European Central Bank acknowledged that he understood the movement without supporting it. Allegedly, the movement Occupy Wall Street had an impact on Ohio residents who voted overwhelmingly to subsequently repeal a state law limiting public workers' collective bargaining rights.

Finally, there is no doubt that the Arab Spring tactics in 2011, especially those in Tahir Square in Cairo, inspired those embryonic movements. The online networks were used to stage pop-up occupations, a strategy also used in British and American cities to spread unrest in the summer of 2011 through 'flash mob' messages. But a social network, like Twitter, also calmed down activists and kept the mobilization peaceful in order to retain the support of public opinion. The global character of such contention came from the presence of onlookers communicating effectively on what was going on to receptive audiences, via social networks, and from international media crews covering the sites of unrest. International decision-making bodies such as the United Nations, the European Union, the Council of Europe in the case of Taksim's Gezi Park, as well as national governments, British Parliament members, the former Hong Kong governor, and the chancellor of the University of Oxford, Chris Patten, in the case of Hong Kong, expressed their serious concerns about the extreme repression of what authorities (local, subnational, or national in the case of China) perceived as public disorder. There were rallies in support of the Hong Kong pro-democratic mobilizations in over sixty-four cities worldwide.

## Divergences

Motivations for mobilizing and then creating public disorder vary. On the political axis gathering grievances due to racial and social segregation, police discrimination, lack of empowerment, and institutional abuse, one finds the 2005 French disturbances, the Ferguson and Baltimore mobilizations, and partly the Gezi Park occupation and Hong Kong. In Gezi Park, not only was there 'anger at government-backed commercial construction encroaching on a rare fragment of public green space'. There were also

> anti-authoritarian and pro-democracy protests and an alliance of 'new proletarians', i.e. the graduates working in telemarketing, with inflation-hit traditional middle classes, both of whom had to go through a set of political turmoils under the AKP rule characterized with Islamisation, Euroscepticism, parochialism, nationalism, polarization, majoritarian democracy and electoral authoritarianism.
>
> *(Kaya, 2016, forthcoming)*

On the economic axis pointing economic conditions, the growth of inequalities and the 'financialization' of global processes, protests staged in 2011 in London (partly), in Zuccotti Park in New York City, and (partly) in Hong Kong enter this category. Like all typologies, the categories are not rigid and some cases may fit in one or the other description. The modes of operation of the occupiers in various parts of the world reveal the institutional culture of place. In Hong Kong, for example, legal and political issues pushed protesters to defend democratic rights by occupying part of the city. But the graduate students and middle-class employees also denounced the overly dominant presence of mainland Chinese taking jobs, apartments, and a number of important positions. In New York City, while economic and financial issues were dominant among a number of grievances, the occupiers did not intend to put an end to the banks. Their widespread discontent meant that they expected more equity, democracy, and justice in the processes impacting on their everyday life.

Elsewhere, the two hundred German demonstrators who set their tents in front of the European Central bank were mostly concerned with economic issues, while

Southern European *indignados* were restless about their future and their perceived lack of job prospects. There were very few demonstrations in France, probably due to the dominant presence of radical political parties denouncing the excesses of the financial system and the fuzzy decision-making process characterizing day-to-day politics. Beyond those immediate grievances, a wide context of discontent with politics as usual motivated activists to search for alternative modes of expression.

## Time

How the notion of time was interpreted by the interacting parties is important. Obviously, time was on the occupiers' side, as long as public opinion supported them. They differentiated themselves in that respect from three-hour public demonstrations or three-night protests. Their resistance is shown in their motionlessness. Such collective inertia is like an anchor replacing the absence of visible leadership and organization and of a specific political content.

That occupiers in Hong Kong were able to occupy the sites for almost three months is a feat in itself. Zucotti Park in New York was occupied for two months or so, while those in Gezi Park could only stay for three weeks. A number of unions, public employees, and justice groups joined in the momentum and contributed to sustaining the occupations.

## Leadership

With these occupations, one may say that a new type of mobilization has appeared. Its internal structuration inhibits any power seizure by a leader. Efforts are made to keep the mobilizations self-governed by their members, although a handful of experienced activists on the ground and acting invisibly on the social media coached them. But their expertise differed according to place. Joshua Wong refused to be considered as leading the Umbrella mobilization, despite the cover of *Time* magazine. But he and a few older characters certainly fulfilled that role when interacting with the local authorities. By contrast, no leaders appeared as such in the Taksim's Gezi Park, and the man standing still was more iconic than anything else during that occupation. During the Zuccotti Park occupations, those who monitored the actions on the ground and on the social media remained invisible.

Contagion has been facilitated by the global coverage of the media and the skilful use of the internet and of social networks by the participants. But, as noted before, no one can say that a global space has been created. Processes and instruments facilitating connections are global, but conversations and exchanges remain linked to local practices and modes of thinking.

Despite their differences, these mobilizations display a lot of commonalities. Their assertion of democratic rights is one of them. There is a demand for equality, for democracy, for justice, and for the respect of people's dignity (Ogien & Laugier, 2014) which is expressed here. These demands are based on an occupation of space given visibility via the social network. This is where the dimension of globalization transforms previous forms of protest into new embryos of short-term social movements. Will they have lasting effects? Only the future will tell. It may be the case in Hong Kong, with an important election taking place in 2017, and in Istanbul, where new events caught attention without ruling out the experience of the Gezi Park and other cities' mobilization. As for Zuccotti Park, it remains emblematic and linked with other worldwide forms of occupation.

It is important at this point, based on an interactive and comparative approach, to study the responses given to those forms of disorder.

# PART II

# 5

# THE POLICING OF PUBLIC DISORDER

In this chapter, order maintenance will be considered via three main cases New York, London, and Paris. Such order maintenance in contentious circumstances is 'an immense challenge' for the police (Metropolitan Police Service, 2012: 116). The police apply the law but they also articulate states' desire and interests in order maintenance. 'Policing of general order is a . . . conservative activity-one bound to the past'. It is also 'a temporally contingent activity-tied to and shaped by the circumstances of a particular time' (Loader & Walker, 2007: 102–4). Policemen are enemies for some and for others (and sometimes the same) saviours. After the terrorist attacks in Paris in November 2015, a citizen spontaneously kissed a police officer, while bystanders gave him an ovation.

A difficulty comes from the fact that the legal concept of public order varies considerably. There is consequently a large diversity of protest policing. France tends to have the broadest definition of public order. Britain's authorities frequently invoke the principle of public interest where the French would use a public order justification (Anderson, 2011). But the main categories of disorderly behaviour in public space may be very similar, in particular regarding violent behaviour associated with political demonstrations and social movements. The priority given to repression of various kinds of disorderly behaviour varies over time, according to particular circumstances and in different national settings, but it displays commonalities.

In this chapter, I firstly examine police practices and tactics deployed in the cases previously studied in order to understand how public order is handled differently according to local challenging contexts. Case studies reveal that interactions between police and protesters are modified by multiple forces, including the media, social networks and bystanders influencing action. Secondly, I retrace the evolution of public disorder management and police forces' methods of disorder management in various metropolises.

My work relies on various types of material: a series of formal interviews with senior officers involved in operations of order maintenance conducted at the Préfecture de police in Paris, at the Metropolitan Police Service (MPS) in London, and at the New York Police Department (NYPD) in New York City; police officers' testimonies when I conducted hearings at the French Police Appeals Commission; direct observations of disorder private conversations with retired public officersand secondary sources.

## A diversity of disorder policing approaches

Despite obvious differences due to national history, the political environment, variations in protest, organizational structures, size, resources, and the savoir faire of the police, there are similarities, shared characteristics, viewpoints, and practices observed in the management of disorder by police forces. They resort to common methods to incapacitate threatening protesters. In the cases examined in this research, how do similarities and divergences reveal themselves, according to circumstances, contexts, and interactions between police and protesters? Are some police forces better prepared to confront new actors of public disorder than others? I have chosen to regroup my observations in three sections – namely, police responses to 'riots' in Greater Paris (2005) and in London (2011); to incidents in Ferguson (2014) and Baltimore (2015); to occupations in Zuccotti Park (2011), Gezi Park (2013), and Hong Kong (2014).

## Greater Paris (2005) and Greater London disorder (2011)

Despite a rhetoric emphasizing major differences in French and English modes of policing, one finds a number of similarities when it comes to the management of disorder, specifically during recent disorderly situations involving a large number of groups taking hold of public space. Despite their efficacy in halting disorder, police forces in Greater Paris and in London have been blamed for similar causes: the poor handling of the initial phase of tensions after deaths resulting from an interaction with the police, the handling of the disturbances management, and the coordination of forces.

### *The initial phase of tensions*

Urban violence, opposing youths in deprived urban communities to police forces in charge of order, had been current in England and in France over the last thirty years. Yet, strangely enough, both in London and in Paris, the police were taken by surprise. In both contexts, early operations were delayed for a number of material and logistical reasons, and numerous observers pointed to a lack of appropriate communication from the police.

In London, the police response was slow. Many officers were at a training seminar at a seaside resort in August 2015. Due to a series of scandals, heads at the top of the Met had been fired. It took one or two days following the shooting of Mark

Duggan for the Met to properly organize forces to confront rowdy agitators, stop looters, and restore street order.

The police were also blamed for not expressing sympathy to the victim's grieving families or their friends in closely knit communities. (The parents of Mark Duggan were not personally informed of his death by police and filed a complaint.) Also at first, strategic errors were made. For example, it was not a senior, experienced police officer who was sent to Tottenham, and the victim's family's expectations were not met. Disparaging comments regarding such perceived neglectful police treatment circulated in the victim's community and beyond. Many youths and their parents sided with the victim from the locality. As a consequence, police cars were burnt as a sign of disapproval of police behaviour. Moreover, in both countries, hostile statements from politicians at the highest levels of power set the boundaries of contention, and the media covered those events with a binary vision of 'us' versus 'them'.

## Disorder management

In France, in the early stages of the social revolt, the mayors from localities hit by disorder had required police backup to the French minister of the interior, but the urgency of their demands was not taken into account. Instead, bureaucratic routine followed, and a decision was made to send highly trained anti-riot police officers to the soccer stadium, Stade de France, for a game attracting antagonist and rowdy supporters and thousands of spectators, with the media covering the game. That first decision at the top was unfortunate, because the disorder in the localities close to Clichy-sous-Bois spread to other localities that very same evening.

But then, the incident at the Bilal mosque in Clichy-sous-Bois had a strong impact for Muslim families when a tear-gas canister like those used by the police rolled through the entrance of the mosque during a most important holy night gathering of hundreds of people (Kepel, 2015). The incident was poorly handled by the Parisian police authorities. A number of outraged Muslim youths, all dressed in long white robes, marched to express their anger. The report of this march circulated on the web. It prompted the intelligence service to issue a statement regarding Muslims' lack of involvement in the riots, in order to calm opinion down and prevent an escalation of emotions, possibly fuelled by Islamophobia (personal interview with former intelligence police inspector, October 2015).

Yet in subsequent stages of operations, French police experience in order maintenance prevailed. For example, police anti-riot units maintained a distance between bystanders and violent actors; they isolated them, allowing journalists to cover the events without being harmed (a situation that changed in 2016 when violent actors took the lead in crowds, cf. chapter 7). Command, and orders were given in real time process by GPS from centres of information and command and from headquarters. Police commanders met twice a day with the minister of the interior, who also went on the field during night operations. New weapons such as those using blintz gas temporarily froze offenders, and a drone was used for detecting whether the large public housing roofs were loaded with missiles meant to hit the police. After November 10, 2005, gradually urban violence receded (personal interview, J. F., at the Ministry of the Interior, June 2008).

In London, once in control, with support arriving from nearby regions (overall 16,000 officers were on the streets of London 4 days after the start of the outbreaks) and the courts' active work, the police arrested around 4,000 individuals; 2,400 were charged for a number of offences.

## Coordination

On the sites of disorder in the Parisian region, the various police units experienced problems of coordination. For lack of intelligence transmission, it seems, police units were unable to connect with each other and to evaluate how large the riots were in one locality or another. Due to a lack of adequate orders, police units arrived late on the sites (the same problem was detected during the terrorist attacks of November 2015 in Paris), and for lack of resources, they were unable to deploy on several sites at once. This harmed the efficiency of disorder control (personal interview with former intelligence service officer, October 2015). Subsequently, police forces were equipped with drones, helicopters, and night vision binoculars (Jobard, 2015: 81).

The same observation applies to London, where the Metropolitan Police Service and other police forces were ill-equipped to monitor youths' coordinated actions. Hooded and masked youths used Blackberry's encrypted instant message service and other social networks and speedily indicated to each other empty streets with no police surveillance. The social media gave protesters the capacity to assemble, plan, and share actions. It took the Met police four days to restore order in some neighbourhoods.

In terms of intelligence resources, the French police were not up to the task, due to an internal reorganization within the services. The merging of former intelligence services (Renseignements généraux – RG) and national police services gave birth to a centralized Directorate of Domestic Intelligence (DCRI – later to become DGSI). The former RG who had years of experienced field work opted for more prestigious bureaucratic work, and a lot of valuable information was no longer transmitted (personal interview with former intelligence service officer, October 2015).

## Arrests

Thousands of young people and adults were stopped, both in Greater London and Paris, placed in custody, and sent to the judges. Lots of them were then set free for lack of serious proofs. But the number of arrests had an impact on the momentum of the incidents. An efficient police strategy consisted of proceeding to early arrests in order to destabilize half-motivated or scared participants. Police units subdivided in fractions, and a small number of police officers, usually working in twos, made arrests sometimes on the spot but usually later, with the use of photos taken by undercover police officers or helicopters.

Those observations support the assumption that, in France as in England, in the first decade of the twenty-first century, police forces in charge of order maintenance could not at first adequately respond to the challenges of new forms of disorder orchestrated by dispersed, rapidly moving, and well-connected protesters. Soon enough, their savoir faire prevailed, and control was exerted in the public space due to the large number of resources mobilized.

## Incidents in Ferguson and Baltimore

The handling of Michael Brown's death by the local police in Ferguson in August 2014, and that of Freddie Gray's by the local police in Baltimore in April 2015, illustrate a lingering racial divide in the United States between local police agencies in charge of order and young minorities occupying public space to express their protest in downtrodden communities like West Ferguson and Sandtown-Winchester in West Baltimore. After those deaths, peaceful and lawful demonstrations gave way to violence, scattered attacks, and destructions.

### Ferguson

In West Ferguson, on August 9, 2014, after crowds formed at the news of Michael Brown's death chanting 'no peace, no justice', local police officers confronted both peaceful demonstrators and rioters with a stunning show of force. For four nights, it was reported that the police forces streamed onto West Florissant Avenue, wearing camouflage and black helmets, carrying assault rifles and ammunition, with slender black nightsticks and gas masks (Bosman & Apuzzo, 2014). They had 'armoured cars with snipers on top pointing military weapons at the crowd, tear gas thrown at participants – and precious little tact' according to an observer (*The Economist*, Aug. 23, 2014). For one week, streets were blocked by the police, and blockades formed to halt demonstrators, some of whom had turned to looting. Molotov cocktails and tear gas were exchanged on both sides. Daily life was significantly disturbed in that neighbourhood.

This tense situation called for authorities to put a halt to disturbances. On August 14, local police chief Thomas Jackson was replaced. Jay Nixon, the Governor of the state of Missouri, installed a more experienced Highway Patrol police chief, declared a state emergency, called the National Guard, and imposed curfews in Ferguson. Other police forces were sent from localities, North of Saint Louis county, for backup. They were loosely coordinated. Crowds were dispersed with tear gas and rubber bullets. Brutal arrests were made, and according to press accounts, some protesters were shot at by the police. 'To the rest of the world, the images of explosions, billowing tear gas and armoured vehicles made this city look as if it belonged in a

chaos-stricken corner of Eastern Europe, not the heart of the American Midwest'
(Bosman & Apuzzo, 2014).

Some Democrat and Republican House representatives expressed their deep
concern over the deployment of military equipment and vehicles. They ignored
that, for more than a decade, the Federal Homeland Security policy and the Justice
Department grant policy had contributed to equip local police agencies with loads
of surplus military equipment. The police in St Louis county received $9.4 million
of equipment. Ferguson benefitted from a $360,000 armoured truck, other vehi-
cles, and body armour protection for officers without apparently any restriction
or training required for their use (Bosman & Apuzzo, 2014). Such military devices
were used during the events.

After a grand jury decided not to indict police officer Darren Wilson for
Michael Brown's death on November 24, 2014, public disorder broke out again in
some areas of Ferguson. The heavily armed police forces resorted to escalated force
and to routine techniques of incapacitation, pointing rifles to peaceful demonstrators and 'erecting a wall of armoured vehicles with snipers on top' (*The Economist*,
Aug. 16, 2014). Four days later, Darren Wilson resigned from the police. Gradually,
disorder receded in Ferguson after having been the number one top news story of
2014, according to the Associated Press.

The demonstrations continued through the fall and winter of 2014, boosted
by media coverage documenting police officers' deadly shootings of minorities in
various parts of the United States and by the activism of Black Lives Matter.

### Baltimore

While the majority of the police force and of the local structure of power are white
in Ferguson, a locality which is three quarters black, in Baltimore, the sixth-largest
city in the United States, the mayor, the chief prosecutor, the police commissioner,
and the majority of the population are black. In the metropolis, however, the police
have a reputation for brutality towards minority members (personal interview with
C. S., a senior scholar doing field work in West Baltimore). Baltimore experienced
extensive riots in 1968. Then, over three decades, the police underwent a difficult
process of integration. In 1984, the city settled a lawsuit that forced the police
department to hire more minorities. Nineteen percent of the force was black at this
time, a rate that rose to 47 percent in 2014. However, tensions had been simmering
between black residents in deprived neighbourhoods, and the police, accused of
institutional racism. Freddie Gray's death in April 2015 was the spark in the tinderbox. For a whole week, the city was shaken with protest, some of it peaceful, some
of it violent. While being transported in a police van, with no seat belt to hold him
and his legs tied, Freddie Gray suffered a fatal spinal injury and subsequently died
in the hospital.

Three nights after the victim's death, in West Baltimore, at the end of a peaceful demonstration through the city, a small number of participants scuffled with
police officers in riot gear outside a baseball park. According to Governor Hogan,

the forces were soon overwhelmed (Le Bars, 2015). On the whole, 15 buildings and 144 cars were set on fire, and more than 200 people were arrested. Nineteen police officers were injured. Facing a chaotic situation, the mayor asked for assistance, and the governor immediately declared a state of emergency in a gesture of institutional cooperation. On the day of Freddie Gray's burial, violence, arson, and looting took place and lasted over the weekend. Three thousand local policemen were deployed, with more support coming from the state police. One thousand members of National Guard troops patrolled a main thoroughfare, the Western district police station, and the touristic inner harbour. Added to the general prosecutor's prompt decision to charge six police officers without delay, the firm institutional response put an end to unrest.

There are various explanations offered for the different police handling of public disorder in Ferguson and in Baltimore. Firstly, the demographics are sharply contrasted. Baltimore is a larger city with more resources than Ferguson. Secondly, the culture in Baltimore is that of a Northern city marked with numerous episodes of confrontations in the past. Over the years, police officers have acquired an experience in disorder management. By contrast, Ferguson is a small Southern community with recently arrived black households. The police institution had not been challenged before Michael Brown's death. Thirdly, the power-decision apparatus in Baltimore is black, sophisticated, progressive, and coherent, a strong contrast with that of Ferguson's, which is white, seemingly parochial, and conservative. Fourthly, Freddie Gray's death occurred after months of national controversy regarding lethal shootings of young minorities by local police forces. The debate impacted on the prosecutor's prompt decision to charge six police officers without delay and prevent demonstrations from lingering as they had in Ferguson. As noted in the next chapter, in both contexts, the justice institution's decisions made a lot of difference.

## Occupy movements

Are there similarities in the evacuation of Gezi Park, of Hong Kong downtown areas, and of Zuccotti Park?

### Similarities

Similarities come first from conflicts regarding the use of public and private spaces, over which police and protesters have diverging views. In the early stages of protest, police officers marked perimeters with metal barricades around the occupied sites. Police officers usually stand inside the metal fencing. Demonstrating on sidewalks is tolerated, but according to local laws on public order, blocking the traffic on roads and streets is not.

Secondly, in those different contexts, institutional biases within police organizations vary, but they reveal stereotypes of active militants who display non-conformist values. In Istanbul, a policeman complained that militants 'do not value national and local people as much as they value environment and trees' (Koca, 2015, 77–78). In Hong Kong, Chief Superintendent Hui Chun-tak from the police relation branch issued a press release on December 1, 2014. He repeatedly alluded to 'radicals' and 'troublemakers' performing 'riotous acts' with helmets, masks, goggles, and umbrellas, indicating that such acts were premeditated and organized. He said that radicals attacked the police, deliberately throwing pepper powder, canned drinks, and eggs at the police, who had no other solution but to use the minimum level of force with pepper spray and batons. He accused troublemakers of eroding the foundation of the rule of law with disorderly conduct in the public space, obstructing police, and resisting arrest. The police chief concluded that 'the police have the determination and capacity to take stringent enforcement actions in order to protect public safety and restore public order' (Press conference, Dec. 2014). During autumn 2014, the police communication carefully used a respectful language in direction of the public, emphasizing the Force's protective role.

In New York, NYPD spokespersons also referred to occupiers as 'outsiders' and sometimes as 'violent' towards police. Some of my interviewees mentioned 'anarchists' and the presence of 'criminals' within the group of occupiers. The police characterized the grievances as incoherent and diversified (from the defence of cats and dogs to the denunciation of capitalism) (Gillham et al., 2013: 97). Both sides revealed a total misunderstanding of each other's objectives.

A third feature comes from the police forces' extensive use of surveillance both during protest events and after. 'Surveillance consists of the collection of real time and static data, which is subsequently "mined" for actionable "intelligence" in both contexts' (personal interview with NYPD intelligence service). Technological innovation used by the police allows the collection of images and sounds emanating from occupation sites. It was less used in Istanbul, more pronounced in Hong Kong, and fully taken advantage of in New York City.

A fourth feature is displayed by the excess of police force as seen on television screens. Television and the social media largely covered the militants defending their right to a park or to more democratic processes, thus raising additional anger and protests. Disrespect 'for protester civil liberties and rights, intolerance of disruptions to public order, excessive use of force' were displayed by police officers deployed to bring back order via arrests (Gillham et al., 2013: 81–82). Contentious efforts to control the production and dissemination of information and unprecedented levels of surveillance were noted in the three cases.

## Divergences

The divergences in the handling of public disorder are probably more important than the common features in the three cases.

In Istanbul, as in Hong Kong, it is likely that some police officers resisted protest in favour of democratic rights because they found them illegitimate. Police forces defended the regimes' concept of order, and their traditional views oppose street-level politics. For them, those who get involved do it at their own risk (Della

Porta & Atak, 2016). In all the studied cases, police chiefs neither talked nor negoti-ated with protest organizers.

While the occupiers' strategies were highly innovative, including artistic expres-sion, the repression exerted by the Turkish and Hong Kong police forces was bru-tally traditional. Escalated force characterized their routine incapacitation strategy. Their repertoire of tactics included massive arrests, beatings, and the use of pep-per and tear gas to intimidate protesters and quell protests. Metal barricades were used in Hong Kong in an ongoing attrition battle opposing police and protesters that lasted several weeks. In the densely populated area of Mongkok, hooded and masked thugs, allegedly affiliated with local triads, as well as paid peasants, molested students and journalists, provoking them and seeking their violent reactions in order to legitimate repression (*The Guardian*, Oct. 4, 2014).

In Istanbul, at dawn on May 28, the riot police fired tear-gas canisters on the occupiers, and two days later, they set their tents on fire. The crackdown was brutal. About one hundred protesters were injured, and two journalists had to be hospital-ized. In the panic, the park's concrete banisters collapsed. On June 1, a protester was shot in the head by a police officer.

The zero tolerance stance against threats to public order appears to be the dominant philosophy of the Turkish police, a militarized police that fight domes-tic wars against the state's enemies and operate under military codes of proce-dure. Roché (2012: 15) defines the Turkish *jandarma* as the fourth army of the country.[1] Amnesty International observers report that police officers, including plain clothes officers and civilians acting in partnership with police, were seen beating suspected protesters, as well as journalists, doctors, and lawyers. Detained women complained of sexual harassment. The pattern of abuse was widespread and systematic, according to the report (Amnesty International, 2016: 18). Water cannons were used as a principal means of dispersing protesters. Vehicles known as TOMAT and 'scorpions' dispensed water, chemical gas, dye, or foam. They also targeted people inside buildings and hotels, through doors and windows, as well as makeshift clinics – namely, the German hospital near Taksim Square. On June 15, 2013, a violent clearing of the Gezi Park by the riot police and jandarma caused numerous casualties. It was reported by the media that 150,000 tear-gas cartridges and 3,000 tonnes of water were used by police cannons during those three weeks.

> Popular uprisings in Turkey 2013 were emblematic of police escalation and culpability conducive to public outrage and eventual mass revolts. Unwar-ranted coercion against a small group of peaceful activists worked as a flash-point and backfired to an unprecedented level as it transformed a minor protests into a countrywide mass uprising. Police-protester interactions laid bare the repressive character of law enforcement as well as the alienation of policemen from the demonstrators and the legitimate reasons that poured them to the streets. Recent developments in protest policing are alarming due to the rising tide of a zero-tolerance approach to civil unrest. Together

with cynical police perceptions, the prevalent strength of the law-and-order discourse is a major obstacle to setting up a more facilitative style of policing.

*(Atak, della Porta 2016)*

On the whole, for the most part, the zero-tolerance police approach was the cause of eleven fatalities and over eight thousand casualties, according to the same source. According to an Amnesty International report (2016: 25, 35),

> the widespread practice of holding people in unofficial detention was adopted by the authorities in cities across Turkey during the Gezi Park protests, violating the rights of detainees. In some cases, it appears that unofficial detention was used for logistical reasons due to the high number of detentions being carried out by police. However it is also apparent that unofficial detention has been used as a method of intimidation . . . without access to lawyers, family members and mandatory medical examinations.

The report emphasized the de facto immunity enjoyed by Turkish police officers and the absence of genuinely independent complaints mechanisms. Amnesty International observers noted that the levels of violence used by police forces in the course of Gezi Park protests clearly show what happens when poorly trained and supervised police officers are instructed to use force – and encouraged to do it unsparingly – safe in the knowledge that they are unlikely ever to be identified or prosecuted for their abuses.

In Hong Kong, the police image has evolved from a corrupted force under British colonial rule to a more progressive one in the 1970s after an Independent Commission against Corruption (ICAC) purged the force. However, recently, there is a perception that the 33,000-strong force is becoming increasingly politicized. 'Officers work for a government that ultimately answers to the Chinese Communist Party in Beijing' (*The Economist*, Jul. 23, 2016: 43). During the 'Umbrella revolution', after nearly three months of confrontations, police officers resorted to aggressive raids, causing numerous casualties. They proceeded to several hundred arrests. Older authorities from Occupy Central like Benny Tai, Chan Kin-Man, and Chu Yiu-Ming begged the students to stop their movement for fear of harsher repression, leading to possible lethal consequences.

In the two cases, in the early stages of the events, unwarranted police violence became a flashpoint and backfired to a spectacular level. What disrupted the routine of the repression was that the abuse of force garnered a great deal of media and social network attention and commentaries which generated widespread protests among the public in Turkish cities, in Hong Kong, and beyond. Conversely, Erdogan's followers on Twitter accused 100 Gezi occupiers of having harassed a young woman with her child for wearing a headscarf at Katabas, a district of Istanbul during the protests, an accusation refuted by security cameras (Ayan, 2016). Some high-ranking officials attempted to no avail to weigh on the Hong Kong and Turkish governments to soften their stance and defend the protesters' civil rights.

The situation was different in New York City, where police forces evolved from a hard stance of escalated force in the 1960s and 1970s to that of negotiated management, accepting the legitimacy of non-violent protests, tolerating the use of public space for expressions of dissent, discussing with organizers about routes and planned events. Yet in the late 1990s, this 'softer' approach shifted towards what observing scholars characterized as 'strategic incapacitation' (Gillham et al., 2013: 83). This strategy was much more sophisticated than that in Istanbul and Hong Kong, it would seem, due to the NYPD operational, intelligence, and technological resources.

Technologically, the NYPD benefited from a $150 million Security Coordination Center located in Lower Manhattan, close to the financial district, protected via two thousand cameras located in the Ring of Steel at the foot of the reconstructed tower at Ground Zero (personal interview with NYPD Intelligence service). During the Occupy Wall Street occupation, the cameras had the capacity to film even inside the tents. Police officers monitored 'live stream' videos running night and day inside the park. I was told by officers at the NYPD that with the help of archived data, real time events were analyzed and scenarios elaborated in order to figure out how the disorder could evolve. Police videographers were on rooftops, behind barricades, and on scaffolding adjacent to Zuccotti Park. They sent images to a central command centre in Lower Manhattan, informing officers on the field on the evolution of the situation. Subsequently, in London, at the Met Police Service, I was shown how these data were analyzed by police experts and used to neutralize protesters or arrest them later on, when a law had been breached (personal interviews at the Met and at NYPD). In New York, the surveillance was exerted from 'a twenty-five-foot mobile Watch Tower with a two-person observation booth equipped with darkened windows, flood lights, video cameras, a permanent closed-circuit television' located at one end of the park and from a mobile surveillance vehicle with a camera affixed to a twenty-foot boom, parked at the other end of the park as well as from fixed surveillance cameras around the park (Gillham et al., 2013). The Technical Assistance Response Unit (TARU) filmed those who entered and left the park and those still protesting, and they sometimes recorded conversations. This information was sent via a mobile communication vehicle to the appropriate NYPD divisions.

The availability and use of operational resources have been negatively commented upon by Gillham and his colleagues when they were on the site, at the beginning of the occupation. My interviews with NYPD officials defending the legitimacy of their approach offer another perspective on the management of the Zuccotti Park occupation. Divergences between the viewpoints come from the tactics used by the New York Police Department, which were diversified.

For example, the police created various zones of space in a strategy of spatial containment: hard zones, free-speech zones, soft zones, and free-press zones (Gillham et al., 2013: 95). The goal of the hard zones was to prevent activists from setting up tents close to the banks, such as the Chase Manhattan Plaza, Wall Street, and the Stock Exchange. Walking corridors were formed for regular pedestrians and clients needing to access the banks and move between steel barricades protected by police officers (personal interview with NYPD). In September and October 2011, those areas became sites of contention, with occupiers attempting to pull the fence down.

Free-speech zones were areas where police allowed the expression of dissent. But 'OWS activists generally elected not to limit their actions to free-speech zones, choosing instead to engage in transgressive and sometimes illegal actions' (Gillham et al., 2013: 95). For example, protesters illegally camped in privately owned Zuccotti Park, a move subsequently tolerated by the police. When a large rally was permitted by the police near City Hall with a march across the Brooklyn Bridge, the demonstrators, narrowly contained within metal barriers, were asked to stay on sidewalks and not on roads. This constraint made walking a lengthy process and discouraged rowdy protests.

The soft zones were zones where people not walking or not staying within the established free-speech zones were prevented from voicing dissent and from assembling by the police. When activists decided to move from Zuccotti Park to Times Square, for example, this move was perceived as a high-risk endeavour by the police in charge of order maintenance. Police officers had indeed to protect tourists, theatre goers, and consumers attending their business as usual, while checking the disorderly conduct from the occupiers (personal interviews with NYPD). Clashes occurred, pepper was sprayed, and arrests were made for disorderly conduct (Gillham et al., 2013: 95). The police squads forming lines pushed the protesters away from Times Square, then from Washington Square, and back to Zuccotti Park.

A problematic group for the police was the media, especially freelance journalists and independent media, without credentials. Their numbers could reach to the hundreds. The police needed to be careful with them as 'they create the environment that makes the demonstration go wrong', Inspector G. remarked (personal interview). The coverage of police practices as depicted in the mass media is sometimes more crucial for the development of contentious interactions than actual police action. Elements of unpredictability need to be taken into account in the analysis of public disorder management. Attitudes during disorderly events shifted constantly; myriads of experienced and inexperienced, united or divided actors interacted, influencing participants' and bystanders' perceptions and actions.

In those large-scale protests, there were a lot of 'unknowns' – the nature of the events was uncertain and the terrain not known to the majority of participants. How and when all this would end was unpredictable. A brief look at history contributes to an understanding of the legacy transmitted to modern police forces.

## The evolution of public disorder management

### Brief historical accounts of city policing

In cities' history, there were always unwanted categories like thieves, crooks, street peddlers, hoboes, non-criminals who did not speak English, and blacks who police suspected of creating disorder in the public space. Authorities were asked by law-abiding citizens and taxpayers to have them checked by the police for the sake of public tranquillity (Johnson, 2003; Kalifa, 2012). How was it done? Who were those suspects?

Historians and criminologists have attempted to answer questions, as the cases of three cities, New York, London, and Paris, illustrate.

## New York City

Historical accounts (Chevigny, 1995; Muir, 1977) report that there was an extreme diversity of populations in American cities' neighbourhoods of the past, with a less clear social polarization than can be the case today, for example, in New York, London, or Paris. Wheeling and dealing, payoffs and local politics played a role in keeping cities from civil strife or at least in damping down the fire.

In New York, in the past as today, patrolling police, on foot or on horseback, kept a mental file of the populations on their beat and watched out for potential mob riots or gangsters' feuds. They were asked to repress the 'enemies of society' (Body-Gendrot, 2000: 13–14). At the end of the nineteenth century, New York was a violent city, firearms already circulated.

> The crime system as a whole was part of the larger rationalization of social relations in nascent capitalism and a new technology of repression emerged to legitimate and strengthen ruling-class control of the work-force and to deal with various redundant, superfluous and marginal populations.
>
> *(Cohen, 1985: 23)*

Public disorders were fiercely repressed with violent crowd-control tactics and the misuse of deadly force (Abu-Lhugod, 2007; Johnson, 2003). In the 1930s and 1940s, social and political unrest led the police to use physical force to control or suppress strikes, demonstrations, and other public political events. The police used agent provocateurs to infiltrate protest groups, and they slandered their victims with allegations of communism or disloyalty to America. Police brutality was linked to various motivations: challenge to their authority, a will for revenge, class or ethnic bias, a feeling of impunity, and the specific culture of the police force. Most of all, police officers knew that the public believed that tough and aggressive street policing is the most effective means of maintaining order, so the use of force remained gratuitous and often excessive.

Since then, police reforms and within the repertoires of protest control, a more 'negotiated management', a softer approach, has been put in practice to pre-empt public disorder. Yet 'policing is part of a larger political, economic and social system that treats some citizens, particularly those from poor, non-white or socially stigmatized groups more harshly than others' (Johnson, 2003: 9). Consequently, tensions between the American police forces and certain groups, in particular racial minorities, linger and the outrage and indignation of police victims' supporters have been given visibility in cities' streets, particularly in 2014 and 2015.

## London

London has a different profile in its disorder management approach. According to Clive Emsley, from whom this account is borrowed, 'the police have always enforced a dominant ideology; they have the power of coercion but they have generally preferred to act by consent' (1991: 5). From the mid-nineteenth century onward, crime and disorder increasingly began to be seen as a nuisance by English society, especially by the upper classes and the ruling elites. As London was becoming a cosmopolitan city, the urge to have an effective, preventative Metropolitan Police, not that exemplified by the French, was clearly articulated by Home Secretary Robert Peel, as early as 1822. Peel is credited with formulating the principle that

> the police are the public and the public are the police, the police being only members of the public who are paid to give full-time attention to duties which are incumbent on every citizen in the interests of community welfare and existence.
>
> *(Lentz, Chaires, 2007: 67)*

In the last seven years, the city population had increased by 19 percent and crime by 55 percent (1991: 24). Peel's Bill was then timely, as fears of rowdy crowds and of radical agitation were openly expressed by constables and beat patrols. But the new police at first raised antipathy, as they reminded Londoners of the army or French-style gendarmerie. Only in the 1840s, when revolutions erupted in other European capitals and when major events or social movements causing some disorder were contained, did the benefits of the Metropolitan Police appear more clearly to the population. Most forces from previous systems, parishes, or boroughs were too small to cope with major disorder. The tranquillity of the city depended on a centralized force with national responsibilities.

When large scale disorder (triggered by the New Poor Law and the Chartist movement) wracked provincial cities in the 1830s and the 1840s, police squads from London were sent to support local constables and prevent direct military intervention. The new police were then seen as an improvement, since they caused less deaths than the soldiers did. They were even better at maintaining order in working-class neighbourhoods, where the street was so much in use for leisure time. While the police operated more arrests for petty crimes,

> street traders were ordered to move along, as were groups of loitering youths, prostitutes and vagrants; street games and street gambling were stopped; drunks were dragged to the police cells to sleep off their inebriation; fighting drunks were dragged with more force.
>
> *(Emsley, 1991: 57)*

But the Met police were frequently less brutal than previous constables, and in the 1850s, the familiar figure of the 'bobby' gained an affectionate image among

Victorian law-abiders. Yet, as Emsley points out, 'there were plenty of "riotous Victorians" in the second half of the nineteenth century and from 1850 onward, the police were generally recognized as the first line of defence when a problem of public order arose' (1991: 62). As a consequence, new forms of militarization within the Metropolitan Police became disquieting for residents.

In other cities, like Nottingham in 1885, the abuse of truncheons and of brutality was attributed to the local police and it triggered an official enquiry. Were the police more brutal because Victorian society was more riotous? This is questionable. Social order was not under threat in those days but, now and then, large scale disorder created moral panics that were dealt with locally.

Large police deployments were unusual, according to historians (Critchley, 1978; Sindall, 1990) but maintaining order in poorer working-class neighbourhoods where the street was an important site for entertainment caused continuous friction. As usual, the police repressed drunks, prostitutes, vagrants, and loiterers, and as they were regularly assaulted, they had to wear cutlasses or other protective devices. Yet the atmosphere was not always hostile. As in New York and Paris (Chevalier, 1958; Monkkonen, 1981: 154), the police exercised discretion and allowed deeds in those urban sections that they would not tolerate elsewhere in the city. Many members of the working class sought respectability and desired orderliness and decorum. They wanted to be protected from crime and to work in peaceful environments. Here also policemen exercised their discretion, ensuring that there was no breach of order. Police were preferred to army by all parties involved.

In the following decades, English police forces have become more centralized. This phenomenon has resulted from a need of uniformity, rationalization, and efficiency. Times of emergency have turned this trend into a necessity, and a return to the status quo has not been achieved. Additionally, the professionalization of the police has pushed local police committees to the margins. Under the conservative rule of Prime Minister Thatcher, the control of protests and public order policies displayed coerciveness and an authoritarian trend. Currently, there is a need for transparency and accountability and emergency situations seem to put the judgemental spotlight on the police even more.

## Paris

Paris was always characterized as a riotous city in the past. The city's big renovation works implemented by Baron Haussmann in the 1860s precipitated the revolt of the lower classes during the Paris Commune of 1871. This type of social revolt was a continuation of a century of popular uprisings and political and social unrest, the consequences of what would be later on be called 'Paris' urban pathology'. All through the nineteenth century, the working class was considered by the dominant classes and by the police as 'the dangerous class' (Chevalier, 1958; Kalifa, 2013). Actually, the proletariat was seen as a race rather than as a class. The word connoted a savage way of living and dying rather than an occupational distribution or economic characteristics. Workers were continuously perceived as fomenting revolts by the ruling classes, and their neighbourhoods were under police surveillance. In 1893–94, following anarchist attacks, the French Parliament voted villainous laws (*lois scélérates*), restricting a number of freedoms and reasserting the established social and political order.

There were divides within the working class, with continuous flows of provincial peasants coming to the city and looking for work and threatening established workers. Animosity between such groups led to frequent outbursts of violence in working-class or craftsmen neighbourhoods.

What was the general philosophy characterizing the French mode of policing disorder then? According to an interviewee,[2] an experienced police officer, the philosophy prevailing until the end of the twentieth century was based on a refusal to call the army to bring back order in public space, as was the case in the nineteenth and the beginning of the twentieth centuries. At that time, the influence of scholars Le Bon and Tarde on crowds' psychology was more strongly felt in police academies than is currently the case. The crowd was seen by Le Bon (1895/1947) as homogeneous, irrational, mindless, and potentially destructive, whereas Tarde argued that crowd action revealed individual characters' personal flaws (Stott and Reicher, 1998: 510).

Democratic values – the Compagnies Républicaines de sécurité, CRS, in principle respectful of the people, were created in 1945 under the influence of the Gaullist and communist lobbies – and gradually imposed to minimize the use of force. On May 29, 1968, as rowdy events were beginning to fade out, then police prefect Maurice Grimaud addressed his officers. He indicated that he understood that when men who have been attacked for long months receive the order to clear a street, their action may frequently be violent. But after the first encounter with aggressive demonstrators that they needed to repel, he added that men in charge of order maintenance should immediately get their self-control back. To hit a man on the ground was to hit oneself, he concluded. More pragmatically, police officers then were not adequately protected to confront rowdy crowds and violent actors.

But in the last thirty years, due to continuous clashes between youth and police in urban peripheries occurring by surprise, such philosophy has changed, negotiated management has been accepted, and judicial and administrative reforms have been enforced. *De jure*, the double authority of the prefect/police chief on one hand and, on the other, of police commanders is alleviated. This authority does not apply to gendarmes accountable to the minister of the interior, since 2003. *De facto*, urban violence requires rapid decisions to be taken on the spot by police heads.

In the last decades of the twentieth century and at the turn of the new century, disorder largely covered by the media has regularly characterized inner cities, the problems of which were increased by a general context of economic insecurity and by flows of poor immigrants moving in deprived communities. Restoring order in the public space of one locality could imply a displacement of problems to another locality.

After terrorist attacks in Paris in 2015, the deterioration of security has led the government to grant extensive powers to the police required to check sources of potential disorder (see chapter 7).

★ ★ ★

These brief historical accounts reveal commonalities in the handling of public disorder by police forces. The evolution is not only due to internal reforms but to changing morals, assertion of civil rights and of victims' rights, and self-awareness that negotiation is less costly for an institution than force (Stott, 2016). Differences in terms of philosophy, accountability, modes of organization, and resources remain huge nevertheless, as will be discussed.

In public management systems, diverse styles of crowd control have oscillated between escalated force, negotiated management, and strategic incapacitation, according to the threat that protest groups carried, the timing of police intervention and government in power, among other factors (Della Porta & Reiter, 1998). The avoidance of physical harm by the police has become a priority, due to the abhorrence of public opinion for violent confrontations resulting in deaths and casualties. But in some places like Istanbul, public indignation did not stop the police who knew that they were unlikely to be identified and prosecuted for their abuse. Policemen, despite their diversity, then meet stereotypes, as 'saturated characters'. But conversely, they also operate according to 'police knowledge' based on representations and stereotypes. As noted by Loader and Walker (2007: 102), 'in their public order and state security role, the police are often set in opposition to the organized an disorganized forces of the Left; [this] tends to encourage or confirm police officers in a political worldview that looks sceptically both on the relationship between socio-economic deprivation and crime and political resistance'.

Case studies reveal that most of the incidents started after a poor handling of an incident by the police. However disorder policing approaches varied, according to the resources allocated to the police forces, to police culture, to the level of centralization or decentralization of the police chain of command, and to logics of contexts. The diversity of attitudes towards repression is revealed here according to the amount of democratic practices and of the central authority prevailing in various regimes.

## Current views on the police management of public disorder

What are the police views on protest policing? Personal interviews and other sources reveal that police forces share common features regarding order, tactics, and strategies, but that divergences also abound. I agree with Roché (2012) that

> four concepts are required to systematically and comparatively study 'police' and their governance: polity (the structural features of a political organization, the distribution of powers and conflict between powers), police ecosystem (at

country level, the mutual links between various police forms), doctrines (the organizational strategies which are guiding police daily work) and accountability (principles and mechanisms as well as managerial techniques used for holding police accountable). Each concept is one of the 'elementary bricks' that define what police are and do, and each of these bricks are made up of several dimensions. Each national police system is a unique combination of those basic bricks. The governance of the police system is constituted of the links between forces and their environment that established and monitors them.

In the following section, the observations made by police officers offer a vivid perception of their interpretation of such concepts.

## Policing disorder at the New York Police Department

The NYPD appears as a well-oiled machine, adjusted to handle disorder with efficiency. Its experienced, well-trained officers and abundant resources (both from intelligence and from technical and legal services) contribute to its reputation of excellence in the United States.

There about five demonstrations a day in New York City, which are of three types. The first type are peaceful ones, such as the anti-war protests, which may gather 150,000 people. The civil disobedience protests form the second type and may include rowdy anarchists, masked militants, and a few agitators. The third type typifies professional violent activists gathering in a site to protest during global summits, for instance, or to express their hostility to the police. There are few summits in New York City, however; maybe due to the intimidating reputation of its police (personal interview with K. S., Legal Services, NYPD, Jan. 14, 2016). When a situation threatens to be out of control, very rapidly, a large number of officers are simultaneously deployed for backup in any of the five boroughs.

### Operational resources

The officers sent to check crowd disorder are trained within a new unit called Strategic Control Response (SCR) made up of 660 men (with an additional 200 to be incorporated subsequently) (personal interview with Inspector D., SCR). The selected men in the unit need to be dependable with an excellent record so that they can be trusted to offer new responses to new threats (Wilson, 2016). Police officers are aware of numerous videos recording police behaviour. Training in disorder control is thus continuous. The SRC, which operates twenty-four hours a day, must be ready to intervene at any moment; officers carry heavy weapons and, if needed, they can benefit from the support of the Emergency Intervention Unit, and from the Special Operation Division. The Emergency Intervention Unit is also heavily armed, walks in public space, and checks places which could be potential targets. The aim of the NYPD is to make them visible to remind the public that there is always a potential danger lurking and to act against amnesia (Body-Gendrot, 2012: 77).

The first goal of the SCR unit is to have orders properly communicated, Inspector D. observes. There is one insigna commander per scene, but if there are two sites of disorder, there will be one commander on each site. The commanders communicate directly with captains who then speak to the lieutenants who lead the sergeants along the chain of command. On average, the police presence represents approximately forty men who arrive in five vans to confront protesters. Lieutenant V., from this division, explains that the protesters are given clear orders via a giant megaphone. Other officers make sure that the warnings are heard despite the background noise, and they give a sign of approval to the commander. The police interviewees report that too often, the defendants have said in court that they had not heard the warnings. The megaphone should clarify the problem. The legal bureau officers are also on the ground and write down the terms of the warnings.

The NYPD officers are given tasers. They do not have to use lethal weapons, they observe, since their numbers are already a formidable resource.

If the rowdy crowd is big or a Type 3 disturbance – a demonstration by Black Lives Matter (BLM) may gather 1,000 people, but some demonstrations 25,000 people – the strategy is then to break large crowds into smaller groups and allow traffic to flow between them. No arrests are made then if no breach of law is observed. Some agitators are known by the police, but unlike in France, they cannot be arrested preventatively. The strategy is to have them followed by officers who can arrest them during action, if they have a reasonable suspicion that the law has been broken. The police strategy is to make arrests as early as possible. 'After visible arrests, the group may calm down, as few of them want to have a file in the police records', Chief M. observes.

Frequently, protesters are surprised when the NYPD officers confront and charge them, which is an approach that not all local police agencies have in American cities.

'The sleeping dragons' tactics is a mode of protest that officers have a hard time with, an intelligence service officer explains. This manoeuvre used by eight or nine protesters consists of participants handcuffing themselves to each other through a PVC pipe using wire and duct tape that they put on their arms in order to make it very difficult for the police to break as 'the duct tape can mess the sawing machine' used to unlock them from each other, Lieutenant S. observes (personal interview with the Strategic Division). The protesters may even chain themselves to objects that the police can only remove with a lot of difficulty. The officers do not want to hurt the protesters who then would denounce police brutality in order to gain sympathy from the public. All the arrests are filmed by the police officers to avoid litigation. With four million people carrying cameras, policemen need also to wear cameras. 'Many do currently', A. S., a General Intelligence counsel for twenty-five years, observes. 'This comes as a post-Ferguson effect' (Personal interview at NYU Law School, Jan. 14, 2016).

## Intelligence resources

The intelligence division is another strength of the NYPD. It is reported to be the largest Intelligence Department in the United States, with an extensive Closed Camera TV network (Gillham et al., 2013: 86, 97). Everyone in this unit remembered the disturbances associated with the Republican convention at Madison Square Garden in 1984. For A. S., the challenge came from the number of participants; this convention attracted 800,000 people. It was well handled by the police, no deaths occurred, and only one policeman was injured. But after the convention, dozens of lawsuits were started by people claiming that they were harmed by police misbehaviour (Interview at NYU Law School, Jan. 14, 2016). More recent confrontations are also memorable, such as those with Occupy Wall Street militants in 2011, those against the United States intervention in Iraq, or those launched by environmental groups and some focused groups (personal interview of Chief of Intelligence G., NYPD, Jan. 14, 2016). An anti-police demonstration may gather 25,000 people. Undercover officers from the intelligence service infiltrate the crowd and send information to the commanders who then can adjust the strategy according to the evolution of the situation. 'We need to learn who these groups are', I was told, a statement also made at the Met Intelligence Service. A reduced group of twenty-five officers within the intelligence service is usually able to anticipate and estimate how many people will show up for a wide-scale protest demonstration. Beforehand, they have tapped into the social networks. They need approval from the police legal services to do so and need to sign an investigative statement. As with the Met in London, and the French services, the intelligence unit infiltrates the groups by sharing conversations on their forums online, watching their videos, or by attending their protests undercover. The work carried by this division is crucial; it allows other branches to anticipate violence if a minority of protesters intends to carry harmful devices at the demonstration.

The channels and networks used by hostile groups change constantly. Lots of protesters come from other states, as Facebook or Twitter publicize the action about to take place. Social media mobilizes followers, and then organizers use such media to widely spread decisions and strategies.

## Technological resources

The NYPD benefits from a $150 million Security Coordination Center located in Lower Manhattan, close to the financial district, which it protects via its 2,000 cameras located in the Ring of Steel at the foot of the reconstructed tower of Ground Zero (interview). The Technical Assistance Resource Unit (TARU) team is also at the site of disorder. Its officers gather intelligence, document police/protester interactions, take pictures, and tweet them to the police commanders. In November 2014, after the decision was made not to indict the policeman allegedly responsible for the suffocation and death of Eric Gardner, a cigarette vendor, hundreds of exasperated militants converged on New York City from all over the country (personal interview, Assistant Chief M., Jan. 14, 2016). Some of them had 'long guns' (rifles). The police knew this fact beforehand due to intelligence and also because they had received many anonymous denunciations.

Among the technical resources from which they benefit, my interviewees frequently mentioned 'aviation' – that is, helicopters located in Brooklyn which can rapidly intervene on a site and send information relative to numbers and the geographical importance of the demonstration, for example. Photos taken from helicopters are sent to ground officers who can instantaneously adjust the strategy during a rowdy demonstration.

Another service, the Legal Division, is on site during the disorder. This division in New York has regular conversations with well-known militants such as Reverend Al Sharpton 'who are anti-police but accessible'. Some 'anti-everything groups' cannot be reached (personal interview, K. S., Legal Division). Approximately 180 legal attorneys advise the police of New York and indicate what can or cannot be done.

It may happen that this well-oiled machine becomes almost burnt out if it receives too many demands for order at the same time, as was the case in Paris during the state of emergency in spring 2016. Here, while the occupiers pursued their actions, the United Nations General Assembly met, the Pope was visiting the city for forty hours, and the president of the country was closing the assembly. Five different locations had to be kept under surveillance at the same time, mobilizing hundreds of officers, mostly from the SRU.

## Policing disorder at the Metropolitan Police Service

The British model of disorder policing works differently from that of France and that of the United States. As noted by Bayley (1979), the police should be defined by the link of forces with a superior authority. This authority could be the people or the government, be it democratic or tyrannical. It is the environment of police. In principle, the British police do not serve the state; they serve the people. British chief officers are accountable to the law rather than to national or local government.

### Operational resources

The structure of intervention in disorder in England has been efficient for the last twenty years (personal interview, New Scotland Yard, November 25, 2015). As a Gold Commander at the Metropolitan Police Service, Deputy Assistant Commissioner P.T. sets the strategy of intervention around specific parameters and resources to adjust to the challenges of the situation. Silver commanders, second in hierarchical position, define tactics on the ground. Then several types of bronze commanders intervene in terms of geography, intelligence, communication, protection, and use of firearms. When disorder is anticipated and preventative actions needed, Commanders talk to the appropriate people, establish contacts on the internet, and contact business owners and the affected communities (see chapter 7). They handle expectations. A range of police tactics enhance police capability for dynamic risk assessment, dialogue, and communication. Some participants may be detained for short periods before or at the end of an event to prevent conflicts and disorderly behaviours. The participants are aware that this possibility may happen. This is often the case during football events. The large number of 'knowns' facilitates police planning and proportionate policing.

Behaviours to be followed during order maintenance operations are inspired by the National Decision Making System, according to silver commander A. B., a Detective Chief Inspector in charge of public order investigation (Personal interview, New Scotland Yard, Nov. 25, 2015). This model emphasizes the importance of the centralization of structures which may be called upon to coordinate, to implement, or simply to assess and advise policy. Its role is to bring the disparate parts of the security agenda together. The main objective is set on information-sharing and the integration of intelligence efforts, with a view to producing threat assessments from a wide range of sources, offering a balanced perspective to governments. It ensures that resources are effectively allocated; reviews the effectiveness of a plan or body; checks the ability of different bodies to continue operating during emergencies; and oversees expenditure, administration, and policies of security agencies.

The impacts that police tactics can have upon crowd dynamics are found in the Elaborated Social Identity Model of crowd behaviour, taking into account the context of crowd (HMIC, 2011: 86). Conversely, the use of force during a large-scale event can only occur if there are enough police resources to do so, which was not the case in 2011, DOC Peter Terry remarks.

## Intelligence resources

Risk assessment at the Met is facilitated by intelligence gathered on the profile of groups involved in violent behaviours, on the possible threats associated with them, and on the local environment in which they move. Intelligence officers tap into the communications of websites and of established social networks (but at the time of writing, as in New York and Paris, they have not been able to break encrypted messages); they listen to telephone exchanges. Commanders are provided with information on the groups' anticipated numbers, their modes of transport, and the likely flashpoints. These elements produced by intelligence services allow them to deliver a tactical plan in the best circumstances, to elaborate contingency and emergency plans, and to assess resources. Then it is possible to distinguish 'the risk participants' from others.

There is a lot of work done ahead by intelligence teams and silver commanders, A. B. observes. He explains how undercover officers go to suspect groups' meetings, form people profiles, and manage to obtain access to useful information from tight circles. The websites and well-established social media are monitored by the intelligence services. As other police forces studied here, the Met must respect the Human Rights Act, defending individual freedoms, and respond with proportionality.

Every week, at the New Scotland Yard, intelligence police officers meet with officers trained in order maintenance, and they exchange information on potential risks and threats (ranked green, amber, or red according to the seriousness of the danger), on potential leaders among radical groups, on the traction they have.

### Technological resources

The various services at the Met insist on English police officers' reluctance to carry firearms. Very few do – less than two thousand, P. K. remarks. They may have to, in airports or as personal protection squads for royalties, for example. The Met has nineteen armed response vehicles to be used in case of persistent disorder. The most common resources for crowd containment are cordons, horse mounted police, and police dog handlers. In principle, the Met does not use water cannons, which are a source of controversy.

## Policing disorder at the Paris Préfecture de police and at the Ministry of the Interior

Public space is under police control in France. As at the Met and at the NYPD, avoiding person-to-person contact is a feature of the French mode of disorder policing, in order to avoid injuring protesters who would go to court as well as to protect the physical integrity of police forces. To avoid personal contact, devices like tear gas, tasers, baton guns, and sometimes water tanks and offensive grenades can form a physical screen. Baton charges are intended to 'create a no-man's-land that prevents person-to-person contact' (Fillieule and Jobard, 1998: 84). But recently, the extensive use of these 'less-than-lethal' weapons has been criticized after a protester lost one eye and went to court as a victim. Other cases are pending.

### Operational resources

Various types of specialized forces intervene on sites of public disorder. First, the gendarmes mobiles are squads which are at the disposal of the Ministry of Interior. The elite unit, GIGN, is an intervention group from gendarmerie nationale, which also acts in case of terrorism or other challenging risks. Second, the CRS (Compagnies républicaines de sécurité), a civilian corps from the national police (unlike the gendarmes, who are military), trained in anti-insurrection and anti-riot techniques are sent all over the country for crowd control and for the repression of public disorder. They were created in 1944, and there are sixty of them nationally. Historically, tensions have characterized the relationship between police and gendarmes, although they now both report to the minister of the interior. Third, the Research and Intervention Brigades (BRI), often called 'Anti-Gang Brigades', are also elite units of the Ministry of the Interior. BRI is a separate National Police unit reporting directly into the Paris Police Préfecture.[3] These forces undergo a hard physical training with regular drills. In principle, as for police forces abroad, the rules are simple: the men have to follow orders given by their hierarchy; they need to act as one, under the command of their senior officers. In practice, in the same way as demonstrators opposing each other, the forces of order do not necessarily act in a unified way – a situation that can potentially result in disastrous loss of time, as seen recently during the November 2015 attacks in Paris.[4]

Regarding the forces' specialization, the gendarme mobile forces and the CRS are not the only ones intervening to check rowdy disorder in the public space. The new trend is to call for a mix of forces made of anti-riot officers (BAC), local units of public safety, horseback police units, and dog brigades. In case of very serious disorder, shock forces like the GIGN (Group of Intervention from Gendarmerie Nationale) or the RAID (Research, Assistance, Intervention, Deterrence) are summoned. Created in 1985, RAID is the National Police counterpart of the National Gendarmerie. Both units share responsibility for the French territory.

Since 2009, RAID and the Paris BRI have formed a task force called 'National Police Intervention Force' (Force d'intervention de la Police nationale – FIPN). Since the terrorist attacks of 2015 and in order to banish inefficient competition between these forces, it has been decided that the force which first arrives on a site of massive disorder will exert its leadership over other forces.[5]

The intensive use of video recording by specialized police analysts allows them to identify potential offenders and to proceed to arrests at a later stage. In cases of space disruption, measures of incapacitation consist in arresting violent protesters even before demonstrations start.

Such was the case during an unauthorized pro-Palestinian demonstration in Paris on July 26, 2014. According to a report from the Bureau of public safety in the Parisian region, police officers made forty preventative arrests. Then rowdy confrontations took place at Place de la République, a site traditionally used for the expression of dissent, and more arrests followed, totalling seventy-six. Out of seventy-six stopped protesters, thirty-one had their papers checked and forty-five were held in custody. After a period of custody, twenty-six were set free, eight were held, nine were retained for more investigation, and two were summoned. Aged between sixteen and forty-two, only six of them had previous police files. Most of the three hundred violent participants, however, managed to run away (Zerouala, 2014).

During public disorder, as seen in chapter 2, rituals of intimidation are important. Heavily protected gendarmes hit their shields, policemen put their helmet visors down, and they all progress in a line or a column. Likewise, hooded protesters hide their faces with scarves and chant hostile slogans. Those are sources of intimidation but also means of communication intended to convince the public that protesters, attackers, and the police defend a righteous cause vying for the redefinition of order. Showing police drills on television ending with a quick police victory over terrorists is a pure exercise in public relations on the part of the minister of the interior. The same can be said with the elite New York Police Unit (the Critical Response Command Team) rehearsing for a terrorist attack for journalists from the *New York Times*.

Policemen still see crowds confronting them as irrational, irresponsible, and dangerous which need to be neutralized as quickly as possible. Police officers, however, establish distinctions between different types of protesters or of rebellious crowds and adjust their tactics proportionally to the various situations. Irresponsible looters will trigger harsher police responses than desperate farmers, who also benefit from judges' leniency.

A 1935 law requires protesters to give the police three days notice when they organize an event. The police can then anticipate what the peaceful organizers' intentions are and discuss details of the route to be followed. The Intelligence Service (DHRI) provides information to other police units regarding the demonstrators' goals, their possible numbers, and their frame of mind. A plan of action can be jointly elaborated with the prefect, namely assigning forces, selecting commanding senior officers and material resources.

In practice, as in London and New York, the law is never followed to the letter. 'If such was the case, two demonstrators out of five or more would be convicted' (personal interview with police officer from the General Inspection of Services, October 2015).

A challenge for senior police officers in the field may come from the control of their own men during protest events. As said before, the overall goal is to avoid an escalation of force between police and protesters. On one hand, both political authorities and public opinion disapprove of disorder and want order maintenance to prevail, and on the other, the management of protest is at the mercy of the weakest link – that is, of young police recruits who are not as disciplined or trained as expected. Their temptation to use force may be strong, and their discretionary power cannot be minimized.

> Non intervention and a dispassionate approach are the two criteria for excellence in the senior officers' view, but their men do not consider the operation a success without some kind of physical confrontation or without having evened the score with the demonstrators.
>
> *(Fillieule and Jobard 1998: 82)*

Another problem which should not be overlooked comes from the possible reluctance of inexperienced police officers to fully confront rowdy participants, such as football supporters or politicized extremists.

## Intelligence resources

The Intelligence Services had a good reputation in France and abroad. Almost four thousand men worked for this unit and studied minutely suspect populations in suspect neighbourhoods, particularly since the 1990s. An internal reorganization within the services took place in 2007 (personal interview with police officer from the General Inspection of Services, October 2015). The goal of the reform launched by the minister of the interior in 2008 was to create a new centralized Directorate of Domestic Intelligence (DCRI), modelled after the US Federal Bureau of Investigation (FBI). It merged former intelligence services (Renseignements généraux – RG) and the rather secret Direction of State Safety (DST), the mission of which was to trace spies. The former RG had accumulated years of experienced field work, especially in deprived, Muslim communities where they talked to imams, social workers, and ordinary people. It is reported that the reformers thought that the RG would influence the culture of the DST, but the reverse happened (personal interview, police officer from the General Inspection of Services, October 2015). Men from the field opted for more prestigious bureaucratic work and a lot of resources were lost – not only many files on suspects but approaches with experienced teams and so forth. The emphasis was put on technology and not on human resources. 'Destroying the RG appears then as a tragic error', a former officer reports. 'A generation of potential terrorists disappeared, files were destroyed, united teams of police officers were split, and the price to pay today is high' (Alonso et al., 2015). Currently, French intelligence is characterized less by a global failure than by a series of dysfunctions in the gathering, treatment, and processing of information, a former DGSE chief remarks.

Among 20,000 suspects recorded by police files, half of them are linked to Muslim fundamentalism. The failure of the DCRI clearly appeared as early as 2012 with the Mohammed Merah case (see chapter 7). This radical Muslim made undetected trips to the Afghan-Pakistan border, connected to Salafist websites, and horded an arsenal of weapons in his home. Not only did he slip through the surveillance of the DCRI, whose headquarters in Paris ignored the Toulouse intelligence service's warnings, but erroneously, he was considered as a lone wolf and a possible recruit as informer. At the end of 2013, a new service, Territorial Intelligence (RT), was created with two thousand men. A new division, the General Directorate for internal security (DGSI), emphasized the use of new technologies and replaced the DCRI in 2014. Porous borders in Europe, however, make a strictly national approach hazardous. Eradicating the distrust and isolating national services from one another in Europe seems an urgent task to confront global threats.

## Technological resources

Better protection and more efficient weapons allow national forces to check violent protesters instead of merely pursuing a 'goal of containment', as was formerly the case (personal interview, police officer from the General Inspection of Services, October 2015). The 2005 events, then those in Villiers-le-bel in the Parisian Region, in 2007, led to a massive police investment in technologies of surveillance: night vision binoculars, drones, devices for listening live to the social networks used by the protesters, and video cameras recording their faces. In Villiers-le-bel, protesters had infiltrated the police internal streams of communication, allowing them to be prepared for police intervention, in most circumstances. Firearms were also used against the police. After two policemen's horrendous murder by a terrorist at their home, a reform in 2016 allowed police officers to keep their arms, even when they are out of service. Two hundred and thirty million euros were allocated to police to upgrade their equipment. This large budget has raised comments regarding the militarization of protest policing and its political economy. Private businesses in charge of devices of police control such as tear gas or stun guns benefit from the sophisticated equipment of law enforcement forces during protest management. In the United States, the narrow cooperation of private sector interests with those of public authorities was denounced a long time ago. In the European Union, 'international cooperation has led towards militarized forms of intervention, as well as a consistent reduction in democratic accountability' (Reiter & Fillieule, 2006). The impressive affluence of the less-than-lethal weapons market is ironic since social unrest and political protests are seen as main 'drivers' of its dynamics, Atak and della Porta (2016: 527) observe. They report that in Europe the market was valued at $287.3 million in 2013, expected to grow at 5.3 percent annually and reach $372.4 million by 2018.

This brief comparison reveals that law enforcers are confident in their operational, intelligence, technical resources and capacity to manage public disorder. Some types of disorder are more challenging than others. The well-oiled machine of the NYPD with its reputation for expertise, resources, and competence seems well prepared for such challenges. The Metropolitan Police Service and the French police struggled during riotous events in the first decade of the twenty-first century. With new forms of terrorist attacks, their capacities and limits are tested again.

Research has shown that whether the police do not just serve the state but are also accountable for their actions and outcomes to the people makes a lot of difference. American and British reports on police reforms all emphasize that proximity, trust, and 'consent' allow police forces to give a better performance, even during acute social tensions. The respect of procedural rules founds the legitimacy of the police and explains why people obey the law (Tyler, 1990). Modes of community policing are not then incompatible with the violent deterrence of contentious activities. This is where the possible reconciliation between various styles of policing takes place.

When disorder occurs in a city, all police forces studied here resort to repressive methods that look strangely similar. They operate through sophisticated weaponry with familiar tactics such as 'kettling' (*nasse* in French), or 'trudge and wedge', pushing and cajoling resistant crowds, with elaborate techniques and tailored tactics. They communicate along the same lines.

The role of the police as a brake to public disorder is thus established and legitimized by authorities and the need to return to order. Yet police officers care about their image. Avoiding sanctions and the verdict of public opinion acts in return as a brake on the unrestrained use of force.

Lastly, it is currently observed that the supposedly silent police institution more frequently than before comes forward, speaks out, and publicly expresses discomfort and fatigue. Too frequently, the part played by the police is negatively or unfairly covered by the social media and the general media after repetitive and hostile confrontations. The city listens and then diverging and unexpected voices are heard, some defending the police, others expressing hostile views. A difficult but welcome dialogue then starts between authorities, police spokesmen, and protesters, with the public watching and listening to what takes place in the city.

The next chapter will explain that police forces are more or less autonomous, according to political regimes, some being very centralized like France or decentralized like the United States, with Britain in between. The cards played by states and judges may then make a difference in modes of order maintenance.

## Notes

1   The Turkish *jandarma* is affiliated to the general chief of staff who is acting as the head of a constitutional power and not answering to the minister of defence. The gendarme protects borders, fights a domestic war against the terrorist organization PKK, and does order maintenance at the same time. Its agents are liable to military courts (Roché, 2012).
2   Exchange of emails with the author and a third party, September 23, 2015.
3   'The police of Paris ... do not exist legally as a force since there are only two national forces in France, the Paris police being part of the national police. However, based on empirical observation and not on law, it is observed that Paris police is a force in itself. It has independent command and control, internal oversight, as well as other features of a national force (including its intelligence services)' (Roché, 2012: 11).
4   Such situations can potentially result in disastrous loss of time, as seen recently during the November 2015 attacks in Paris. Due to a delayed information, the anti-riot police arrived rather late at the Stade de France in Saint Denis. An anti-riot squad located next to the concert hall where massacres took place was not asked to intervene, whereas a more distant one was called. Investigations will probably reveal why such decisions were made and will be kept confidential.
5   In early 2015, the seven regional units of the National Police, previously known as (GIPNs), were permanently integrated into RAID and called 'RAID branches'. Such units were then subdivided into sections and then in smaller fractions in order to ease arrests when trespassers were caught in the act and given summary summons, in cases of vandalism or assault.

# 6

# STATES AND JUSTICE

This chapter examines how states via the police, the courts, and other institutions deal with public order and disorder. The idea is not to provide a catalogue of all the public measures that can be taken to maintain order and to check public disorder, but to give some examples of the range of tools that states and judges have at their disposal at any given time to do so. In democracies, emergency laws, executive orders, reinforcement of coercive powers, accelerated judicial processes, the creation and/or coordination of enforcement services, freedom restrictions, and investigative commissions all fill such a purpose.

Are states' powers regarding security weakened or strengthened by current global processes? Is the states' sovereignty changing with the competition of multiple actors involved in security? In the first section of the chapter, I review states' and judges' responses to disorder in the three types of case studies discussed earlier (chapter 3). Those cases are not comprehensive, but they are samples of the complex responses given to public disorder by state's authorities and they allow for comparisons. Then, in the second section, I draw more general observations on states' and judicial stability and on how they adjust to the context of globalization and global communication.

## Authorities' and judges' responses to public disorder

### The Paris and London cases

#### Paris

The resources developed by the French state are both material and symbolic. In 2005, President Chirac declared a state of emergency for twelve days, extending it on November 9 to three months, allowing the state to wield its sovereignty over the law in an extraordinary situation. This measure was uniformly approved by the

French. It authorized prefects to impose nightly curfews, to permit search and sei-zures, to ban public assembly, to deport undocumented foreigners involved in the banlieues' outbursts, to ban the sale of petrol cans to youths, and to have bars and entertainment halls close early in the problem areas of twenty-five geographical departments.[1]

Rhetorically, from the initial moment of disturbance and through their devel-opment, authorities' provocative statements revealed their confidence that the media would serve their cause. To deflect attention from embarrassing questions regarding the shortcomings of policies addressing problems in downtrodden ban-lieues, the official communication, appealing to law-abiding citizens, focused instead on rebellious youths' behaviours and on their differences compared with the mainstream population. The day after the two youths' deaths in Clichy, at a press conference, Interior Minister Sarkozy declared that it was during an attempted burglary that the youths ran from the police. Prime Minister Villepin confirmed his suspicion that the burglars were caught in the act, before adding that (their death) was a terrible human tragedy (Mauger, 2006: 31). Earlier, Minis-ter Sarkozy had controversially said that he would ensure that poor banlieue areas would be cleaned of scum (*racaille*) with a power hose (*kärcher*). At one point, dur-ing the riots, he hinted at a plot: 'What we witnessed in the Department of Seine-Saint Denis tonight (November 2) was by no means spontaneous, it was perfectly organized. We are currently searching by whom and how' (Bertho, 2009: 67). Later, Sarkozy declared at the National Assembly that '75 percent to 85 percent of the rioters were well-known delinquents' and that the riots expressed 'the will of those who turned delinquency into their main occupation, to resist the ambi-tion of the Republic to restore its order and its laws on the territory' (Mauger, 2006: 42). (The general prosecutor of the Paris Appeals Court alluded to the acts of 'organized bands'.) Sarkozy reinforced cultural divides in remarking that 'there are more problems for a child of an immigrant of black Africa or of North Africa than for a son of a Swede, Dane, or a Hungarian, because culture, because polyg-amy, because social origins bring more hardships for him' (Sciolino, 2005). The head of the conservative party in the National Assembly, and one of the country's most eminent historians added that polygamy was the reason why youths were not in school but on the streets, due to overcrowded flats with several wives. These innuendos and the constant blaming of Islam in some media, adding to the propaganda of the extreme right and playing on fears, partly succeeded, since after 2005 the global index measuring tolerant attitudes (and ethnocentrism) in France marked a drop, losing five points from sixty-five to sixty (Commission nationale consultative des droits de l'homme, 2014: 160, 165). Other factors may have influenced the rise of intolerance, such as a very high unemployment, and an increased competition for meagre resources.

Most media praised the bureaucratic and political responses given to public dis-turbances in three hundred neighbourhoods. They shared the police interpretation of events, according to the victims' lawyers.

Regarding the police management of public disorder, what was said in chapter 5 need not be repeated. It should, however, be emphasized that

> the 2005 riots did not mark a break in the French approach to order maintenance, all the more so as French police [including national gendarmerie] think and claim to have victoriously met the strong challenge to which they were confronted during the three weeks of Autumn 2005. One does not change a winning team and the Minister of the Interior heading the two forces [police and gendarmes], since 2009, has hardly changed anything.
>
> *(Jobard, 2015: 75–76)*

How does one measure success? For officials, that there were no casualties was a success. Compared with the Los Angeles riots, for instance, ending after fifty-four deaths and two thousand casualties, there were no deaths in Clichy caused by the police, besides the two electrocuted youths. The official rhetoric of the French minister of the interior, carefully controlling his media communication, emphasized that no death was reported by the media. The second aspect in favour of the French police management of the 2005 disorder concerns the spatial containment operated by police forces. It is indeed less costly for governmental authorities (i.e. the prefects) to have disturbances contained within the strict borders of a *cité* – sink estates with huge, cheaply built public housing at the periphery of main urban centres – than to let them reach the core of Paris or other large cities where the perceived destruction of wealthy assets, public and private buildings, and general transportation would be costly materially and symbolically. Even the cost of cars burned by youths during confrontations with the police is taken care of by the French All-Providing state, according to a law unanimously passed in 2008 interpreting arson as a norm, a risk, rather than as a breach of order. 'Everyone knows how dreadful it is, for a modest family living in a low-income estate, a banlieue place, often badly served by the public transportation system, to see its car set alight', a Parliament Member asserted (reported by Jobard, 2014: 140). Jobard points out how such a law emphasizes the circular rituality of riots occurring in France and the apparent repetition of the same patterns both on the part of the angry youths and that of police forces, despite a diversity of local contexts.

State authorities could count on 30,000 well-trained and supervised anti-riot units (CRS) and on subnational forces which could easily rotate when they showed signs of exhaustion, which was not necessarily the case for protesters. Mass arrests contributed to the decline of riots, as shown by both curves falling, day after day. However, on the field, there was difficult police coordination, as previously noted. One noticeable consequence of this awareness was to subsequently boost anti-riot police equipment. Acknowledging that, on the field, operations had been hard to conduct in 2005 and that the police needed better and more appropriate material support, Minister of Interior Sarkozy allocated '450 baton guns, 2,800 tear-gas canisters, 6,700 "bliniz" missiles [prohibited after 2014] and a series of protective devices like bullet-proof helmets' to the police in December 2005 (Dufresne, 2010: 66). Improved technologies of surveillance to facilitate night operations and better anticipation were also provided. After discovering that their own communication channels had been hacked, police investigators were allowed to tap into the youths' channels of communication.

Concerning judicial efficiency, state authorities were supported by prosecutors who were asked to be tougher than usual. In that respect, they were efficient. The curve of extensive arrests indicates that summary processes translating into large sentencing reduced the amount of rioting. However, according to a judge from Bobigny in the Parisian region, in more than one-third of the cases – a much higher proportion than usual – charges were dismissed because police evidence was not convincing enough. Most of the offenders were accused of throwing rocks and missiles at the police; others were indicted for arson or vandalism. They were sentenced on average to four months of incarceration, including two-and-a-half months of suspended sentencing, a milder judicial decision than in the English case. A lot of French judges are convinced that prison does not work for juvenile street activism, and some of them write editorials in national newspapers to support this view (Sultan, 2010).

At the local level, active mayors of urban deprived areas mobilized their local forces, made use of public and private security agents, summoned anti-violence commissions, and engaged in a dialogue with public housing managers. Silent marches, as symbolic demonstrations of unity and solidarity, showed that residents are not without resources. But there is a time for civil mobilization, which can only occur after civil unrest. Other mayors merely observed the status quo.

After the events, French national authorities were reluctant to institute a major public inquiry that would have circulated on the internet, possibly starting a debate on inequalities and racism in French society. 'Before the events, the government did not want to know what was wrong with the banlieues; they did not want to know afterwards', Roché observes (2006: 184). Maybe they did not want police officers to talk. Maybe elites were cynical enough to bet on the French lack of empathy for those revolting 'others'. Despite a revolutionary legacy, only 4 percent of the French approved 'the fact of causing material damages' to express opinions or claims (Brouard & Tiberj, 2005). Hardly any call denunciating troublemakers were reported by the media, and civil society was not asked to cooperate into the return to order. Ironically, the Stock Exchange kept rising between October 28 and November 8, 2005 (Roché, 2006: 214; 56), revealing the elites' indifference and the marginal position that the banlieues occupy for the mainstream, except in terms of unspecified insecurity.

## London

In London, as in Paris, a lot of care was put into governmental communication regarding the disturbances, at the eve of a global event, the Olympic Games.

Rhetorically, Prime Minister Cameron as Nicolas Sarkozy (as Prime Minister Erdogan in Istanbul and Chief Executive CY Leung in Hong Kong) chose to demonize the rebellious youths involved in the disturbances to deflect attention from embarrassing questions. He highlighted the moral decay and 'sick culture' of the looters, denouncing 'criminality, pure and simple . . . people with a twisted moral code, people with a complete absence of self-restraint . . . behaving as if your choices had no consequences. Children without fathers. Schools without discipline. Reward without effort' (Newburn, 2016b).

Prime Minister Cameron did not spare the police management of the 'riots' either. Rumour circulated that an American police chief, Bill Bratton, who had accumulated renowned experience in New York, then in Los Angeles, by apparently claiming the disorderly streets back thanks to his methods of police management and zero tolerance, could be appointed to head New Scotland Yard. The Home Office strongly opposed such an idea. The Metropolitan Police Service acknowledged their poor management of the initial disorder. Five lives were lost, allegedly over 15,000 people were involved in the disturbances, more than 2,500 shops were looted, and the cost of the damage ran into the hundreds of millions of pounds (Winlow et al., 2015: 135), However, once in control, with support arriving from nearby regions (overall 16,000 officers were on the streets of London, four days after the riot began), the police were in a position to check disorder. Within two months, the ten forces most heavily affected by the rioting had made approximately four thousand arrests, a police activity that the government could count on as well as on that provided by the courts.

'In the first year after the riots, of the more than 2,000 people sentenced by the courts, two thirds received an immediate custodial sentence – the normal sentencing having been suspended – with sentence being on average almost five times the usual length', that is, seventeen months each (Newburn, 2016b). This heavy sentencing may be explained by the offenders previous interactions with the police: according to the Ministry of Justice (2011), 80 percent of adult defendants and 62 percent of juveniles brought to the courts had committed almost a combined twenty thousand previous offenders'. Courts fulfilled the role they were asked to fill by the state and contributed to the decline of disorder. Other governmental measures, overtly punitive, addressed the conservative voters. They advocated the suppression of family benefits and the eviction of delinquent families from public housing units. Local authorities and methods to do so via images caught by CCTVs called for civic denunciation, while innovative collective actions to repair the streets were encouraged.

Major public inquiries were launched and the reports circulated on the internet. Their recommendations opened the path to police reforms. They filled 'the various practices of a restored social order, complete with a series of rituals including investigative 'commissions', 'findings', public shaming and finally, the much awaited white paper to forestall the fire next time' (Brotherton, 2014: 234). Yet, as in France and the United States,

> the UK chose not to look too long and too hard at itself, at the state of its economy, the increasing stratification of society, the declining standards of public education, the enormous cynicism among youth, the rising prison

population, the deleterious impact of consumerism and celebrity culture, the large swathes of the country now virtually criminalized and the increasing feelings of precariousness among the working and middle-class population.

*(Standing, 2011 in Brotherton, 2014: 229)*

The government's response to disorder was to settle for courts' decisions and test a strategy of 'Othering' and scapegoating focused on convenient subjects, the young, the poor, and 'minorities', truncating debates which might have taken place, as they did in Britain, at the time of Lord Scarman and his inquiry on the Brixton disorder in 1981. He had published a report on the kinds of reforms that British society should look towards, a move similar to that of the Kerner Commission in the United States after widespread disturbances shaking the country from 1965 to 1968.

## American tools against public disorder

Unlike the previous cases, law and order is a states' and local prerogative in the United States, and it is at this level that the analysis of the US riots must begin before turning to the federal arena.

### *Local actions against public disorder*

Three of the case studies in this research are located in the United States, where law and order is an issue handled by states' jurisdiction. The federalization of the issue, tightly related to public concerns, however, explains why the federal level also intervenes in such local matters.

In Ferguson, as in Baltimore, Republican governors Jay Nixon and Larry Hogan were within their rights when, by executive order, they declared a state of emergency, called the National Guards, and imposed night curfews to stop public disorder in 2014 and in 2015. Those were powerful tools that contributed to quell outbursts coming from angry minority youths exasperated by repetitive police lethal shootings. Although disturbances took place in other cities, all the urban constituencies were not mobilized. But the president and US attorneys repeatedly had to intervene to indicate their support to social justice. Justice played an important part both in activating and/or checking local expressions of outrage.

In the Ferguson case, as noted, the role of the local prosecutor did not seem impartial to a number of observers, and he was accused by the media of having sided with the police. The Republican governor of Missouri refused, however, to replace him, ignoring the pressure of groups seeking what they perceived as fair justice. Protesters' claims favoured independent prosecutors who would be appointed to investigate the circumstances of local police officers' lethally firing at minorities. But more time may be needed for this reform, and its implementation will vary according to state.

The popular jury's verdict after the death of Michael Brown also started a general debate on popular juries in the country[2]. As the verdicts related to the Rodney

King case in Los Angeles and the Trayvon Martin case in Seminole county, Florida, revealed, Caucasian or Latino jury members who acquitted police officers lived in the same suburban communities, they shared middle-class values, and they could not adequately judge the circumstances of incidents taking place in deprived neighbourhoods that they only know by hearsay and via the media. In the Brown case, there were allegedly problems of neutrality involved, but due to the tense local context, the verdict was not nullified.

The situation was different in Baltimore, Maryland, where the attorney general, Marilyn Mosby, responded rapidly to the outrage caused by the police lethal misconduct towards Freddie Gray. On May 1, 2015, the six involved policemen were charged for improper behaviour and one of them for a serious crime. However, letting the police investigate their delinquent police officers was a costly error of the prosecutor; it led to the dismissal of charges against all six police officers by the judge. Despite Mayor of Baltimore Stephanie Rawlings-Blake's firm handling of the disturbances, however, her reputation was tarnished by the events. So was prosecutor Marilyn Mosby's handling of the cases.

## Federal actions

At the federal level, the involvement of both the president and the US attorney general was more than lip service. In light of the Ferguson events that exposed rifts in the relationship between local police and the communities they serve, on December 18, 2014, President Obama signed an executive order and created a nine-member task force on 'Twenty-First Century Policing', asking it to identify best practices.[3] In May 2015, important recommendations were made. Building trust and legitimacy on both sides of the police/citizen divide was advice based on the findings of Tom Tyler (1990), a scholar who examined why people obey the law. People are more likely to obey the law when they believe that those who are enforcing it have authority that is perceived as legitimate by those subject to it. Law enforcement agencies should have a guardian rather than a warrior mindset and should adopt procedural justice as their guiding principle, establishing a culture of transparency and accountability to build public trust. There should be clear and comprehensive policies on the use of force (including training on the importance of de-escalation), on mass demonstrations (including the appropriate use of equipment, particularly rifles and armoured personnel carriers), among others (such as external and independent investigations and prosecutions of officer-involved shootings and other use of force situations and in-custody deaths).

Law enforcement agencies in the United States are encouraged to conduct peer reviews of critical incidents separate from criminal investigations and to establish civilian oversight mechanisms with their communities. The federal Office of Justice Programs (OJP) and Office of Community-Oriented Policing Services (COPS) can provide assistance and incentives to local police agencies (as is currently the case in Ferguson). Besides an emphasis on technological training, community policing, quality training, and education, the creation of bodies at the federal level to boost such efforts was emphasized by the task force (President's Task Force, 2015). This commission's influence may appear limited, but some of its members were eager to implement reforms as soon as they were back to their constituencies (personal interview with T. M., one of the commission members, December 2015). More states currently require their police officers to wear cameras, a difficult reform to implement due to the resistance of local police agencies.

At the head of the US Department of Justice, President Obama successively appointed two minority members known for their commitment to racial justice as well as progressive judges at the Supreme Court. The investigations led by the Justice Department's Civil Rights Division brought at least twenty civil rights lawsuits against delinquent municipal police departments. As noted, regarding Ferguson, the scathing federal report resulting from a lengthy investigation pointed to its broken criminal justice system and on its money-making local power apparatus. The report circulated all over the world via the internet and sustained a lot of indignation from progressive observers. Federal and local authorities spent months negotiating a settlement with new guidelines on arrests without probable cause and the misuse of stun guns by local law enforcement. An ordinance punishing jaywalking was prohibited, and police shooting on moving cars was forbidden. At first, the city rejected an agreement to overhaul its criminal justice system using the costs of the reform (appointing an independent monitor and better paying police) as an excuse not to step forward. But in March 2016, the city council changed its mind and avoiding an expensive legal fight with the federal government, it signed a consent decree. It will cost Ferguson less than a lawsuit.

In terms of justice at the federal level, numerous decisions support fundamental rights such as the freedom of expression as well as basic institutions as the police. Recent decisions from the US Supreme Court (*Plumhoff v. Rickard* in 2014 and *Comnick v. Thompson* in 2011) make it extremely difficult, if not impossible, to convict police officers and their local employers, the cities, in the case of civil rights violation and power abuse. Two journalists (Park and Lee, 2016) examined eleven recent cases which had fuelled outrage and heightened racial tensions after allegedly unjustified police lethal shootings on black men, caught on video. In all the cases, accused officers were placed on administrative leave or reassigned, a routine step. In four cases (Arlington, Texas; Cincinnati, Ohio; Prairie View, Texas; and North Charleston, South Carolina), they were fired. Criminal charges were brought in five of the cases against involved officers. In four cases, including Baltimore, grand juries declined to bring charges. The cities did not admit any wrongdoing, yet they offered large settlements to the victims' families in the range of $5–6.5 million. Four of these cases incited the US Department of Justice to open civil rights investigations into the practices of police department (Baltimore, Chicago, North Charleston, and Ferguson). The case of the Occupy protesters in New York illustrates a range of judges' decisions regarding their responsibility and that of police officers generally.

## The Occupy movements

### *New York City*

Despite the global visibility of the Occupy Wall Street mobilization which lasted three months and the strong support that it received, the City of New York revealed its strength in restoring order in 2011. Mayor Bloomberg asserted that he supported the right to protest as long as it was within the law. When he felt that the time was ripe to end the occupation, that conservative news dailies, radios, and television channels had evidence against the deviance going on in the park, the mayor commanded David Kelly, his police chief, to evacuate the park. As time went on, the support for OWS and their denunciation of neo-liberalism, banks, corruption, and economic insecurity had become less innovative for the media.

Both City Hall and the police communicated powerfully on the legitimacy of their position. They skilfully mastered public relations techniques.

> The NYPD actively shaped the production of information by the press and other commentators by framing OWS protesters as potential and actual threats to American society and national security. . . . OWS grievances were frequently characterized as unrealistic, incoherent, overly simplistic, part of a 'blame game', job destroying and harmful to the middle class. The Zuccotti encampment was referred to as a den of criminal activity including sex crimes, drug use and gang-related activity as well as a dumping ground for the chronically homeless, mentally ill and unemployed 'who just needed to get a job'.
>
> *(Gilham et al., 2013: 97)*

This portrayal appealed to the working population hostile to supposedly idle, middle-class youths in dreadlocks, occupying the park. 'In America, there is a long-running animosity towards ideology as such, and communism and socialism in particular', Winlow et al. rightly point out (2014: 161). Even in New York, majorities are not ready for a revolution and city officials were well aware of it. Mayor Bloomberg could then command his police chief to clear the park, saying that health and safety conditions had become intolerable. The police had considerable resources to do so (chapter 5). A total of 7,700 OWS participants were arrested between September 2011 and June 2013 (Brotherton, 2014: 225). In the end, the mayor thus appeared as the proud supporter of the city that wins (and never sleeps) due to its work ethic. The police, for their part, publicly emphasized their professionalism and their restraint when handling disruptive and potentially dangerous activists. The media, confined to a free-press zone, could not cover the eviction live from the park. After the event, the judges took over.

After arrests were made in Manhattan in connection with Occupy, including seven hundred of them on the Brooklyn Bridge on October 1, approximately half of all defendants accepted offers from the Manhattan District Attorney's office to dismiss charges if they avoided arrest for six months. Hundreds more pleaded guilty to get a lighter sentence. Overall, less than 3 percent of the total (i.e. fifty-three cases) resulted in convictions (Ax, 2012). Even when they felt that their arrests were illegitimate, many protesters preferred not to go to court, which was a lengthy and costly process. A few cases lingered and lasted more than ten times as long as the occupation itself did. The vast majority of arrested protesters were charged with minor infractions, such as disorderly conduct or blocking traffic.

In a few cases, the protesters received support from justice. In a written ruling, a federal district judge believed the marchers when they said that they did not receive proper warning by the police that if they walked on the Brooklyn Bridge on October 1, they would be arrested (CBS, May 2, 2012; June 7, 2012). 'Indeed, the plaintiffs' video shows what should have been obvious to any reasonable officer, namely, that the surrounding clamour interfered with the ability of demonstrators as few as 15 feet away from the bull horn to understand the officer's instructions', the judge remarked. He said that the videos offered by both sides showed that the police officers 'exercised some degree of control over the marchers, defining their route and directing them, at times, to follow certain rules'. But 'no reasonable officer could imagine, in these circumstances, that this warning was heard by more than a small fraction of the gathered multitude'. However, he discarded the claim that arresting protesters was a deliberate policy by the city to discourage protests. The judge cited the contributions of people such as Thomas Paine and Martin Luther King Jr., saying 'what a huge debt this nation owes to its 'troublemakers'. 'They have forced us to focus on problems we would prefer to downplay or ignore', he said. He continued:

> Yet, it is often only with hindsight that we can distinguish those troublemakers who brought us to our senses from those who were simply 'troublemakers'. Prudence, and respect for the constitutional rights to free speech and free association, therefore dictate that the legal system cut all non-violent protesters a fair amount of slack.

Police officers 'did training in disorder control about how to break up mass protests and did not do training in First Amendment policing', he added.

This judge summarizes the position frequently taken in this research, showing that disorder can be a healthy signal of institutions' dysfunctions.[4]

## Gezi Park

After the Gezi Park occupation and evacuation, the return to order in Istanbul was handled by the mayor, Kadir Topbas, at the end of spring 2013. The police received the order to evacuate the park, but its poor training and supervision and the brutality of the crackdown, watched live on television and on social media, triggered an outcry from the outraged public, according to media reports. The absence of consultation between the mayor and his constituents was notorious, and the destruction of a landmark in the park displayed a top-down process after the conclusion of an independent commission on the transformation of the park as 'not serving the public interest', had been flatly rejected by the mayor.

With the transformation of Gezi Park, the stake was a visible recentralization of urban policies in Turkey. 'Such transformation is led by the central power, in its own interest, short-cutting local mechanisms of decision-making and control' (Pérouse, 2013). In the debates and negotiations which had taken place since the beginning of May 2013, neither the Beyoglü district mayor nor the mayor were players, a sign of their powerlessness. Gezi Park was not a unique case. All the major transportation programmes intended to make Istanbul a global city were handled at the centre by the Justice and Development Party, the AKP.

According to French scholar Jean-François Pérouse, the mechanisms of civic participation which had been set by local laws passed in 2004 and in 2005 were not implemented as counter-powers. Associations and trade organizations were marginalized. President Recep Tayyip Erdogan's and the AKP's goal is to make Istanbul attractive for international tourists, most of all consumerist and religious upper- and middle-class Muslims. For Kaya (2016, forthcoming), Prime Minister Recep Tayyip Erdoğan's intention of building mosques in Taksim Square and Camlica Hill was only one example of his will of raising 'religious and conservative youth', urging mothers to give at least three births, directly intervening in the content of the Turkish soap operas, and banning alcohol on university campus, thus marking his control on Turks' paths of life.

With Gezi Park, the aim was to revive the Ottoman past. With the reconstruction of the military barracks built early in the nineteenth century, then destroyed in 1940, with the renovation of the park designed by French architect Henri Prost and with the pedestrian zoning of Taksim Square, the goal was to change the balance: public space would no longer be shared by the whole population; the Ottoman reference would benefit the privileged. Since June 2013, two hundred sites from the Ottoman era have been marked for renovation. Once more, space is an issue of contention revealing power relations and public and private interests' strategies for appropriation. Next to Taksim Square, nine census tracts were bulldozed at the end of 2012 and impoverished tenants pushed out, not an unusual phenomenon in large Western cities.

Politically, as in Hong Kong, the confiscation of public space by public authorities is more a scheme for silencing dissent than for alleviating car traffic. For conservative decision makers, the park cannot 'serve deviant uses which would disturb the urban and moral dominant economy' (Pérouse, 2013). In Istanbul, Taksim Square was traditionally used for the demonstrations of unions and political parties. But the use the park to celebrate May 1 was banned after 1978. In 2013, it was announced that Taksim would no longer be appropriate for public demonstration. This decision is to be understood in a context of conservative moral order that also bans the consumption of alcohol and sexual freedom in public space.

In his communication on Gezi Park, Prime Minister Erdogan, at various times, demonized the occupiers. 'We cannot sit and watch a few hooligans coming to the square and provoking the people' (Amnesty report, 2016: 5). 'The state will have to consider every individual (there) as members of terrorist organizations', he mentioned in a speech on June 15. Appealing to religious conservatives, Erdogan also labelled occupiers 'drunkards' and 'alcoholics'. Addressing a rally of the Justice and Development Party (AKP) on June 24, 2013, he added the following:

> The limits of tolerance have been exceeded. I told my minister of the interior: within 24 hours, you will clean up the Atatürk Cultural Center. You will clean up the square. You will clean up the statue. After that, you will clean up Gezi Park.

He also called 'legendary' the response given by police to the Gezi Park occupation. With a few exceptions, official statements have exonerated the police of wrongdoing and given a vision of them as the victims of violence. The Amnesty International report (2016: 36) observes that 'the encouragement at the highest levels of the use of force and the excuses offered when it has been used excessively, have undoubtedly contributed to the scale of the police abuses that have accompanied the Gezi Park protests'.

The context contributes to the understanding of the authorities' position. The governmental elites support a Haussmanian vision of Istanbul, sanitized, segmented between 'clean', international, and 'moral' spaces, appealing to educated Muslim upper- and middle-classes on one hand and, on the other, marginalized, crowded, traditional neighbourhoods. The centralization of the management process of order and of the prime minister's authoritarian character, already distinguishable, was also obvious in this case.

According to observers working for Amnesty International (2016), the authorities' response to the Gezi Park protest has been characterized by an extreme level and sustained nature of abusive use of force by law enforcement officials during the demonstrations. Not for a generation has the level of police violence against demonstrators been so pronounced, they noted. On July 10, more than eight thousand people had been injured at the scene of demonstrations. Three people were killed by police, one of them through brutal beating. The minister of the interior announced on June 23 that there had been approximately 4,900 detentions from the scenes of protests. All summer, the police continued to detain and question individuals unofficially across Turkey. Complaints were not seriously investigated. Impunity prevailed. Many investigations regarding police misbehaviour were closed by judges. In the end, members of Taksim Solidarity association were investigated under anti-terrorist laws, and the risk of counter-charges against those complaining led many of them not to report abuse. Most of the time, impunity prevailed.

The Amnesty report points out that Turkish authorities have displayed – with some exceptions – a blatant disregard for the right to peaceful assembly as set out in international and national law. The government has repeatedly sought to discredit the protesters' motives, integrity, and behaviour.

Yet democratic institutions played their part. A coalition of over one hundred non-governmental organizations, political groups, and professional bodies formed rallies against police brutality which, at first, were tolerated. It is estimated that, in various parts of Turkey, two and a half million people participated in such rallies, marches, and forums. The strike launched by trade unions in support of the protesters was not forbidden either, and the workers' march gathered several thousand people around the country.

However, democratic counter-powers were light by contrast with the central power's ambitions. Many public and private interests supported Istanbul's future global status.

## Hong Kong

The handling of public disorder during the Occupy mobilizations is intriguing. It displays a mix of democracy inherited from Hong Kong's close ties with Britain, and of brutal repression due to China's increasing interference in the territory's local management. The way the Legco handled the so-called Umbrella revolution reflects such ambiguity. It displays democratic processes but also the constraints of the pressures exerted by China on this institution. For example, although in principle chief executive CY Leung agreed to meet the students for a discussion, he never did and let his representative Carrie Lam meet them; as expected by those siding with the students, nothing came out of the discussion. The difficult position of the Legco, itself divided, came both from the non-violent character of the protest and from the disruption of local economy. A democratic decision was to replace the Hong Kong anti-riot police, perceived by the public as too brutal, and have the unit sent back to their barracks early on, at the beginning of the mobilization. Television channels were not censored and could report various police crackdowns.

However, according to the Amnesty International report (2016),

> police in Hong Kong formally arrested 955 people who had taken part in the 79-day pro-democracy protests. . . . A further 48 were summoned. Among those arrested were opposition lawmakers, the three co-founders of the 'Occupy Central' civil disobedience campaign, and leaders of two student groups, Alex Chow of the Federation of Students and Joshua Wong of 'Scholarism'. A pattern of long intervals between initial arrests and the decision to prosecute meant that only a small proportion of the protesters who had been arrested were convicted by the end of 2015 and that more was to come.

In October 2015, Ken Tsang Kin-Chiu, a pro-democracy activist whose beating by police during the protest in 2014 was caught on camera by a local TV channel, was charged with one count of 'assaulting police officers in the due execution of their duties' and four counts of 'resisting a police officer in the due execution of his duty'. The seven police officers normally assigned to fight triad gangsters were filmed when carrying out the beating and charged with 'causing grievous bodily harm with intent' on the same day. 'It did not help the force's image that it took the police a year to lay charges against them' (at the time of this writing, their trial has been adjourned; *The Economist*, Jul. 23, 2016).

Law professor Benny Tai was sanctioned for his handling of anonymous donations related to the protests; according to the administration, he violated university procedures. The university's governing council rejected as well the nomination committee's choice to appoint Johannes Chan Man-Mun, a professor of law, and also that of the former dean of the faculty of law as a pro-vice-chancellor, allegedly in retaliation for the two academics' support for the 2014 'Umbrella' protests. Three leaders of the student-led demonstration, Joshua Wong, Nathan Law, and Alex Chow, were found guilty of charges stemming from their roles in the events in July 2016. Facing heavy penalties, they were ultimately given lighter punishment.

What characterizes the return to order in Hong Kong are the pressures exerted by China. It is unusual in a democratic state to allow the police to use two hundred members of major triads in support of police repression. The triads' presence was openly acknowledged by Andy Tsang, the police commissioner, during one of his numerous press conferences. (The Hong Kong police opened a website for its communication to counter that of students' on the social networks.) The censorship exerted on the freedom of the press was another sign of China's influence. According to a Reporters without Borders' classification, Hong Kong fell from rank 18 in 2002 to 58 in 2013, then to 70 in 2015 in terms of press freedom. As for China, it is ranked 176 out of 180. Since 1996, Hong Kong journalists have been the victims of twelve attacks, including physical attacks with knives, arson, and incarceration, in China (*Le Monde*, Apr. 23, 2016: 5).[5] There are then insidious and long-term consequences in the follow-up given to the return to order in Hong Kong after the 2014 mobilizations. The episode is not over, since important elections will take place in 2017.

★ ★ ★

What do these various responses by state authorities, police, and judicial systems reveal on states' and judicial systems' strength in restoring 'order' in an age of globalization? First of all, what representations and understandings are conveyed by the term *state* associated with *order*, and how do they vary from one country to another?

## The notion of state[6]

Carl Schmitt (1988: 15–16) defines '*order* as an effect and a major accomplishment of state sovereignty. State authorities are the depository of "order"'. They have an exclusive competence, and they are empowered with a monopoly of 'legitimate force' (or 'legitimate violence', depending on Max Weber's translation). It would seem that, with the monopolization of force, states have full sovereignty granted by the people to define and enforce order. Historians view this monopolization as a key institutional development in the consolidation of modern states. Police are thus the institution most closely associated in the development of the modern state.

Citizens expect national states – and in a federal regime, federate states – to protect them from all kinds of threats and risks, including large-scale public disorder. In Europe, this expectation goes back to the Middle Ages when sovereigns were responsible for protection granted to all their residents within their territorial domain. To explain the relationship between policing and the rise of the modern state, Pierre Bourdieu (1994: 4) develops the concept of 'meta-capital' detention that gives the modern state its unique features. 'The state is the culmination of a process of concentration of different species of capital: capital of physical force or instruments of coercion (army, police), economic capital, cultural or (better) informational capital, and symbolic capital', he says. 'It is this concentration as such which constitutes the state as the holder of a sort of meta-capital granting power over other species of capital and over holders'. Previously, Bourdieu had explained that the unique position of the state was due to the fact that it had gradually eliminated its rivals and dispossessed them of their legitimacy, of their instruments of physical violence and of their rights to use them. At this point, in his lecture at College de France, Bourdieu quotes Norbert Elias (1939/2000) and the notion of a civilizing process.

Elias develops the idea that the rise of the modern state with the professionalization of two bodies, police and army, took away the duty that civil society had had until then to solve its private conflicts by resorting to physical violence. Bourdieu remarked, though, that Elias had missed the importance of the state's symbolic capital. The *tour de force* operated by the state comes from the production of an amnesia relative to its own genesis (Bourdieu, 2012: 198). Consequently, an alleged disinterest on the part of the state conceals the state's own interests and its sites of power struggles.

Bourdieu asserts that the concentration of armed forces and of financial resources via the collection of taxes is accompanied by the concentration of a symbolic capital of recognition. Capital has changed from relatively private hands (the king) to relatively public hands. At the top, an interdependent and complex network of powerful, competing power-holders in various sectors surround the state. But because the process of legitimation is lengthy and differentiated, it does not threaten the state's monopoly of domination. 'A gets his/her legitimacy from B who gets his/her legitimacy from C, etc. who grants legitimacy to A' (Bourdieu, 2012: 224). Functionaries who contribute to the advance of the universal then also defend their private interest 'in the public interest'. Three dimensions of the sovereign state thus overlap: the judicial (the state being founded on a social contract), police (state as public force), army (state as sovereign nation), a construction leading to notions such as the reason of state, *raison d'état* (bypassing laws), surveillance (of movements, groups, or other nations [Clavel, 2014: 13]), which all contribute to the production of a modern political order.

In a unique historical way, the French 'model' is defined by a legitimacy directed primarily to the state, a broad definition of the police mandate, and a centralized command structure. For French philosopher Foucault (2004: 58), the state is a set of technologies of power, with its own institutions, tools, apparatus, procedures, dispositions, and agencies where calculations, analyses, and strategies are elaborated, based on various types of knowledge. States define what is normal, legal, and acceptable, or not. They regulate behaviours via processes of socialization, categorization, regulation, and corrections, as much as via public security measures, surveillance, identification, and sanctions, which vary according to national contexts (Foucault, 2004: 236–37). As seen in the previous case studies, policing results from its differentiation from other social structures and from its re-concentration under the protection of a concentrated state authority. According to Manning (1997: 20–21), 'the police role conveys a sense of sacredness or awesome power that lies at the root of political order, and authority, the claims a state makes upon its people for deference to rules, laws and norms'.

## States' actions supporting order

What do states do, and how do they do it? Their first mission, as noted, is to protect, not just to defend constituents, but also, in a risk society, to confront threats, vulnerabilities, and dysfunctions. Their second mission is to control populations, places, and flux in the public interest. Associated with the detention of a symbolic capital, states communicate and there is hardly any questioning when they declare a state of emergency, as was the case after 9/11 in the United States, and recently, 11/13 in France. In times of uncertainty, states display their powerful symbolic mission of cementing the nation, launching investigations, task forces, and commissions. They provide budgets to army, police, justice, and defence in charge of the sovereign task of order maintenance, and they produce executive orders.

How does globalization affect such state sovereignty and monopoly of force? To answer this question is an analytical challenge. Many scholars have claimed that the state was hollowed out. It depends which state. A centralized state? A laggard state? A state supported by a majoritarian or by a consensual democracy? This question is all the more difficult to answer in the context of policing. To think how globalization transforms states, the people cannot 'cut off the king's head' (to quote Foucault), as there is nothing to replace the state with. If one admits that the function of control is currently changing from a hierarchical, vertical chain of command within 'disciplinary societies' to that of more horizontal, anonymous, reticular processes within 'control societies' (Garland, 2001), it appears that the state buttressed its hold on the security issue.

Using global technology – including predictive algorithms – the state apparatus operates its controls at a distance, as revealed by Edward Snowden disclosing the National Security Agency (NSA) hidden modes of behaviour. States also rely increasingly on private actors (using competitors of Google or other technological giants to get the data that they want), when they anticipate potential global threats emanating from micro-territories, closely knit communities, or more opaque local groups. Are there are too many expectations placed on technology to ensure security? This issue is currently debated. In the case studies discussed in this book, intelligence investigations, stops and checks, and the usual management of public disorder appeared as more sound resources than would technology. Approaches adjusted to contexts and experienced law enforcers are needed to de-escalate tensions in increasingly heterogeneous and anonymous societies. But the private market of technology exerts more influence and a better marketing on governments and parliament members than bureaucratic reports requiring a reorganization and a better allocation of funding to police services.

The regulating function of the state suggests that state sovereignty depends on adjusted responses to global dynamics. For Sassen (2006), global forces are not entities, over in cyberspace, eroding states' power; they are entwined with state dynamics. States are embedded and realigned in global structures, and they are influenced by international processes, with national elements of policing and of the judiciary acting as a go-between and impacting on institutional transformations. The state is not a supra-entity; it is disseminated in multiple loci, under different forms and actions. Williams (2016: 188) observes that:

> The assembled nature of the contemporary security field, consisting of a multitude of public/private, global/local actors with different forms of capital may also alter the conditions of security politics. While the state by no means disappears as an actor or as a locus of politics, it is located within networks that cut across and through it.

In the end, are states then up to the task of checking substantial public disorder? Are they hampered by global processes? Answers to these questions can only be formulated within specific national and local contexts and timing.

### States' capacities

Regarding the case studies relating to France and Britain, the regime stability was not shaken by the forms of public disorder that it confronted in 2005 and in 2011. States and governments kept the upper hand, and few decision makers asserted that they bore some responsibility for those events. The police arrested offenders and prosecutors sanctioned them. Public resources, mobilized for halting public disorder, however, did not address the structural and contextual causes of disorder: the dysfunctions of mass public education; the decline of employment opportunities for inner-city residents, especially the youths, with their slow mobility and precariousness; and pervasive institutional and societal discrimination and racism. In France, the growing importance of Islam was generally ignored by the central state and by local mayors, except in reinforcing secular laws. Leaders felt no need to come back on the headscarf issue or on demands for halal meat in public school lunch programmes. Multiculturalism was not seen as a strength but as a liability. Inserting Islam's values into France's core values and giving a place to (rather than inserting) populations from the South was not an option, partly due to the electoral strength of the far Right in the forthcoming elections. The political framing of the issue and of the public responses revealed the deep crisis of representative democracy. In the meantime, the Middle East and other conflicts took on localized, ethnicized, and essentialized forms (Body-Gendrot, 2016). In the ten years following the events, besides an urban renewal policy at a cost of 600 million euros, which sought to transform the physical appearance of downtrodden neighbourhoods but not their social problems, no comprehensive governmental policy alleviated the banlieues' social and economic deterioration with more jobs and public services. Both Right and Left governments announced a series of measures designed to improve job opportunities in the banlieues, but unemployment, especially for youths, kept rising year after year. Despite expenditures amounting to $57 billion in the first decade of the twenty-first century to raise living conditions and employment, the job situation in banlieues like Clichy remained miserable (Crumley, 2012).

Numerous band-aid policies at a cost of 43 billion euros addressed territorial problems under the auspices of politique de la ville (urban policies), but according to a poll of February 10, 2015, only 10 percent of the French regard it as fruitful (Devecchio, 2015). 'Visible minorities'" political representation has hardly improved in the banlieues. At the top, authorities remain short-sighted and confused about what to do in the long term. In that respect, the 2005 events produced few changes, except for the reinforcement of law and order policies as the main strategic option.

The model of policing in the banlieues aiming at catching suspect youths rather than at protecting them was never questioned. Centralized police unions are usually hostile to 'balkanized' community policing. The ides of police officers having ties to the place where they work goes against the concept of a public service for all. Interviewed police officers say that they are not in the neighbourhoods to meet social goals. Community policing for them is not real police work. They think that they have nothing to learn from populations whose expectations are too diverse and incoherent. The police's shared motto is that citizens should never be partners of policemen, even less their advisors (Mouhanna, 2012).

Neither the weak minority representation within police forces nor the lack of procedural justice based on those invisible institutions so dependent on trust and fairness was debated. Minister of the Interior Sarkozy received significant public support for his handling of law and order, and it may have contributed to his victory in the subsequent presidential election.

In Britain, structural causes supporting disorder were also ignored. Seventy percent of those sent to the courts in 2011 were living in the 30 percent most deprived areas of the country, and the majority of them came from the 10 percent lowest income areas. They suffered from exclusion and from no full participation in society (Riots, Communities and Victims Panel, 2011: 11–12). There was no pledge from the government that this situation should be redressed. On the contrary, austerity policies were reinforced by the conservative team in power. The poor relationship of some communities with the police was not addressed either, and hostility to the police was mentioned in the polls as a factor accounting for disorder.

How to prevent the police loss of control of the streets was subsequently addressed by the police, emphasizing the need for partnerships involving community leaders and accountability, trust, and fairness. Police tactics oriented towards the disruption of disorder and interception of leaders were also debated according to the testimony delivered by Her Majesty's Chief Inspector of the Constabulary Denis O'Connor to the Home Affairs Committee (O'Connor, 2011). The dialectics of order and disorder operated. The state kept the upper hand; police and justice functioned as expected to buttress order. The revolution was not at the corner.

## A path of dependency

The political and bureaucratic responses to the events however reveal a 'path dependency' – that is, the tenacity of nationally particular and idiosyncratic ideas, which impedes internal adaptation to problems (Favell, 2001: 8).

In the United States, federate states and local authorities displayed a fluctuating capacity in the management of public disorder. In New York, the disorder caused by space occupation and by its evacuation was firmly handled with the resources allocated to the police, culture, 'dictionaries' of general approaches to police work, and 'recipes for action' (Chan, 1997). After two months, order was restored, a move positively publicized by the media. The management of the case remained local, but it was also interpreted with a global lens, reassuring investors, consumers, tourists, and city users.

Ferguson is another story, and it forced the federal administration to intervene in local matters. As noted, the task force convened by President Obama indicated that there was a profound awareness that the criminal justice system was deeply broken in certain states. Presidential candidates in 2016 echoed that statement. But in a federal regime, progressive reforms may take a long time due to subnational authorities' strength and resistance to change. It is likely that tenacious, lengthy litigations will slow the reform of local law enforcement agencies, unless new local leadership keeps the need for reforms, regarding the selection, training, and supervision of police officers and minorities' constitutional rights, on the agenda. A new police chief in Ferguson in 2016 seemed determined to push for this type of reform. Future will tell whether the new Ferguson police chief can contribute to a change in the local police culture. The profile of Anthony Batts, the Baltimore police chief, is intriguing and says a lot about the difficulty of reforming police. A champion of procedural justice and against maximum force, he was disavowed after Freddie Gray's brutal death. What transpired is that changing a police culture is a long and complex process. There was resistance to change among a distrustful rank and file. The idea that changing attitudes between the police and the public could be done in a couple of months was just not reasonable. Batts may have had to pay for his too progressive attitudes (Rosenberg, 2016).

Finally, both in Hong Kong and in Istanbul, decision makers', police's, and judges' resilience was demonstrated, sometimes painfully, in terms of deaths, casualties, and governance image. While opponents to decision makers elicited a lot of support and sympathy around the world, the determination of the ruling bodies and of the upper levels in those cities and in those countries to counter dissent has not been shaken, and it may even have grown.

What my next chapter indicates, however, is that maybe such case studies already belong to the past. The new context of homegrown terrorism and the lethal danger it represents for cities and countries dwarfs events of public disorder in contexts of peace. A more pressing question is: are national institutions, including those of the United States, up to the task of confronting global, death-wishing actors engaged in a kind of asymmetric war?

## Notes

1  Only eighty-two localities in seven departments took advantage of night curfews for eleven days. The mostly symbolic measure, the state of emergency, is also to be understood in the context of a political rivalry between the prime minister and the minister of the interior, both vying for the monopoly of authority in order to attract conservative voters, on the eve of a presidential election in 2007.

2  These institutions were established in England in the twelfth and thirteenth centuries to counter the king's and powerful people's unfair prosecution and to yield more protections to citizens. It explains why deliberations are kept secret. Their opponents claim that popular juries are no longer appropriate institutions for cases involving police officers, which should not be kept secret. The handling of police shootings should be separated from local grand juries. It is unfair, they say, to ask jurors to handle cases involving local police officers on whom they rely every day (Adams, 2014).

3  The task force was chaired by the Commissioner of Philadelphia Police Department and by an academic at George Mason University.

4  Some Occupy lawsuits, like the one that accused police officers of wrongly arresting people walking on a sidewalk in the East Village, have resulted in the city's paying significant settlements. But others were dismissed. The city of New York agreed to pay a total of $332,500 to six Occupy Wall Street protesters who said police unjustly blasted them with pepper spray in an episode that helped propel the movement into the spotlight. The settlements reached ranged from $52,500 to $60,000 per person in cases arising from Occupy's early days in September 2011 (CBS, May 2, 2012; June 7, 2012).

5  During a sit-in in October 2014, a bag of animals' rotten viscera was thrown on Jimmy Lai, the head of the Next media and a supporter of the students' protest. Well-known brands boycotted his journal, the *Apple Daily*, for fear of displeasing China, a powerful client.

6  For lack of space, actions at the local level by public authorities and by the private sector cannot be addressed here. See Body-Gendrot (2013).

# 7

# IS GLOBAL TERRORISM AN EXTREME CASE OF PUBLIC DISORDER?

This chapter is set apart from previous chapters because recent public disorder created by terrorists in Paris and in Brussels is unique in nature, intensity, and casualties. It does not fit in a typology, and it cannot be compared with the public disorder caused by violent anti-police protesters. The responses provided by the European Union, states, police, and judges to that form of disorder are also singular and exceptional. Those events mark a before and an after, they are unique, they point to the end of a world, yet because they could happen again, they can almost be conceptualized. *The Concept of 9/11* is the title of a book of dialogues between Jacques Derrida and Jurgen Habermas (Borradori, 2003). The 9/11 event showed that a great city could be brought to a halt by chaos and shock. Within a flicker of time, catalytic terrorism caused the city to shut down not just airports and bridges but large institutions, schools, the UN building, and so on (Savitch, 2008: 27).

No one will deny that terrorism is the very symbol of a disorder created in a city by hypermobile, global actors acting within secretive networks. Not detected beforehand, terrorist acts question the efficiency of states' power and public interventions from the highest levels of command and control to the lowest micro-territory levels. New forms of terrorism give credence to my assumption that, to an extent rarely met before, global actors challenge national (and international) institutions' legitimacy. Such a challenge opens a new era. Currently, cities are attacked as a consequence of conflicts developing within Muslim communities in barely governed countries – conflicts that reverberate in many parts of the world.

It would seem then that we are in the middle of a significant transition. There is no going back to the handling of disorder as it was done ten years ago, and we do not know what the situation will be like ten years from now. A zone of extreme uncertainty and indeterminacy has been reached, in which old tools are eroded in terms of efficacy and new tools like international intelligence that would be appropriate for understanding contexts and for taking action do not work, in part due to national states' resistance, bureaucratic blocks, and a general lack of trust and of vision.

In this chapter, mostly focused on France,[1] enigmatic terrorists and the nature of their global/local acts is first examined, an analysis supported by journalists' interviews of terrorists in prison or still in Syria or Iraq; then, the study turns to states' loss of clear vision to confront terrorism and their overreaction possibly leading to further violence: it ends on the assumption that we have entered an era of *Unsicherheit*, indeterminacy and uncertainty with more questions than answers (Bauman, 1998). Information in this chapter comes from investigative journalism published in French, British, and American national newspapers; from information provided by other media; from the French Intelligence Agency (DGSI); and from police and court reports detailing ongoing investigations.

## Homegrown terrorists as enigmatic enemies

Terrorism is a thorny subject. There is no universal definition of the phenomenon. Over two hundred definitions of terrorism have been suggested since 9/11. For the US Homeland Security Administration, terrorism is a calculated use of violence or a threat of illegal violence, meant to provoke fear with the goal of constraining or intimidating governments or civil societies for usually political, religious, or ideological goals. What is important for our purposes is the nature of the act, along with the identity of the perpetrators and the nature of the cause.

> The fear created by terrorists may be intended to cause people to exaggerate the strengths of the terrorists and the importance of the cause, to provoke governmental overreaction, to discourage dissent, or simply to intimidate and thereby enforce compliance with the demands.
>
> *(Savitch, 2008: XIV)*

The term 'intimidate' is important: terrorists want to instil fear. They also aim at displaying their enemies' weaknesses and at triggering states' overreaction. The new terrorists, with their digital skills, use publicity to compensate for their weak numbers by magnifying the damage inflicted to their targets. They also use 'the other side of publicity, the cult of heroes and martyrs, to heighten support for their actions. Thus, even though terrorism has mutated, publicity is still one of its choice weapons' (Manin, 2015: 29). Terrorism is framed as a form of global, local, and unpredictable asymmetric 'war', led by enigmatic enemies who ignore conventional rules (Body-Gendrot, 2012: chapter 3). The term *war* is questionable, as will be seen. Using such a term promotes terrorists to the status of warriors and, possibly, heroes.

Why do three quarters of terrorist attacks target cities?

> If . . . cities make and master space, the tactic of terrorism is to undo that supremacy by decontrolling urban territory. The . . . objective of the terrorist is to put a halt to city function – preventing it from crystallizing its creative

energies, breaking down its rich mosaic, upsetting its natural rhythms, and
sabotaging its economic generation, shutting it down in a flicker of time.

*(Savitch, 2008: 95)*

Terrorists target spaces in global and major Western cities because these cities offer
them the best returns: lives, disorganization, fear, and media attention. Recent religious terrorism is all the more lethal, as it sanctifies suicide. Since November 2015,
twenty terrorist attacks occurred on five continents. Old terrorist forms caused few
deaths; new terrorism aims at creating as many deaths as possible (Rapoport, 2006,
IV: 4). Besides Europe, terrorism recently hit Grand-Bassam, Istanbul, Bali, Bagdad,
Lahore, and previously Egypt and Tunisia. In each context, the disorder took a
specific shape, the claims were different, and so were the responses. For attacks emanating from ISIS (Islamic State in Iraq and Syria), also called Daesh, taking hybrid
forms in its changing evolution, the claim is a long-term and ambitious one, that
of a world power within a caliphate exerting its global sovereignty. Such ambition
doesn't allow for negotiations.

It should be emphasized that some of the most durable examples of terrorist
groups such as the FARC and Sendero Luminoso in Latin America do not have
any visible global relations, networks, or communications. However, in this research,
those terrorist groups who masterfully access and utilize globalized communication
are the focus of attention.

## Waves of terrorist attacks

Are Islamic terrorist attacks new? France confronted several generations of Islamic
terrorists. Waves of terrorism alternated with periods of tranquillity.

As early as 1954–62, during the 'Algerian war', domestic terrorism did not spare
France, and public space was placed under specialized forces' heavy surveillance. French
authorities responded to terrorist attacks with a state of emergency in 1955 and with
specific measures endowing institutions with more adjusted tools. Between 1979 and
1987, the anarcho-communist group *Action Directe* committed eighty acts of terrorism, numerous assaults, and several murders of well-known officials, in the name of
the proletarian revolution. It was supported by approximately two hundred militants.

In 1986, fourteen terrorist acts took place in the name of the Committee of
Solidarity with Arabic and Middle East Political Prisoners.

An anti-terrorist law was then passed by the French Parliament, blurring notions
of external and internal threats and giving institutions better tools to confront
both of them. Several agencies, emanating from the French Ministries of Foreign
Affairs, the Interior, and Justice coordinated with one another. A central anti-terrorist branch was created within the Ministry of Justice. Nine anti-terrorist judges
presided over the cases.[2]

After 1986, nine years went by without any attack. Then, in 1995 and in 1996,
a plane was hijacked in Algiers, landed in Marseille, and three hostages and four
terrorists were killed. An Algerian radical Islamist group (GIA) launched a bomb
in a Paris subway, causing eight deaths and 117 casualties, including young terrorist

Khaled Kelkal. In 1998, 138 people were indicted for these offences. That first generation of Muslim terrorists had close connections with North African countries; they had fought French colonial occupation.

Distinct from previous scattered attacks, those after 2000 – such as 9/11 and Madrid (2004) – were carefully planned by the Al-Qaida organization, and only the best minds were selected to carry out plans first elaborated in Muslim countries (Body-Gendrot, 2007).

With Mohammed Merah, the rise of a third generation came to light. In March 2012, in Toulouse and Montauban, south of France, Merah murdered three Jewish pupils and their teacher and three army personnel (a fourth was wounded) of North African origin. Although he apparently acted alone, he was locally supported by his radical Muslim family and coached by his older brother and sister and by their radical acquaintances. His actions 'placed France in a space of universal Jihadism in which social dereliction, colonial past, political disenfranchisement and an Islamic exacerbation overlap' (Kepel, 2015: 113). French intelligence services which had prevented terrorist attacks from happening in France for sixteen years did not grasp then the new type of global actor that Merah embodied. They 'were unable to anticipate the fusion the Merah case revealed between a foreign Islamic ideology, the social networks and the new political sociology of French radical salafism doctrine' that was attracting a minority of committed Muslim youths in French deprived neighbourhoods and in prisons (Kepel, 2015: 24). Such articulation is of major importance for understanding why global Jihad became such a threat to order in European societies.

Another 'lone wolf' Jihadist, back from Syria, was Mehdi Nemmouche from Molenbeek in Belgium. He killed four people at the Jewish Museum of Brussels in May 2014. But Belgian investigations suggest that he had probably been in touch with the authors of the November attacks in Paris. Allegedly a network helped him escape from Belgium (Stroobants, 2016). He was subsequently arrested in Marseille on May 30, 2014.

### Why terrorism is unusual

A number of scholars (Cusson et al., 2016: 8) ask why terrorist attacks are so rare. Terrorism caused the death of 149 people in Paris in 2015, then of 84 on Promenades des Anglais in Nice on Bastille Day when families watched fireworks. By comparison, in France, each year, the number of homicides fluctuates between 650 and 800. Those scholars list six reasons why terrorist acts are unusual: (1) moral inhibitions prevent a lot of people from killing innocent people (Collins, 2008); (2) few people will accept becoming suicide bombers; (3) few people are fanatics, ready to kill, except during revolutions or wars; (4) internal conflicts frequently make terrorist groups split; (5) anti-terrorism is efficient, in terms of surveillance and penetrations, even though maximum security is given to infrastructures like airports or nuclear plants; and (6) the rapid responses of specialized police units may kill plots before they develop. In France, according to the minister of the interior, eleven plots were discovered and their authors arrested in 2015. Do all those reasons 'make terrorist acts look like mosquito bites on the back of democracies', as claimed by Albert de Swaan (2016)? 'They shudder but they are not mortally wounded'. Those points are examined in the following sections.

## In search of motivations

The third Jihad generation is a product of deep mutations in the Middle East as well as in France. Religion has become an anchor in downtrodden neighbourhoods inhabited by poor Muslim families. Besides religion, is there another motivation for some of their children to join Jihad? Kepel (2015) asserts that a minuscule number of them have been inspired by radical fundamentalism, accepting martyrdom for a cause they embraced. Olivier Roy (2005) disagrees with Kepel's thesis. For him,

> the Western-based Islamic terrorists are not the militant vanguard of the Muslim community; they are a lost generation, unmoored from traditional societies and cultures, frustrated by a Western society that does not meet their expectations. . . . They find their cause in the utopia of a universal *ummah*, in an abstract and pure Islam, in the same way that the Left radicals in the 1970s – the Baader band or the Red Brigades – opted for terrorism in the name of the 'world proletariat' or of the 'Revolution' without caring for its consequences.

In other words, for Roy, violent and angry youths find a cause to express their anger and negative feelings in Islam, whereas for Kepel, in poor European neighbour-hoods such as Molenbeek, idle youths become indoctrinated by salafist/Waahabist preachers, then recruited by ISIS, sent to Iraq or Syria for training, and back to perform suicide-bombing duty in Europe. Specific neighbourhoods like Molen-beek in Belgium provide them with a niche to hide from authorities. Probably, both scholars are right. In spring 2016, the French minister in charge of cities remarked that there were presumably one hundred Molenbeek in France, pro-voking reporters to investigate poor Muslim communities like Saint Denis, Lunel, and Roubaix (Carzon, 2016). Retrospectively, Molenbeek, a neighbourhood of Brussels, was a convenient basis for ISIS in Europe, due to the concentration of Belgian and French salafist (radical) groups. The potential recruits were submitted to the same propaganda and to the same modes of communication (via borrowed cell phones for example), they shared apartments and hung out in the same places. They were the perfect illustration of the local/global merging. Muslim radicals liv-ing in Molenbeek had known each other for years. They formed a network which attracted Syrian and Iraqi recruiters because Belgium was then loosely protected against terrorism by its failing institutions. For over a year, the country, divided between Flemish and Wallon communities, had no government.

   For some of these young people, the end of adolescence is marked by vulner-ability, mental problems, and delinquency. Psychoanalyst Fehti Benslama (2016) observes that Jihad recruiters take advantage of these youths and offer radicaliza-tion as a treatment for their problems. Lots of people think of death. Every year in

France, ten thousand individuals commit suicide, including one thousand young people. In fanatic groups formed around religion, individualism recedes and a fusion occurs with a mystical body, Benslama (2016) adds. Physically, the young Muslim is alive, but subjectively as an individual, he/she has ceased to live. *Passage à l'acte* (acting out) and martyrdom then become a solution. Benslama calls such youths 'over-Muslims' (*surmusulman*), haunted by guilt and the temptation of sacrifice. They are in a continuous overbidding to prove their loyalty to their faith.

All observers emphasize the fear inspired by small numbers. 'The fear of small numbers is intimately linked to the tensions produced by the forces of globalization' (Appadurai, 2006); in our case, the number of individuals tempted by Jihad is minuscule. Terrorist acts emanate from the margins of the Arab-Muslim world attempting to occupy the centre. As a dark side of globalization, currently, such margins reach out for the margins of Europe in opaque spaces such as prisons, parts of banlieues, inner cities or training camps, and they impose themselves on the world (Garapon, 2016: 28).

As nations become more peaceful, compared with a past marked by devastating wars and massacres, and as democracies are more open and apparently borderless, the power of nuisance and disruption of such very small minorities reveals nations' and democracies' vulnerability and an absence of anticipation.

### *The digital communication of global radicalization*

Spanish-Syrian thinker Abu Musad al-Suri played a major role in inspiring a whole generation of violent actors via global networks (Kepel, 2015: 52). A veteran of the war in Afghanistan, he was also connected to Algerian radical militants. After tumultuous experiences, he moved to London, where he attended the Finsbury Park radical mosque. He regularly wrote a newsletter at first sent by fax, then via YouTube, to radical mosques. In 2005, he launched his *Call to a World Islamic Resistance* and broadcast his vision of a borderless Islam. In his call, he recommended the renouncement of a top-down organization like Al-Qaida's, which had failed after Bin Laden's death and to opt instead for a 'Jihad of proximity' (Kepel, 2015: 52) via the creation of secret grassroots networks with Muslim homegrown radicals trained to launch destructive attacks from the bottom up.

Disenfranchised Muslim youths attracted by Suri have been called 'the Y generation', maybe because of the shape that the wires of their earphones take when hanging from their ears! Socialized since childhood with video games, they easily communicate via Twitter, Facebook, or YouTube. On social networks, leaders like Suri offer them a new dignity: they would become warriors and heroes to their 'followers'. As in video games, the Jihad cybervision symbolizes what globalization can achieve (leadership, management, efficiency, success). Such a vision blurs the boundaries between the virtual and the real, as happens to some youths addicted to their smartphones or iPads. These youths act in a fantasy world. They see themselves as knights defending a global, imagined community, while exerting revenge on their enemies for their humiliations. Their violence draws lines between the dots of political violence and those of civil violence. Their form of terrorism emanates from an imagination reconstructing the West and Islam under the influence of globalization and of video games.

Court reports reveal, however, that terrorists more often used meetings and cell phones to communicate with one another than the internet. What is striking in the November attacks in the Paris area and in those of Brussels soon afterwards is indeed that those highly mobile and well-connected operators were trained to use old-style cell phones and an encrypted programme called True-Crypt to hide their connections with Syria. Such a programme has not been disencrypted by investigators at the time of this writing. European recruits used USB keys, encoded with serial numbers which were identified by Jihad leaders abroad. Those keys contained CCleaner, a programme erasing the user's online history, then they were thrown away (Callimachi et al., 2015). This process kept those operators undetectable.

The November attacks in Paris were operated by French Salah Abdeslam, living in Belgium and helped by a chain of participants in Belgium and other European countries (Germany, Britain, Spain), moving easily from one city and one country to another, finding access to arms and human support. According to investigative journalist Elise Vincent, French-Belgian cooperation had been at work in previous terrorist attacks in Casablanca on May 16, 2003 (resulting in 45 deaths, including the 12 suicide bombers) and in Madrid on March 11, 2004 (resulting in 191 deaths). This cooperation involved drug dealers operating from the Rif rebellious region in Morocco. The organization had cells in Italy, Britain, Canada, the most active of them being in France and in Belgium (Vincent, 2015). At the end of 2015, according to the French minister of the interior, the number of Jihadists in France was approximately 3 percent of Muslims and the number of radical mosques 150 (versus 30 in 2005) out of 2,449 prayer rooms (536 in 2000) (Guehenno, 2015).

In brief, new patterns reveal a 'rhizome' syndrome – the reticular way in which underground roots invisibly link with each other – for deviant purposes. The dark network resilience in a hostile environment has generated an abundant literature (Burcher and Whelan, 2015; Dupont, 2015; Everton and Cunnigham, 2015). The Islamic state has opted for a network mode of operation rather than for the type of pyramidal chain of command previously used by Al-Qaida in several regions of the world. The extreme cases of destruction and disorganization, perpetrated by minuscule numbers of violent actors, illustrate in which way global modes of thinking, communicating, and operating increase such operators' potential for nuisance and their capacity at renewing usual repertoires in the 'asymmetric war' that they have launched within the Muslim world and against the West.

## States' and judges' resources

Unusual measures such as a state of emergency (*état d'urgence*) hide the confusion and embarrassment that institutions face with those new types of threat. Chapter 6 has shown that states and judges have resources and experience to put an end to forms of mobilizations and occupations resulting in public disorder. But here, a new story reveals the limits of states and of justice. Nothing in the French Constitution addresses terrorism. Issues regarding the duration of the state of emergency and its conditions, guarantees, and limits do not bring clear answers. Could the *state of exception* become the common rule? This is a debated issue.

Are emergency laws efficient? Do they promise much and accomplish little? Emergency laws display their inefficiency when they are used for political aims and create controversies, as illustrated in the case of France. A Left government is more prompt to censor itself and use emergency law to restore order in times of social contest, giving the impression of a lack of authority and of legitimacy. Police forces, and other forces of the sovereign state, express resistance at being used without restraint.[3] And, finally, overreaction betrays a state's core weakness.

### *Emergency laws*

With its revolutionary past, France has a long history of serious public disorder. The country has always been able however to find appropriate resources to restore an internal order, after bloody episodes of turbulence. Among their resources, strong institutions enable the president to gather all the representatives of the nation in times of distress in order to receive their consent at yielding him a large amount of unchecked power to restore order. The symbol of French elected representatives gathered in a Congress room in Versailles around the chief of state is a powerful symbol of unity, as was the unanimous consent given by US Congress to the Patriot Act, yielding significant power to the president of the United States after 9/11.

Unlike January 2015 when, after the attacks, not everyone identified with the satirical journalists of *Charlie Hebdo* killed by suicide bombers, in November, most French people were deeply shaken by the deaths of so many young people in a concert hall, in restaurants, and cafés' *terrasses*.

They rightly felt that their values, cultures, and modes of living had been challenged. Consequently, there was hardly any opposition to declaring that the country was meeting a 'state of exception'. Then when France was horrendously hit again in Nice in July 2016, the population staggered. Unlike in New York, Madrid, or London, it had not had the nine months allegedly necessary to recover from the January 2015 and then the November 2015 attacks.

The idea associated with the emergency law regime is that, for the sake of fighting terrorism, citizens' security will be considered in a system of general surveillance buttressed by specific resources allocated to police forces. Acting in full sovereignty, the state fills its symbolic function, indicating that it can respond to a threat quickly and powerfully, even bypassing laws if necessary.

As observed by Bourdieu (2012: 57), in hard times, it is unusual for the public to question state operations, because the state has framed minds in such a way that they take for granted what is enunciated at the summit of the state as its *raison d'état*, and ignore particular interests, contingencies, and conflicts. Bourdieu asserts,

> To obtain this effect of de-particularization, this set of institutions that we call 'the state' needs to dramatize what is official and universal; it must give

the spectacle of public respect for public truths in which the whole society is supposed to recognize itself.

Communication is what matters, before long-term efficiency. As an example, when the Climate Conference met in Paris at the end of November, exceptional measures were taken to ensure the security of hundreds of visitors, and there was hardly any objection to these measures (see insert).

---

## SECURITIZING THE CLIMATE CONFERENCE IN PARIS IN 2015[4]

The Climate Conference, COP21, was held in the Paris suburb of Le Bourget (Seine Saint Denis) between November 29 and December 12, 2015. The conference illustrated how the French police can be at their best in their preventative mission, when they are given time for planning and resources. (The information provided here is based on a personal interview with H. W., responsible for the security of the conference, and J. F., a French prefect, January 2016).

A COP (or Conference of the Parties) is a meeting held to discuss climate change. A total of 196 countries are involved, plus the European Union, which negotiates on behalf of its 28 member states. A COP has been held every year, usually between November and December, since 1995. At each COP, the 196 parties negotiate targets and measures to limit climate change. The talks deal with topics like the reduction of greenhouse gas emissions, adaptation by developing countries to climate change, the financing of mitigation and adaptation initiatives, and technology transfers.

The COP is the supreme decision-making body of the United Nations Framework Convention on Climate Change (UNFCCC), which was signed by the 196 Parties at the Rio Summit in 1992. The three founding principles of the UNFCCC are the principle of precaution, the principle of the right to promote sustainable development, and the principle of common but differentiated responsibility.

France asked to be the host of the twenty-first Conference of the Parties (COP21), and its foreign minister, Laurent Fabius, presided over the conference. His role was to welcome the conference participants and facilitate the negotiations – a crucial and complex mission, since all decisions had to be ratified by unanimous vote. Given the high stakes, France set up a special intergovernmental team specifically for COP21.

Prioritizing security at the climate conference was decided as early as January 2014. However, the momentum accelerated in November 2015, after terrorist attacks hit Paris. There was indeed fear that this summit would be used by terrorists to hit France again, a fear that had been raised in January but that was unspoken until November. Due to its international commitment to fight

Islam fundamentalists, and to its defence of secularization, the country had been a priority target for the last few years.

The security authorities' first move was to create an aerial bubble over the country, protected by war planes. Military drones were assigned to detect other drones, invisible on the radar screens. On the ground, there were also people in charge of detecting hostile drones.

As early as November 6, 2015, the minister of the interior announced that the borders would be closed for a month to prevent a number of malevolent groups from hampering the smooth development of the conference. Closing the borders required the instalment of several hundred check points along the borders with Belgium, Germany, Switzerland, and Italy. The Schengen Treaty of 2006 allows such closure in case of 'a serious threat for public order or for issues concerning domestic security'. Before a global summit, border closing is systematic, as was the case for the NATO summit in Strasbourg in 2009, the G8 in Deauville, or the G20 in Cannes in 2011. The terrorist attacks in November made it easier for France to convince the European Union to allow an unusual duration for borders' closure (Borredon, 2015).

On the domestic front, it was difficult to determine what administration would be in charge of the issue of safety and security at the conference, which would include the presence of a hundred heads of state and numerous organizations. At first, the minister of foreign affairs kept the upper hand, but after the terrorist attacks in November 2015, both branches of the minister of the interior, the DGSE (the Office of External Security), and the DGSI (the Office of Internal Security) were brought in. The DGSE was asked to evaluate the threats and to communicate with services abroad, while the DGSI was expected to exert territorial surveillance. Theoretically, they had to transfer information to a command unit, which is held by the Paris Police Prefect heading the Regional Defence Zone. As such, the prefect coordinates the army, the fire brigades, the territorial security branches, the judicial police, and all the anti-terrorist branches. In contrast with the US federal fragmentation of anti-terrorist units, the French National coordination agency takes on a pyramidal shape. In practice, the top-down line of command is blurred and bureaucratic manoeuvres contribute to the retention of information, so that the flux is never fluid.

The border patrols (PAF – Police des frontières) were asked to control borders. They received information from neighbouring countries in terms of potential suspects. Fears of the highly organized black bloc, which has characterized each global summit since Genoa (1991), did not materialize. What was hazardous, though, was the checking of the flow of migrants converging to Europe at that time. Covert information had been received at the interior ministry for several months, indicating that terrorists could hide among them. Incidentally, two terrorists involved in the November attacks entered France among that flow of migrants.

It was agreed that the Police Prefect would be given leverage to handle road traffic logistics, block highways to Le Bourget airport during the summit, and head all order maintenance regarding public space. Additional police officers were assigned to that task. At Le Bourget itself, UN forces were in charge of VIP security. Elsewhere, within the Parisian periphery where crowds can be rowdy (see chapter 3), the anti-crime brigade kept watch. If serious disorder was to occur, judicial police officers on site could mobilize water cannons (carrying cameras), require helicopters to take pictures, and ask the Police Prefect for further orders.

By decree, due to the state of emergency, all forms of demonstration were forbidden. A large march, planned to open the summit on November 29 with 130 organizations, non-for-profit associations, and trade unions, was eventually forbidden. A total of 57 police units and 5,500 police officers were assigned to order maintenance in anticipation of that march.

A few hundred French violent protesters already known by the French police (environmentalists, anarchists, alternative militants, etc.), highly organized and unpredictable, were closely tracked by police officers before the time of the conference. The emergency law gave the police the capacity to put some of them under house arrest a few days before the start of the conference and until December 12. Executive orders stipulated that 'as the police were assigned to respond to the terrorist threat, they could not face the risks of disorder in the public space that the conference generated at the same time'. In that case, 'there were serious reasons to think that some individuals' behaviours were a threat for public safety and order', justifying house arrest (Borredon & Pecout, 2015). A total of 1,600 home searches were ordered without a judicial warrant. None of them led to a terrorist track. Both house arrests and home searches were motivated by order maintenance and ultimately, security.

Nevertheless, the social network Facebook was used to organize a march on November 24, calling for disobedience and challenging the state of emergency. The call gathered 4,700 participants. No disorder occurred. Other peaceful assemblies took place in the suburb of Montreuil, and they were left alone by the police. Environmental organizations met there, and no visible disorder disrupted their three-day meeting.

It is interesting to reflect on such events and on the efficiency of the emergency law then. In the spring of 2016, the state of emergency will not be invoked to prevent violence during demonstrations against a labour law, and we will attempt to understand governmental reasons.

As the conference host and facilitator of negotiations – a role that required a great deal of work well before and during the conference – France was widely praised by all the participants from the start to the finish of the COP.

## The interference of political calculations

The use of the state of emergency following the attacks of November 2015 and then Nice in July 2016 is, however, anything but convincing. Machiavelli (1515/1908, chapter 17: 1) asserted that when the people turn to the Prince for protection, at the same time, they dread an abuse of power that would jeopardize their liberties. Under the cover of a response given to a massive threat, intertwining issues of national security addressing terrorism and those of domestic and community safety, political calculations are a temptation for those who govern, and judges had to cancel some of the measures that were decided, such as house arrests for environmentalists who had nothing to do with terrorism.

An example of the political use made of the emergency law concerns the failed terrorist attack on the Thalys train in July 2015. The terrorist who had boarded the train joining Amsterdam and Paris was unable to trigger his gun. He was disarmed and neutralized by three American military officers travelling on that train during their vacation. The French Parliament passed a law, punishing serious threats to public security, a definition including frauds in public transportation, which is another matter. To prevent a demonstration which could turn into serious public disorder, is it legitimate to eavesdrop on phone conversations and have suspects tracked before the event? How precise are the criteria leading to such police actions? Those are questions asked by human rights advocates.

According to a Parliamentary control commission after the November attacks, 3,579 searches were ordered by the Ministry of the Interior, leading to only 6 cases of 'malefactors' association with a terrorist enterprise'. A total of 404 house arrests did not just concern potential terrorists but environmental agitators who then went to court to question the legitimacy of their arrest. Six months after the attacks, sixty-nine of them still had to report to the police on a daily basis and stay home at night (Alonso, 2016). The authorities' goal was to prevent protesters known as violent from joining demonstrations against a proposed labour law. Their lawyers defend freedoms to come and go, and the thin accusations based on intelligence services' secret scribbled 'white files' (*notes blanches*). The coverage of those political decisions by the media unveiling political calculations diminishes the status of the emergency law against terrorism meant to protect the country from lethal threats.

## The Left and social violence

Another example of the disrespect of the emergency law comes from the management of social unrest by a divided Left. Historically, the Left is uncomfortable in dealing with police and order maintenance. The 'security issue' is viewed as right wing hunting grounds. Born in the French 'culture of excuse', many left militants reject demands for law-and-order–type policies. In numerous localities, police officers and prosecutors are symbolically present in partnerships born of prevention policies but kept at a distance. In the spring of 2016, after nearly a decade of nearly 10 percent unemployment, the test for the Left government came from a labour law bill intended to spur hiring and growth. The reformist Left in government wanted to give preference to workplace rules over those of labour branches, introducing more flexibility and contracts approved by a majority of employees, loosening rigid codes, thus weakening centralized and inflexible unions' power. Currently, less than 8 percent of French workers are unionized. According to the French government's statistics office, the General Confederation of Labour (CGT) comprises less than 2.8 percent of them. The more unions are weak, the more they tend to radicalize in order to survive. In this case, a very weak union confronted a very weak government. The government's proposal of technical changes in the labour code was not properly explained to the public. The timing for the change was poor, after four years of internal divisions between the old and the new Left and a dwindling support for the government within its own ranks.

With continuous labour demonstrations all over France, why did the Left government hesitate to use the emergency law, invoking the dangers of terrorism to forbid wide-scale use of public space, and why did they let disorder take over the streets over several months? It is likely that the government wanted to avoid accusations of power abuse and mark their distinction from an authoritarian Right. Yet, one year away from presidential elections, letting the coverage of street violence be seen by millions of media viewers, the deeply unpopular government appeared weaker, confused and divided, as seen with Nuit debout ('Night Standing Up').

---

## NUIT DEBOUT (2016)

The occupation of a symbolic space, Place de la République in Paris, night after night, since March 31, 2016, is another example of the difficulties of the governmental Left in dealing with social unrest and restoring order. After several hundred thousands of students and labour union members marched together to protest the change of labour laws, a group of young people decided not to go home and spent the night on the square. Those heterogeneous groups, in a Woodstock atmosphere, drinking and playing music, expressed all kinds of social and political frustrations criticizing business-friendly policies, consumerism, and short-sighted politics. Some weekends, several hundred people met there just to debate, but gradually, less and less people showed up.

The police were not given firm orders about those occupiers' status. The state of emergency was not invoked to prohibit crowds from assembling. Gradually, as with previous occupation movements already analyzed, there were complaints in the neighbourhood about noise, dirt, and violence as the Nuit debout occupiers seemed overwhelmed, in terms of order maintenance and tolerance. Attempting to give their status more legitimacy (and led undercover by experienced organizers, remaining anonymous), they expressed a willingness to join with traditional workers' unions which were demonstrating against the proposed labour law. At the time of this writing, this 'embryo of a movement' is no longer visible in public space.

## The issue of 'casseurs'

As the labour demonstrations occupied large cities' streets, gradually a new phenomenon appeared – that of a large number of violent 'casseurs' (destructive protesters) acting like the black bloc, and taking the lead in demonstrations instead of coming last at the very end, as was usually the case with previous large-scale demonstrations. Those destructive protesters assaulted police officers, union members, and students, breaking shop and bank windows, bus shelters, street lights, and once setting a subway entrance on fire. Such disorder occurred repeatedly in April and May 2016. Usually, the union fighting hardest like the General Confederation of Labour (CGT) has staff experienced in order maintenance. Even police forces are impressed by their experience (Fillieule & Tartakowsky, 2013). But for reasons that will eventually be clarified, this time, the union staff was unable to stop the casseurs, and they were beaten up as well. Why did not the government give the police clear orders to stop those destructive protesters, as they had during the climate conference?

Who are those 'casseurs'? An imaginary category created by the media? According to a few interviews, they do not come from the banlieues; they are frequently young, with time to spend in political activism. They may be advanced students, unemployed, or part-time employed. Lots of them belong to 'ultra' radicalized groups close to the far Right or to the far Left and recruiting middle-class youths. They defend violent 'direct action' as a strategy. Some of them claim that their goal is to bypass the physical barriers formed by police forces and judges' decisions in order to put capitalist society down (Pascual, 2016c). But they have no revolutionary alternative to offer as a substitute to representative democracy. Those who talked tend to minimize violence, saying that material destruction is not violence. They look at it with relativism, adding that violence should not be judged from a moral perspective, but as a strategy. Their testimonies confirm the observations by scholar Weenink (2014) reported in chapter 2. Weenick emphasized that violent actors recognize each other under their hoods. They share behaviours and looks. The minuscule number of 'casseurs' who talked to journalists referred to themselves as black bloc, specifying that they used the term not to refer to a group but to a strategy consisting in assembling and circulating with masked faces in order to destroy the symbols of the state and of capitalism.

In May 2016, out of ten people on house arrest, nine were released by a judge, defending the freedom to come and go in a democracy. 'One cannot use an emergency law against a terrorist risk to regulate domestic social order and ease police work', a lawyer remarked (Gonzales, 2016). Those people had been put on housing arrest because they had a violent profile, and according to the police, they could have caused havoc in the coming wide-scale labour demonstrations. The day following their release, allegedly, some of them violently attacked a police car. On prime time news, the audience saw a hooded youth destroying the driver's window with a blow from his metal-edged shoe, then throwing an iron bar on the windshield, while another masked youth, also dressed in black, was breaking the car's rear window in order to throw a fire canister inside, to inflame the car. None of those youths were caught in the act, despite a small crowd surrounding them.

They were subsequently arrested and brought to a judge who set them free. When asked why those youths belonging to an anti-fascist organization had been allowed to participate in the demonstration in the first place, the judge replied that he had been asked to maintain their house arrest until May 17 but that the police car attack occurred on May 18. The police request had not been precise enough, he said. As for the second judge who set the youths free after the police car attack, the proofs in their files were not convincing enough, the main witness being a retired police officer. This episode illustrates tensions between police and justice in France. Many judges complain that the state of emergency has pushed them aside for the benefit of administrative judges. Some of them and prosecutors as well are eager to become more visible and they forcefully express their malaise on the media.

## The limits of police forces

The limits of national states' resources are a problem, as noted, revealed by the management of post-terrorism by weak and divided governments.

Firstly, the failure of both French and Belgian intelligence services at detecting homegrown terrorists was denounced by a large number of observers. When in January 2015, Amedy Coulibali and the Kouachi brothers killed seventeen people, journalists, police officers, and Jews, the investigation revealed that, since 2012, they had been tracked by DGSI and DGSE. But bureaucratic bungles and a lack of vision made the services powerless at detecting, analyzing, and stopping this new form of terrorism – withdrawn, opaque, and efficient. After the January attacks, the public expected that strong measures would be taken to reorganize intelligence services. But for one year, nothing happened, as if the Left government were embarrassed by structural reforms. As early as 2014, though, rumours had circulated that the next Paris attacks would target a rock concert hall. But among thousands of rumours, intelligence services did not particularly pay attention. DGSI, composed of three thousand agents, remains handicapped by internal – political and labour – conflicts. Its police culture is short-sighted (only 15 percent of the staff is made up of university graduates, linguists, economists, and experts in general) (Le Devin, 2016). The sixteen intelligence services in France remain compartmentalized and need a thorough overhaul. To be fair, one should emphasize the efficiency of private and public security forces, which in November, barred terrorists access to the Stade de France, sparing the lives of eighty thousand people, including that of the French president.

Secondly, on the operational front, French police forces show signs of exhaustion. They have been asked to carry out thousands of house and administrative searches, to ensure order during the climate conference and labour demonstrations, to contain the activists of Nuit debout as well, while maintaining a culture of results and modernizing themselves. Police unions claim that their members are specially hurt by continuous pressures, a lack of protection given both to their image, and to their missions by the state and by an absence of clear orders from the top. A unique feature of the French police emanates from the continuous interference of political authorities in order maintenance situations. When the police are ordered not to intervene at the sight of farmers destroying a prefecture's protective fence or of thugs robbing peaceful demonstrating students, the government's justification is that police non-intervention avoids further confrontation. One explanation of this caution comes from the deep fear of re-enacting the trauma caused by the death of Malik Oussekine when public opinion turned against the police.[5]

On May 18, 2016, police officers publicly expressed their outrage on the Place de la République. Due to a lack of clear and firm orders from the minister of the interior to the police chain of command, they were ordered not to move, sometimes for hours, while watching radicalized youths equip themselves and chant their wish for police officers' deaths during many demonstrations in Paris and elsewhere. During the first semester of 2016, no less than 3267 police officers have been wounded while performing their duty. Demonstrators claim that over thirty protesters were seriously wounded and that a student lost one eye with the weapons used by the police. Investigations are being carried by the General Inspection of the Police and by justice.

The police demonstration addressed the government's apparent weakness and political hesitation. Three or four hundred violent individuals' names are allegedly in the police files. While approximately one hundred of them have been arrested by the police, few are sanctioned by judges for lack of clear evidence. The use of space by multiple users – occupiers from Night Standing Up, union leaders, police demonstrators, intellectuals, and average bystanders reveal the uncertainty of its status. Public space is fragile as it carries groups' strong but conflicting ambitions.

## A new time of uncertainty and unpredictability

'Democracies die behind closed doors', Judge Damon Keith warned in 2002 (Cole, 2016: 437). After political calculations interfering with the state of emergency and the limits of state resources to confront terrorism and ongoing street disorder, another danger should be emphasized. It comes from the confusion and uncertainty surrounding the notion of war rhetorically used by political elites, in response to terrorist attacks. After November 2015, both the French government and Parliament imitated the Bush administration by overreacting to the November Paris attacks in declaring publicly that France was at war, thus incorporating the fear that terrorists wanted to provoke in the French response.

According to the International Court of Law's definition, the Paris attacks could have been qualified as a crime against human kind, that is, 'a generalized or systematic attack, launched against a civilian population and knowingly, by a state or by an organization designing such an attack' (Delmas-Marty, 2015). An attack or an act of war? Is the Islamic state a state? Are not its suicide bombers non-state actors? What does a state of war imply?

### An act of war?

When the attacks occurred on September 11, 2001, the United States qualified them as 'an act of war' in order to grant full powers to the president of the United States. A state of 'exception' is invoked at the federal level in the United States when a state of war is declared. Declaring a state of exception does not require international control. A posteriori, numerous observers link the formation of ISIS to the American decision of intensifying the war in Afghanistan and then launching a war in Iraq as a response to 9/11, in 2003 (Cusson et al., 2016). These commentators claim that this military decision was an overreaction with irreversible consequences. When no international control is exerted, states are tempted to overreact to a threat. 'States don't have the capacity to engage in ordinary policing when the threat emanates from abroad, and so may be inclined to adopt extraordinary measures, as President Bush did in the wake of the 9/11 attacks on the United States' (Cole, 2016: 440).

The situation of the rule of law is different in France, according to legal scholar Delmas-Marty (2015). The anti-terrorist tools provided to the French state were elaborated before globalization turned sovereign states into interdependent entities. France cannot launch a war against transnational terrorism alone. Its response to ISIS and Al-Qaida's attacks should thus be transnational since walls and borders no longer secure national populations from attacks. Technology and human resources may provide new (limited) resources, but they also raise new questions in terms of human rights.

The United States, which has been spared large-scale terrorist attacks since 9/11, seems to indicate that digital technology has been efficient. It better equipped police forces and protected sensitive infrastructures. It challenged Google and opened encrypted messages with the help of hired experts, in order to track terrorists and their social media after the San Bernardino attacks which caused fourteen deaths in California in 2016. This turned the country into a formidable fortress. Nevertheless, David Cole (2016: 434) warns of the danger of being excessively confident about what technology can do. It leads political leaders in the name of national defence, to violate democratic values. He asks:

> Does the doctrine of self-defence permit the killing of those who are not engaged in immediate attack, but are planning future clandestine attacks, where other measures of countering the threat are infeasible? When does terrorism justify a military response, and when does it call for a law enforcement response?

Cole questions the use of massive data, accumulated by police searches. If the data is collected by a subcontracting private sector, how is it regulated? The documents disclosed by Snowden revealed that the NSA and the FBI monitored Muslim civil rights leaders without any apparent basis for suspecting them of terrorism, he remarks. Here we see how political calculations again interfere with the legitimacy of genuine security goals. It is fair to say that the Obama administration has implemented several reforms since Snowden's disclosure. The NSA needs judicial approval before any search of its telephone database. The courts have also currently more leverage to hold the government accountable if they secretly eavesdrop on millions of phone conversations without the holders' knowledge. So far, Google and other data holders respect the privacy of communications. It will be seen whether they will be able to defend this right in the long term.

### The European level

In Europe, clear strategies in support of member states attacked by terrorism are still in progress. It would be hazardous for Europe to launch a war in far-distant countries in order to confront enigmatic enemies. So far, with the doctrine of the 'third pillar', the choice has been to buttress defence nationally. The intergovernmental 'third pillar' goal was to maintain and develop the European Union as 'an area of freedom, security and justice'. But at the same time, the European Court of Justice 'ensured that member states [would be] able to retain a high degree of national control over the development of policy and the adoption of implementing instruments' (Baker, 2010: 189).

National reforms are needed in the short-term, for example, in terms of surveillance services, the conditions of prison, the circulation of people and of goods (including drugs and military weapons), the protection of sensitive infrastructures, and the identification of risks. Can the European Union accelerate national reforms?

The answer is ambiguous. European efforts to find a logical solution to alleviate global threats associated with the Islamic state are dwarfed by national self-centred logics of sovereignty. The filtering of terrorist suspects across borders is deeply lacking. There is no efficient centralized anti-terrorism agency. Central databases like the European Information System (EIS) or the Schengen Information System (SIS) are fed irregularly by member states, and for a long time, there was a reluctance to create a Passenger Name Record (PNR) of airplane travellers. Member states do not trust each other in sharing their information, a phenomenon also seen within countries: the gaps in the transmission of information are not bridged.

The Europeanization of anti-terrorist policies, although slow to be implemented, is however gradually taking place. At the time of writing, after the Nice massacre and attacks in German cities, it is too early to define how European policies, decided in 2016, will fare, but global conferences and numerous reunions among chiefs of state and their prime ministers indicate an urgency for action.

In the end, such arguments indicate that the new type of religious terrorism hitting cities does not fit into the categories of public disorder defined in this study. In my initial definition, public disorder is intimately linked with public space. In the cases of the Paris and Brussels attacks, terrorists were less interested by space and by material destructions than by acts of violence perpetrated on civilians and non-combatants. With limited resources, terrorists used weapons capable of inflicting extensive damage on an unprecedented scale. Consequently, the nature of their acts, their intensity, and their intent are different from those previously studied in this research. Via 'terror', such acts are indeed designed to have an impact on an entire nation and beyond. A large impact is critical to the political dimension of terrorism (Manin, 2008). National authorities' responses summoning states' sovereign powers in a situation of emergency involve countries beyond their national borders. Such a response is different in nature, width, and intensity from those previously studied here.

New forms of terrorism challenge familiar categories, such as those separating intelligence gathering from criminal investigations or external security from internal security. It forces authorities to find new responses, but it also reveals their limits. The extensive use of the emergency law in France has clearly shown its limits, promising more than it could deliver. A lot of people do not understand why many potentially disruptive events are tolerated in the public space if, as continuously repeated by authorities, France is the first target of terrorism in Europe.

'Emergency institutions are designed for national dangers, not for borderless threats. The emergency paradigm, then, is fundamentally inappropriate for confronting the present terrorist threat' (Manin, 2015: 33). For political scientist Bernard Manin, to be consistent with constitutional values, short duration is a necessary condition for emergency measures. He adds (2015: 35) that

> we cannot count on ending a phenomenon that can be brought about by any small group in a world of seven billion people . . . Constitutional democracies should not employ emergency institutions to deal with today's terrorism . . . It is not the right method to rely on the end of the danger when this end is so uncertain and hard to determine.

All the existing legislation should be mobilized, and new ones should be initiated within the rule of law, as the best strategy to confront new emerging challenges.

Where to go then? To quote Tocqueville (1856), we are clearly in the middle way with a worry regarding the past and an uncertainty regarding the future.

## Notes

1   For lack of space, local levels' leverage and the private sector's role will not be addressed here.
2   The number of cases was 157 in May 2015.
3   For lack of space, the case of the French army will not be dealt herewith. The French army has been used extensively since 2015 for military operations abroad (Africa, the Middle East). Domestically, Vigipirate, the anti-terrorist alert programme, mobilizes over 10,000 military personnel, and 950 sensitive sites like synagogues are under continuous surveillance of army and police forces.
4   Préfet Hubert Weigel, adjunct secretary of COP21, kindly shared this information with the author.
5   In 1986, when Minister of the Interior Charles Pasqua, a hard-line Gaullist, had to confront large-scale demonstrations from students against a proposal to make entry to universities selective, a student in fragile health, Malik Oussekine, was pursued by mobile police on light motorcycles (*voltigeurs*) and, suffocating from asthma, died in the Latin Quarter of Paris. 'The government suffered political damage to the extent that it dropped the reform proposal, setting back university reform by over twenty years', M. Anderson remarked (2011: 388).

# 8

# CONCLUSION

In focusing on public disorder and globalization, terms with multiple meanings, my research has explored the intricate interaction between on-the-ground action and online communication on one hand, and, on the other, the online and on-the-ground responses that public disorder conveys in a context of globalization.

How much does order need disorder for its regeneration, adjustment, and survival?

Do episodes of public disorder as those analyzed in this book represent the necessary steps in the adjustment of former situations to new ones?

To answer such questions, I have utilized interactionist theories through a comprehensive analytical framework.

How much do cities' space, social media, and globalization mould public disorder and responses? What conclusions have been reached?

## Contentious spaces

The book has focused primarily on cities' public space and on its capacity to assemble heterogeneous people, at certain times for more or less different reasons. The issue of territorialism is omnipresent in all the local contentions examined here: space is understood by researchers as a composite of multiple differences. It influences social practices, ideologies, and power relations. Space is not static, it is not independent, it is evolving. 'The spatial is social relations stretched out' (Massey, 1994: 2). If we consider that large cities concentrate a growing share of disadvantaged populations, it becomes obvious that 'cities have become a strategic terrain for a whole series of conflicts and contradictions' (Sassen, 1999: 105), which can be heard and seen via public space. Sassen often refers to cities as frontiers, as spaces of contact between different worlds within cities, which my case studies illustrate. Sassen claims that cities' incompleteness allow them to outlast other more powerful and organized systems of power. Let us remember, though, that not all cities provide shared open spaces. Numerous American cities, for instance, have replaced their public space by pseudo open spaces like commercial malls set within heavy CCTV (closed circuit televisions) surveillance. There, marginalized categories of people may be aggressively policed, rejected, and robbed of opportunities to articulate their needs.

But then how does public space neutralize differences and ambivalences in assembling very different individuals and creating moments of shared exaltation, akin to electricity, the 'moments of collective effervescence' that Durkheim (1912/1965: 162) observed? People can be educated to do so. Acting 'under conditions of ambivalence and uncertainty, born of difference and variety', as Bauman (1998) suggests, 'is a difficult art' and needs social maturity. 'Mature persons grow to need the unknown, to feel incomplete without a certain anarchy in their lives' and to learn 'to love the otherness among them' (1998: 46–47). Unpredictability is a strength that cities have. The political power of physical space is frequently ignored, perhaps particularly so in an information age, when so much is relegated to the ephemeral zone of social media. Yet the 'sense of place empowers protests' (Kimmelman, 2011). Public space, buildings, monuments, and bridges, for example, mobilize both memories of the past decades (or, in Europe, of the past centuries) and the power of place to offer a site of dissent and expressivity. Arendt (1958: 199) suggests that 'the space of appearance comes into being wherever men and women are together in the manner of speech and action', adding, however, that 'whenever people gather together, it is potentially there, but only potentially, not necessarily and not forever'.

How is public space recomposed by disorder? What meaning does it acquire and for whom? Local mobilizations in parks, malls, streets, and squares express a sign of democratic vitality and demands for progressive changes. They reinterpret local public space and organize a global drama in a context of marked and contentious territories.

The current political use of public space in cities like Hong Kong, Istanbul, New York, Paris, and London provide illustrations of what can be done by the apparently powerless. To compare and contrast the meaning of 'Whose city?' in Pahl's time (1970; Mayer, 2016) now leads to a critical reflection not only on the changes neo-liberalization has wrought on urban landscapes but also on changes occurring in cities' public space relative to these transformation processes. Public space helps create a political stimulus so that people feel they can exercise a right to peaceably assemble, occupy public space, and create a process for addressing problems. People are moving, regaining political presence; space is a platform for political action and their actions resonate globally. Examples from this research support this point.

The case of Occupy Central in Hong Kong is particularly fascinating. The Hong Kong occupiers, with apparently weak resources, in an asymmetric struggle, challenged China's power of intimidation and its will to extend its domination over this semi-autonomous enclave, after 150 years of British rule. China's use of violence against demonstrators via the local police supported by two hundred members of triads eventually eroded the strength of the movement. However, despite its physical disappearance, the Umbrella mobilization keeps haunting people's imagination. Recent votes in the Hong Kong legislature show that the protest movement was not in vain. Such events appear to reveal something of the kind of leverage some urban groups, with the support of social media, have managed to achieve over their own governance institutions, at least temporarily.

Similarly, in France, in 2005, the young 'rioters' were accused – mainly by comparison with the May 1968 generation – of being 'silent' and more or less absent from political expression. They were often depicted as leaderless and unorganized. But another interpretation is possible. To a certain extent, silent disorder may appear as a healthy form of empowerment by opposition to social alienation. 'Rioters' did not need words to express themselves, since they did not seek to negotiate with power holders from whom they expected nothing. Imposing their presence in the public space via their movements, destructions, and confrontations was enough. They were connected. Their resistance resonated in other groups and other contexts. People can make profound changes with very superficial tools. The social makes space.

Suspending public order is a weapon, a weapon that the 'unheard' have, to quote Martin Luther King Jr. What is currently new is that public disorder resonates with public emotions. Urban sites of protest embody globalization's social failures and give it its confrontational dimension without immediately generating political claims. One cannot deny that such emotions and actions are temporary and will not bring a revolutionary change. What do they achieve? We don't know yet, but we may come to recognize and acknowledge such activities over time.

## Social media and space

In some of the studied cases, the media and the social media marked a difference from previous decades when events were encapsulated in the local. 'An act of protest being tweeted or sent on Facebook rapidly reaches a global audience to such an extent that was unimaginable a couple of decades ago' (Atak & della Porta, 2016: 521). This remark is applicable to the Occupy movements and to the Ferguson and Baltimore cases, which were supported by the mobilizations of Black Lives Matter and other advocacy organizations communicating via social media. The social media has been an activator of disorder at a distance, introducing shifts within a routine order opposing protesters and police forces. For spontaneity to unfold, there was indeed covert scene-setting on both sides, conducted by a nucleus of core invisible organizers, without whom the events would not have crystallized or received broad resonance (Gerbaudo, 2012: 164). The issue then is how accountable are those invisible organizers if something goes wrong?

The social media adds several challenges to police work, but police officers also use the social media to their advantage. Operating under video cameras registering their actions, the police are obliged to follow the rules, but they also have the leverage not to intervene if crowds are openly hostile. To the video of a police officer hitting a protester, another video showing the violence of the protester a few minutes earlier can respond. As shown in the interviews reported in this book, police officers need to strike the right balance between competing rights over space and the protection of people and property, to appreciate concrete situations on the street and to distinguish between the 'good' guys and the 'bad' guys, all dressed the same. Such complex choices were illustrated by the Paris, London, and New York cases. Police work is difficult in conditions of acute tension. In France, where political authorities intervene in order maintenance, policemen acting in defence of order are expected to remain silent. Currently, they tend to express their malaise at being asked by political authorities to fill too many tasks. 'Our mission is not to repair society', the author heard one of them say. The city listens.

The 'invisible' whose culture has been moulded by images are also eager to be heard – not just as people, but for the cause they defend as well, they want their implied messages to be transmitted and amplified and sense to be made of their actions. Authors of disorder depend on the reflection of their own image via the use of video cameras and of social networks. Thus, local events take a global dimension; they are mirrored, they feed imitation and contagion, and they sustain emotions and desires for further mobilization. A link is established between the local and the global.

## The acceleration of globalization

My study confirmed the 'time/space compression' (Bauman, 1998: 2) that globalization operates, changing both the value of space and of time, giving unique and singular events a general value. New hierarchies of centralities and of marginalities are set, paths of mobility and freedom are open for some, while paths of cruel immobility encapsulate and separate others. When boundaries are blurred or illegitimate, violence increases (Tilly, 2003), which is currently the case. But the mere use of violence as a strategy is morally unacceptable in democratic societies, and the so-called casseurs (destructive protesters), hooligans, or black bloc are disapproved of by public opinion and its political representatives defending order. Policemen are seen as victims in such cases, and more sanctions are required from prosecutors and judges (cf. chapter 7).

This research shows how, in some cases, hopefully, public disorder generates positive local change. In the United States, a debate on institutional racism cannot be ignored, the subsequent electoral time providing a window of opportunity to voice minorities' demands. At various levels, efforts are being launched to make local law enforcement agencies more accountable. A new African American police chief has been appointed in Ferguson, and the federal administration officially exerts control over the police-citizens' local relationship, via a consent decree. In Baltimore, prisoners travelling in police wagons are now buckled up and cameras record what happens inside. The Baltimore Police Department is under investigation from the Department of Justice for possible civil rights violations. Active minorities' organizations exert a watchful presence at the city, state, and national levels, using intimidation and numbers. The future will tell whether a genuine change happens, diminishing police and justice racial discrimination, with the support of American majorities. Legewie and Fagan (2016) argue that a proportional representation of minority groups in police departments mitigates group threat and thereby reduces the number of officer-involved killings of African Americans. In a testimony to the President's Task Force on Twenty-First Century Policing, Fagan pleaded for stronger and visible accountability mechanisms. Instead of awarding over $1 billion to settle police misconduct (since 2000) with taxpayers' money, he advocated returns on experience by police departments and their learning from their mistakes. He supported fewer police officers, with higher salaries and better skills to meet the challenges ahead (President's Task Force, 2015).

In London, Paris, Istanbul, and Hong Kong, history is still in the making. In the short term, mobilizations and occupations have been a learning experience for a young generation. Public disorder called for a mobilization of resources within specific, fluid, indeterminate contexts, which were vulnerable to change. The study emphasized that participants' calculations, interests, values, and aggregations intervened in tension-filled contexts. Despite the rules governing specific milieus, the disorder evolved and shifted, owing to interactions between protesters and their opponents. Interactionist hypotheses have been confirmed, also supporting Tilly's (2003) argument that boundaries between opponents are not fixed and that they shift in a course of action. The case studies developed in this research have confirmed those analytical hypotheses.

What this research does not show is the articulation of vertical and horizontal dimensions in protesters' minds. Most of the studied forms of disorder emanate from mobilizations which are 'horizontalist', and that may point to their limitations.

## Are macro-analyses helpful?

Theoretically, disorder can be interpreted, in some cases, as a signal that the accumulation of dysfunctions in the way capitalism works is beyond repair. It is then too early to say whether local, low-stratum, dispersed, uncoordinated protesters and occupiers will find windows of opportunity to generate any new order. Their efforts of transition to a new order may take thirty years or more. It seems indeed that 'disorganized capitalism is disorganizing not only itself, but its opposition as well, depriving it of the capacity either to defeat capitalism or to rescue it' (Streeck, 2004: 48).

One should remember that, after mass protest marked the 1960s in European and American cities, the corporate world and its established allies kept pushing the disadvantaged who were losing their 'right to the city' to the margins (Lefebvre, 1967). Neo-liberalism did not become destabilized by the denunciations of 'the dispossessed', unable to ally with 'the discontented'. More fragmentation, more individualization, more displacements, and more evictions worked against a successful unified opposition to the pursuit of global processes. With deregulation, financial domination, and the blurring of the borderline between public and private interests, neo-liberalism in the past fifty years has reinforced itself with no opposition to confront it. It has become anarchic, with no one at the helm under strong winds.

For some scholars (Winlow et al., 2015), the new types of public disorder created by the Indignant or Occupy movements are entirely powerless. Revolution is out of the picture for masses of people preferring meaningful reforms in terms of more equity rather than a revolutionary change. Pessimistically, Žižek (2006) asserts that

> If one truly wants to subvert the neo-liberal state, it is better to stand mute and refuse to be active than to engage in an endless cycle of pseudo-activity that ultimately legitimises parliamentary capitalism, enabling it to keep on presenting itself as subject to the democratic will of the people.

Badiou would not disagree. Recently, after 150 people were killed by terrorists in Paris in November 2015, he explained that the fascist trend of nihilism that the terrorists displayed came from an evil that went beyond immigration, Islam, the dilapidated Middle East, and plundered Africa. It came from the historical failure of communism as an alternative to contemporary capitalism (Badiou, 2016).

Is radical political posture of muteness to be preferred to the 'aggressive passivity of the contemporary Left', continuously making sure that 'nothing will change, that nothing will really change' (Žižek, 2006: 223)? With its current excess and its social system in chronic disrepair, will capitalism die, not because another system will replace it, but from overdose?

This debate reveals a lack of consensus among scholars. Not all scholars agree that nothing will change. Inspired by Podemos in Spain and Syriza in Greece, Chantal Mouffe (2016) asserts that only an articulation of the Indignatos' claims with forms of involvement at the Parliamentary level may support a Left populism embodying resistance to neo-liberalism.

Mouffe and others agree that capitalism is in a critical condition. It cannot be denied that the decline of economic growth, the rise of public indebtedness, and the ascent of inequality of income and of wealth feed majorities' powerlessness and disenchantment and the will of some to use illegal force to express their discontent. States are accused by progressive observers to be in the grip of money-making industries, with an increasing stake in runaway financialization. Political decision making is seen as privileging corporate and wealthy key actors. The current crisis, then, would come from the political sphere, from its framing of problems, from its ignorance of people's living conditions.

> Among ordinary people, there is a pervasive sense that politics can no longer make a difference in their lives. . . . One result is the declining electoral turn-out combined with high voter volatility, producing ever greater electoral fragmentation, due to the rise of 'populist' protest parties, and pervasive government instability.
>
> *(Streeck, 2014: 41)*

Yet there is no straight assertion that public disorder, globalization, and change are correlated. Multi-faceted, 'wicked' issues defy simple solutions, and there is neither agreement on their nature nor on solutions.

Is it worth trying something then? Opposing the development of current trends marked by inequalities, corruption, and stagnation with spatial protest and dissent on the social media is not enough. What should alternative proposals be? By whom? As apparent in many countries, the political sphere needs to be reframed so that a democratic Europe based on citizens' debates on the institutions that they want is possible (Moufffe, 2016). The shortcoming of horizontal movements needs to be emphasized. They ignore that democratic states are issued from institutions created to think, deliberate, and orient common affairs: the Parliament monitors the political debate, justice puts a halt to mob lynching, and unions buttress labour and work conditions. All those institutions are instruments which have transformed people into citizens. 'We, the people' emanates from a Constitution; it does not spring up naturally (Rousseau, 2016: 21).

Democratic capacities should thus be restored as a counterweight to the power of private forces, but at this stage, we do not know how. Can counter-forces based locally and nationally confront the one percent of the richest and those who will succeed them if they leave? Evidence is provided by numerous experiences from non-for-profit organizations and progressive think tanks that there are opportunities for improving living conditions in the world, eradicating poverty, respecting environmental resources, and restoring the autonomy of the political frame. Is a large democratic consensus needed to support such actions an illusion? Is the power of the Facebook and Twitter generation a mirage and space protest a vain exercise? I do not believe so, and I think that disorder is a healthy signal sent to disjunctive democracies. It shows democracies' resistance to what threatens their values. As US Supreme Court Justice Brennan once observed, liberty is fragile. Just as night does not fall abruptly, it is just the same with oppression. In both cases, first dusk takes place during which nothing seems to change. Yet it is during dusk that one should worry about changes that take place.

## The new story

What has just been said holds for a number of conflicts. But another story is currently being written in Western countries, with a number of unknowns and silences. I am referring to the threat of terrorist attacks. We, as scholars, were on more or less firm ground in our interpretations of public disorder, but these views need to be revised intellectually in the future.

The recruiters of violent suicidal actors creating mayhem in cities have skills and technical support to act destructively and to communicate what they do and why they do it, on the internet, with such mastery that they frequently give the impression of being ahead of states, in terms of organization, coordination, determination, and flexibility. The social media provides them with a logic of aggregation and the capacity to summon potential supporters from a distance. Such operations cannot be done without the construction of a collective identity, 'the identification of an enemy, the definition of a purpose and an object at stake in the conflict' (Melucci, 1996: 72). As the different elements come together to form a new system of relations, the original fragments change their meanings. The actors' fluidity challenges states' traditional modes of defence.

States' uncertainty regarding the path to follow have been commented upon frequently since 9/11. Sometimes, states' preventative organization works, as it did at the Stade de France in Saint Denis, in November 2015, when suicide bombers could not get into the stadium, were stopped by public and private agents, and then blew themselves up. Success also characterized the organization of the climate conference in Paris in December 2015, and then the Euro Soccer Championship in the spring, in terms of security. But states' organizations also fail. Huge gaps in the detection of terrorist plots by Belgian and French intelligence services have been noted, and intelligence apparatuses need a thorough overhaul. If the dialectics of order and disorder operate, organizational change with technology in the background and human resources (including more data analysts) at the forefront should follow. Currently, however, conceptual tools are lacking to make sense of the new patterns emerging both in terms of threat and of possible responses. Calling 'enemy combatants' young people animated with a death wish, with a will to communicate and destroy, is not enough. Linking people's political disenchantment with political leaders' lack of capacities (except in terms of repression) is not enough either.

Those difficult issues need to be explored further. There is more resilience in people than opinion polls or political commentary suggest. Pain and Smith believe (2008: 249) that 'Everyday life always and already speaks back, resists and challenges . . . the politics embedded in the scalar, top-down view of fear assemblage'. Cities are increasingly the terrain where people oppose globalization and its tendency to flatten cultures into sameness. As states become more interdependent, resilient cities come to the rescue. They preserve the way people use cities and interact with them. New, frequently invisible, forms of involvement – some of them quiet and personal, others large-scale and spectacular, characterize such engagements. Alternative change, or at least ideas for it, may happen via empowered citizens forming a watchful presence. Within global processes and with technologies of communication, local actors, some of them illiterate, may connect to other actors in the same city or country or elsewhere, via NGOs, to find solutions. Betting on citizens' involvement has its dangers. Populism from the right or the young people's rejection of representative democracy may lead to a repetition of the tragic errors of the past. Progressive forces are still there, even after the collapse of the Arab Spring, but what paths will be followed is unknown. It may take decades for the disenfranchised to join with the dispossessed and with others and to make history. It will depend on the openings that are made. More research, more conceptual tools are thus needed to tackle emerging patterns and possibly the new ways of looking at the current dialectics of order and disorder.

The last words of Chateaubriand in his *Memoirs from Beyond the Grave*, in 1848, come to mind: 'I found myself between two centuries as at the confluence of two rivers; I plunged into their troubled waters; regretfully leaving the ancient strand where I was born, and swimming hopefully towards the unknown shore where new generations will land'. We seem to have reached this moment.

# BIBLIOGRAPHY

Abu-Lhugod, J. (2007) *Race, Space, and Riots in Chicago*, New York and Los Angeles: Oxford University Press.

Adams, E. (2014) 'Police abusing black men', *International New York Times*, 6–7 December: 7.

Alonso, P. (2016) 'Ma vie d'assigné à résidence', *Libération*, May 28: 16.

Alonso, P. Fansten, E., Le Devin, W. (2015) 'Les filets percés du renseignement', *Libération*, 26 November: 3.

Amnesty International Charity Ltd (2016) *Annual Report, 2015/2016*, London: Amnesty International Ltd.

Anderson, E. (1999) *Code of the Streets: Decency, Violence and the Moral Life of the Inner-City*, New York: W. W. Norton & Cy.

Anderson, M. (2011) *In Thrall to Political Change: Police and Gendarmerie in France*, Oxford, UK: Oxford University Press.

Anonyme (2002) 'Haro sur l'ennemi intérieur: l'antimondialisme', *Acrimed*, August 23.www. acrimed.org/article679.htlm?var_recherche=Haro+sur+l/percent27ennemi+int/ percentE9rieur.

Anonymous (2011) 'Black Bloc scatanati. Blindato in fiamme vetrine rotte, auto in fiamme, petardi e molotov', *La Repubblica*, 16 October.

Appadurai, A. (2006) *Fear of Small Numbers: An Essay on the Geography of Anger*, Durham, NC, Duke University Press.

Arendt, H. (1972) *Du mensonge à la Violence*, Paris: Calmann-Levy.

Atak, K., della Porta, D. (2016) 'Popular uprisings in Turkey: Police culpability and constraints for dialogue-oriented policing in Gezi Park and beyond', *European Journal of Criminology, 13(5): 610–625.*

Ax, J. (2012) 'Slow pace of justice wears down Occupy Wall Street defendants', *New York Times*, July 11.

Aylan, K. (2016) 'Insurgent Citizens of the Occupy Gezi Movement' in B. Axford, D. and S. Buhari-Gulmez (eds), *Bridging Divides: Rethinking Ideology in the Age of Flobal Discontent*, London: Routledge, forthcoming.

Badie, B. (2011) 'Printemps arabe: un commencement', *Etudes*, 415, 17: 7–18.

Badiou, A. (2016). *Notre mal vient de plus loin: Penser les tueries du 13 novembre*, Paris: Fayard.

Bagguley, P., Hussain, T. (2008) *Riotous Citizens: Ethnic Conflict in Multicultural Britain*, Aldershot, UK: Ashgate.

Baker, A. (2010) 'Governing through crime: The case of the European union', *European Journal of Criminology*, 7(3): 187–213.

Balibar, E. (2006) 'Uprisings in the banlieues', *Lignes*, November: 50–101.

Ball-Rokeach, S. (1973) 'Values and violence: A test of the subculture of violence thesis', *American Sociological Review*, 38: 736–49.

Bauman, Z. (1998) *Globalization: The Human Consequences*, Cambridge: Polity Press.

Bayat, A. (2000) 'From dangerous classes to quiet rebels', *International Sociology*, 15: 533–57.

Bayley, D. H. (1979) 'Police function, structure, and control in Western Europe and North America: Comparative and historical studies', *Crime and Justice*, 1: 109–43.

Beaud, S., Pialoux, M. (2003) *Violences urbaines, violence sociale. Genèse des nouvelles classes dangereuses*, Paris: Fayard.

Beauregard, R., Haila, A. (2000) 'The unavoidable continuities of the city' in P. Marcuse, R. van Kempen (eds) *Globalizing Cities: A New Spatial Order*, Oxford, UK: Blackwell: 22–36.

Beech, H., Rauhala, E. (2014) 'The voice of a generation', *Time Magazine*, 8 October.

Benslama, F. (2016) *Un furieux désir de sacrifice: Le surmusulman*, Paris: Le Seuil.

Benyon, J. (1987) 'Interpretations of civil disorder' in J. Benyon, J. Solomos (eds) *The Roots of Urban Unrest*, Oxford, UK: Pergamon: 23–44.

Bertho, A. (2009) *Le temps des émeutes*, Paris: Bayard.

Bertho, A. (2014) De l'émeute au soulèvement, la révolution n'est plus ce qu'elle était. *Revue internationale et stratégique*, 93(1): 73–80.

Bittner, E. (1970) *The Functions of the Police in Modern Society: A Review of Background Factors, Current Practices, and Possible Role Models*, Washington, DC: National Institute of Mental Health.

Bittner, E. (1974) 'Florence Nightingale in the pursuit of Willie Sutton', in H. Jacob (ed.) *The Potential Reform of Criminal Justice*, Beverley Hills: Sage, 17–44.

Bjorgo, T. (2005) 'Conflict processes between youth groups in a Norwegian City: Polarization and revenge', *European Journal of Crime, Criminal Law and Criminal Justice*, 13: 44–74.

Blumer, H. (1936) Collective behavior. In R.E. Park (ed) *Principles of Sociology*, New York: Barnes and Noble.

Blumer, H. (1978) Social unrest and collective protest. In N.K. Denzin (ed) *Studies in Symbolic Interaction*, Englewood Cliffs, NJ: Prentice-Hall.

Body-Gendrot, S. (2000) *The Social Control of Cities? Comparative Perspectives*, London: Blackwell.

Body-Gendrot, S. (2004) Police race relations in England and in France: Policy and practices. In G. Mesko, M. Pagon, B. Dobovsek (eds) *Policing in Central and Eastern Europe: Dilemmas of Contemporary Criminal Justice*, Slovenia: University of Maribor.

Body-Gendrot, S. (2007) 'Urban violence in France: Anything new?' in L. Cachet (ed.) *Governance of Security in the Netherlands and Belgium*, Den Haag, Netherlands: Boom Legal Publishers: 263–80.

Body-Gendrot, S. (2010) 'Police marginality, racial logics and discrimination in the *banlieues* of France', *Ethnic and Racial Studies*, 33, 4: 656–674.

Body-Gendrot, S. (2012) *Globalization, Fear and Insecurity: The Challenges for Cities North and South*, Basingstoke, UK: Palgrave Macmillan.

Body-Gendrot, S. (2013a) 'Urban violence in France and England: Comparing Paris (2005) and London (2011)', *Policing and Society*, 23(1): 6–25.

Body-Gendrot, S. (2013b) 'Place, space and urban (in)security' in S. Body-Gendrot, S.M. Hough, K. Kerezsi, R. Levy, S. Snacken (eds) *The Routledge Handbook of European Criminology*, London: Routledge: 222–40.

Body-Gendrot, S. (2013c) 'Violence in the city: Challenges of global governance' in J. Stiglitz, M. Kaldor (eds) *The Quest for Security*, New York: Columbia University Press: 260–75.

Body-Gendrot, S. (2014) 'Public disorders: Theory and practice', *Annual Review of Law and Social Sciences*, 10: 243–58.

Body-Gendrot, S. (2016) 'Making sense of French disorders in 2005', *European Journal of Criminology*, 13(5): 566–572.

Body-Gendrot, S., Savitch, H.V. (2012) 'Urban violence in the United States and France: Comparing Los Angeles (1992) and Paris (2005)' in K. Mossberger, S. Clarke, P. Jones (eds) *Oxford Handbook of Urban Politics*, Oxford: Oxford University Press: 501–19.

Body-Gendrot, S., Spierenburg, P. (2007) *Violence in Europe*, New York: Springer.

Booth, C. (1889) *Life and Labor of the People of London*, London: MacMillan.

Borradori, G. (2003) *Le concept du 11 septembre: dialogues à New York avec Jacques Derrida et Jurgen Habermas*, Paris: Gallilée.

Borredon, L., Pécout, A. (2015) 'Les militants de la COP21, cible de l'état d'urgence', *Le Monde*, 28 November: 8.

Bosman, J., Apuzzo, M. (2014) 'The militarization of America's police', *International New York Times*, 16 August: 5.

Bottoms, A. (2009) 'Disorder, order and control signals', *British Journal of Sociology*, 60: 49–55.

Bourdieu, P. (1977) 'Une classe objet' *Les actes de la recherche en sciences sociales*, 17–18: 2–5.

Bourdieu, P. (1984) *Questions de sociologie*, Paris: Ed. Minuit.

Bourdieu, P. (1994) 'Rethinking the state: Genesis and structure of the bureaucratic field', *Sociological Theory*, 12(1): 1–18.

Bourdieu, P. (2012) *Sur l'Etat. Cours au College de France (1989–1992)*, Paris: Le Seuil.

Brodeur, J.P. (2010) *The Policing Web*, Oxford: Oxford University Press.

Brotherton, D. (2014) 'The criminalization of Zuccotti Park and its lessons for the UK riots' in D. Pritchard, F. Pakes (eds) *Riot, Unrest and Protest on the Global Stage*, Basingstoke: Palgrave Macmillan: 222–36.

Brouard, S., Tiberj, V. (2005) *Français comme les autres? Enquête sur les citoyens d'origine maghrébine, africaine et turque*, Paris: Presses de Sciences Po.

Broussard, P. (2016) 'Dans la peau d'un hooligan', *Le Monde*, 14 June: 16.

Browning, R., Marshall, D., Tabb, W. (1984) *Protest Is Not Enough*, Berkeley: University of California Press.

Buckley, C. (2014) 'Leaders of Hong Kong protests urge students to leave camps', *International New York Times*, 3 December.

Buckley, C., Wong, A. (2014) Hong Kong removes last democracy protests site, *International New York Times*, 16 December.

Burcher, M., Whelan, C. (2015) 'Social network analysis and small group "dark" networks: An analysis of the London bombers and the problem of "fuzzy" boundaries', *Global Crime*, 16 (2): 104–22.

Callimachi, R. (2016) 'In Europe, ISIS sowed its seeds', *International New York Times*, 30 March: 1, 4.

Carzon, D. (2016) 'Contre-enquête sur les Molenbeek français', *Libération*, 11 April: 1–7.

Chan, J. (1997) *Changing Police Culture: Policing in a Multicultural Society*, Cambridge: Cambridge University Press.

Chevalier, L. (1958) *Classes laborieuses, classes dangereuses à Paris pendant la première moitié du XIX e siècle*. Paris: Plon.

Chevallier, J. (1997) 'Présentation' in *Désordres*, Centre universitaire de recherches administratives et politiques de Picardie, Paris: Presses Universitaires de France: 1–14.

Chevigny, P. (1995) *Edge of the knife: Police violence in the Americas*, New York: The New Press.

Chomski, N. (2014) 'Occupy Wall Street has created something that didn't really exist in the U.S. solidarity', *Democracy Now!* Access 15 November 2014.

Christie-Miller, A. (2013) 'In Turkey, echoes of US-style clashes over glitzy redevelopment', *Christian Science Monitor*, 10 June.

Ciccheli, V., Galland, O., de Maillard, J., Misset, S. (2006) *Enquête sur les violences urbaines. Comprendre les émeutes de novembre 2005. L'exemple d'Aulnay-sous-bois*, Paris: Centre d'analyse stratégique.

Clavel, G. (2014) *La gouvernance de l'insécurité: la pénalisation du social dans une société sécuritaire*, Paris: L'Harmattan.

Clover, J. (2016) *Riot, Strike, Riot: The New Era of Uprisings*, London: Verso.

Cohen, L. (2004) *A consumers' republic*, New York: Vintage.

Cohen, S. (1972) *Folk Devils and Moral Panics: The Creation of the Mods and the Rockers*, London: MacGibbon & Kee.

Cohen, S. (1985) *Visions of Social Control*, Cambridge: Polity Press.

Cole, D. (2016) 'Countering transnational terrorism: Global policing, global threats and human rights' in B. Bradford, B. Jauregui, I. Loader, J. Steinberg (eds) *The Sage Handbook of Global Policing*, London, Sage: 429–442.

Collins, R. (2008) *Violence: A Micro-Sociological Theory*, Princeton: Princeton University Press.

Collins, R. (2009) 'The micro-sociology of violence', *British Journal of Sociology*, 60(3): 566–576.

Commission Nationale Consultative des Droits de l'Homme (2014) *La lutte contre le racisme, l'antisémitisme et la xénophobie: Année 2013*. Paris: La documentation française.

Cornevin, C. (2014) 'Hooliganisme: Beauvau veut faire le ménage', *Le Figaro*, 12 August.

Cortesero, R., Marlière, E. (2015) L'émeute est-elle une forme d'expression politique? *Agora*, 70, 2: 57–74.

Coser, L. (1956) *The Functions of Social Conflict*, New York: Free Press.

Courtois, S. (2015) 'Banlieues: "apartheid" et amnésie', *Le Monde*, 27 January.

Crary, D. (2014) 'AP poll: Police killings of blacks voted top story of 2014', *Associated Press*, 22 December.

Craspey, E. (1872) *The Nether Side of New York*, New York: Sheldon.

Critchley, T.A. (1978) *A History of the Police in England and Wales*, London: Constable.

Crumley, B. (2012) 'The problem of Clichy: After 2005 riots, France's suburbs are still miserable', *Time World*, http://world.time.com/2012/12/07/the-problem-of-clichy-after-2005-riots-frances-suburbs-are-still-miserable. Access 25 April 2014.

Cusson, M., James, J., Hassid, O. (2016) 'Antiterrorisme et sécurité intérieure', *Revue internationale de criminologie et de police technique et scientifique*, 1: 3–18.

Dal Lago, A., De Biasi, R. (1994) 'Italian football fans: Culture and organization' in R. Giulianotti, N. Bonney, M. Hepworth (eds) *Football, Violence and Social Identity*, London: Routledge: 73–89.

Davies, J.C. (1969) 'The J-curve of rising and declining satisfactions as a cause of revolution and rebellion' in T. Gurr, H. Graham (eds.) *Violence in America: Historical and Comparative Perspectives*, New York: Praeger: 415–36.

De Biaso, R. (1998) 'The Policing of Hooliganism in Italy' in D. Della Porta, H. Reiner (eds) *Policing Protest: The Control of Mass Demonstrations in Western Democracies*, Minneapolis: University of Minnesota Press: 213–27.

De Certeau, M. (1984) *The Practice of Everyday Life*, Berkeley: University of California Press.

De Changy, F. (2014) 'A Hong Kong, l'opposition hésite sur les suites de son action', *Le Monde*, 29 October.

De Changy, F., Pedroletti, B. (2014) 'A Hong Kong, les nouveaux visages de la contestation', *Le Monde*, 3 October: 6.

Decker, S., Pyroos, D. (2014) 'Les gangs et la violence' in J.P. Guay and C. Fredette (eds) *Le phénomène des gangs de rue*, Montréal: Presses de l'Université de Montréal: 95–114.

Della Porta, D. (1998) 'Police knowledge and protest policing: Some reflections on the Italian case' in D. Della Porta, H. Reiner (eds.) *Policing Protest: The Control of Mass Demonstrations in Western Democracies*, Minneapolis: University of Minnesotta Press: 228–52.

Della Porta, D., Reiter, H. (eds) (1998) *Policing Protest: The Control of Mass Demonstrations in Western Democracies*, Minneapolis: University of Minnesota Press.

Della Porta, D., Tarrow, S. (2001) 'After Genoa and New York: The antiglobal movement, the police and terrorism', *Items & Issues*, 2:9–-11.

Della Porta, D., Zamponi, L. (2013) 'Protest and policing on October 15, global day of action: The Italian case', *Policing and Society*, 23: 65–80.

Delmas-Marty, M. (2015) 'Le droit d'exception risque de devenir la règle', *Le Monde*, 18 November: 16.

De Swaan, A. (2016) *Diviser pour tuer: les régimes génocidaires et leurs hommes de main*, Paris: Le Seuil.

Devecchio, A. (2015) 'Politique de la ville et erreur de diagnostic', *Le Figaro*, 2 March.

Diani, M. (2014) 'Les désenchantements du printemps arabe sous le prisme de l'epistémé', www.lescahiersdelislam.fr, June 22.

Dobry, M. (1986) *Sociologie des crises politiques*, Paris: Presses de la Fondation nationale des sciences politiques.

Dollard, J. (1974) *Frustration and Aggression*, New Haven, CT: Yale University Press.

Dufresne, D. (2010) *Maintien de l'ordre*, Paris: Hachette, reprint.

Dupuis-déri, F. (2003) *Les black blocs*, Québec: Lux Editions, 3rd pr.

Elias, N. (1939/1994) *The Civilizing Process*, Oxford: Blackwell.

Elias, N., Dunning, E. (1986) *Quest for Excitement: Sport and Leisure in the Civilizing Process*, Oxford, UK: Blackwell.

Eligon, J. (2014) 'After Ferguson demonstrations and challenges', *International New York Times*, November 29: 10.

Emsley, C. (1991) *The English Police: A Political and Social History*. Hemel, Hampstead: Routledge, UK.

Everton, S. F. (2012). *Disrupting Dark Networks* (Vol. 34), Cambridge: Cambridge University Press.

Everton, S. F., Cunningham, D. (2015) 'Dark network resilience in a hostile environment: optimizing centralization and density', *Criminology, Criminal Justice Law & Society*, 16, 1, 1–20.

Fagan, J. (2012) *Floyd et al. vs. City of New York et al.* Second Supplemental Report. 08 Civ. 01634 (SAS).US District Court, Southern District of New York, 29 November.

Favale, M. (2011) 'L'inferno dei black bloc citta sgregiata 90 feriti', *La Repubblica*, 16 October: 2.

Favell, A. (2001) *Philosophies of Integration*, New York: Palgrave Macmillan.

Federici (1791/2008) *Flagrants délits sur les Champs-Elysées.* Presentation and notes by A. Farge. Paris: Mercure de France.

Felson, M. (2014) 'Les gangs et les guêpes' in J.P. Guay, C. Fredette (eds) *Le phénomène des gangs de rue*, Montréal: Presses de l'université de Montréal, 115–34.

Festinger, L. (1968) *The Theory of Cognitive Dissonance*, Stanford, CA: Stanford University Press.

Fillieule, O., Jobard, F. (1998) 'The policing of protest in France: Toward a model of protest policing' in D. della Porta, H. Reiter (eds) *The Policing of Protest in Western Democracies*, Minneapolis: University of Minnesota Press: 70–90.

Fillieule, O., Tartakowsky, D. (2013) *Demonstrations*, Halifax, Canada: Fernwood.

Fischer, M. (2013) 'The photo that encapsualtes Turkey's protests and the severe police crackdown', *Washington Post*, 3 June.

Fisher, C. (1972) 'Observing a crowd: The structure and description of protest demonstrations' in J. Douglas (ed.) *Research in Deviance*, New York: Random House: 187–211.

Fleming, J. (2015) *Police Leadership: Rising to the Top*, Oxford: Oxford University Press.

Forsythe, M., Buckley, C. (2014) 'Protesters look beyond setbacks in Hong Kong', *International New York Times*, 2 December.

Foucault, M. (2004) *Abnormal: Lectures at the Collège de France, 1974–1975*, New York: Picador.

Freeman, J. (2002) 'The Tyranny of structurelessness' in Dark Star (collective ed.) *Quiet Rumors: An Anarcha-Feminist Reader*, Oakland: AK Press.

Gamson, W. (1975) *The Strategy of Social Protest*, Belmont, CA: Wadsworth.

Garapon, A. (2016) 'Un réveil en sursaut', *Esprit*, 421: 26–9.

Garland, D. (2001) *The Culture of Control*, Chicago: University of Chicago Press.

General Direction of Renseignements généraux (2005) *Report*. November 23rd. Quote published in *Le Parisien*, 12 July.

George, S., Wolf, M. (2002) *La mondialisation libérale*, Paris: Grasset-Les échos.

Gerbaudo, P. (2012) *Tweets and the Streets: Social Media and Contemporary Activism*, London: Pluto.

Gillham, P., Edwards, B., Noakes, J. (2013) 'Strategic incapacitation and the policing of occupy Wall Street protests in New York City, 2011', *Policing and Society*, 23: 81–102.

Goffmann, A. (2014) *On the Run: Fugitive Life in an American City*, Chicago: University of Chicago Press.

Goffmann, E. (1963) *Behavior in Public Places: Notes on the Social Organization of Gatherings*, New York: Free Press.

Goffmann, E. (1970) *Strategic Interaction*, Oxford, UK: Blackwell.

Goldstone, J. (1991) *Revolution and Rebellion in the Early Modern World*, Berkeley: University of California Press.

Gonzales, P. (2016) 'Voiture brûlée: pourquoi les casseurs ont échappé à l'interdiction de manifester', *Le Figaro*, 20 May: 10.

Goodwin, J. (2001) *Passionate Politics: Emotions and Social Movements*, Chicago: University of Chicago Press.

Greenberg, M. (2012) 'What future for Occupy Wall Street?', *New York Review of Books*, 9 February.

Guehenno, J.M. (2015) 'Le salafisme, un courant antimoderniste divisé entre "quiétistes" et djihadistes', *Le Figaro*, 21 November: 4.

Guigni, M., McAdam, D., Tilly, C. (eds) (1999) *How Social Movements Matter*, Minneapolis: University of Minnesota Press.

Haenni, P. (2006) 'France facing its Muslims: Riots, Jihadism and depolitization', *International Crisis Group*, Report Europe, 172: 9.

Hall, S., Critcher, C., Jefferson, T., Clarke, J., Roberts, B. (1978) *Policing Crisis: Mugging, the State, and Law and Order*, London: Macmillan.

Hamidi, C. (2009) 'Riots and protest cycles: Immigrant mobilization in France, 1968–2008', in D. Waddington, F. Jobard, M. King (eds) *Rioting in the UK and France*, Cullompton, UK: Willan: 135–46.

Harcourt, B. (2001) *Illusion of Order: The False Promise of Broken Windows Policing*, Cambridge, MA: Harvard University Press.

Her Majesty's Chief Inspector of Constabulary (2007) *Adapting to protest: nurturing the British model of policing*, HMIC Press.

Her Majesty's Chief Inspector of Constabulary (2011) *The rules of engagement: A review of the August 2011 disorders*, HMIC Press.

Heymann, P. (2003) *Terrorism, Freedom and Security: Winning without War*, Cambridge: The MIT Press.

Hirschman, A.O. (1970) *Exit, Voice, Loyalty*, Cambridge, MA: Harvard University Press.

Hobsbawn, E. (1959) *Primitive Rebels*, Manchester, UK: Manchester University Press.

Hochstetler, A. (2001) 'Opportunities and decisions: Interactional dynamics in robbery and burglary groups', *Criminology*, 39: 737–63.

Holston, J. (2008) *Insurgent Citizenship: Disjunctions of Democracy and Modernity in Brazil*, Princeton, NJ: Princeton University Press.

Home Affairs Committee (2011) *Policing Large-Scale Disorder: Lessons from the Disturbances of August 2011*. 16th Report of Session 2010–12, London: TSO, HC 1456–1.

Hornqvist, M. (2014) 'The fluid legitimacy of the Husby riots', *Newletter of the European Society of Criminology*, 13(1): 4–7.

Hough, M., Jackson, J., Bradford, B. (2013) 'Trust in justice and the legitimacy of legal authorities: Topline findings from a European comparative study' in S. Body-Gendrot, M. Hough, K. Kerezsi, R. Levy, S. Snacken (eds) *Routledge Handbook of European Criminology*, Oxford, UK: Routledge: 243–65.

Hunt, A. (2014) 'Racial divide in US defies easy change', *International New York Times*, 25 August.

Hunter, A. (1985) 'Private, parochial and public social orders: The problems of crime and incivility in urban communities' in G. Suttles, M. Zald (eds) *The Challenge of Social Control*, Norwood, NJ: Albex: 230–42.

Innes, M. (2004) *Signal Crimes and Reassurance Policing*, Guilford, UK: University Surrey.

IPCC (2012) 'Report of the investigation into a complaint made by the family of Mark Duggan about contact with them immediately after his death', *Independent Investigation Final Report*, London: IPCC.

Jacquin, J.-B. (2015) 'L'état d'urgence soumis au Conseil Constitutionnel', *Le Monde*, 13 December: 13.

Janowitz, M. (1999) 'Collective racial violence: A contemporary history' in H.D. Graham, T. Gurr (eds) *Violence in Ameutrica*, Beverley Hills, CA: Sage: 261–286.

Jobard, F. (2013) *Police et science politique: Approches empiriques*, Paris: Institut d'Etudes Politiques.

Jobard, F. (2014) 'Riots in France: Political, proto-political or anti-political turmoils?' in D. Pritchard, F. Pakes (eds) *Riot, Unrest and Protest on the Global Stage*, Basingstoke: Palgrave Macmillan, 132–50.

Jobard, F. (2015) 'La police en banlieue après les émeutes de 2005', *Mouvements*, 83, 75–86.

Jobard, F., King, M., Waddington, D. (2009) 'Conclusions' in D. Waddington, F. Jobard, M. King (eds) *Rioting in the UK and France: A Comparative Analysis*, Cullompton, UK: Willan.

Johnson, M. (2003) *Street Justice: A History of Police Violence in New York City*, Boston: Beacon Press.

Kalifa, D. (2013) *Les bas-fonds. Histoire d'un imaginaire*, Paris: Seuil.

Kaminski, D. (2016) *Des objets impénétrables à la connaissance ou des chercheurs rendus impuissants par leur désir de dévoilement*, Revue internationale de criminologie et de police technique et scientifique, 69: 277–288.

Katz, M.B. (2012) *Why Don't American Cities Burn?* Philadelphia: University of Pennsylvania Press.

Kepel, G. (2012) *Banlieues de la République*, Paris: Gallimard.

Kepel, G. (2015) *Terreur dans l'Hexagone*, Paris: Gallimard.

Kessel, J. (2014) 'High school student embodies new political activism in Hong Kong', *International New York Times*, 2 October: 8.

Kimmelman, M. (2011) 'Sense of place empowers protests', *International Herald Tribune*, 17 October.

Klein, N. (2000) *No Logo*, London: Flamingo.

Kneebone, E. (2014) 'Ferguson, Mo. Emblematic of Growing Suburban Poverty', *Rethinking the Metropolitan Areas*, Washington, DC: Brookings Institute, 15 August.

Koca, A.E. (2015) (in Turk) *Protest Policing between Order and Mayhem: Gezi Events from Police Perspective*, Ankara: Atif Yayinlari.

Kokoreff, M. (2008a) 'Sociologie de l'émeute. Les dimensions de l'action en question', *Déviance et société*, 30: 521–34.

Kokoreff, M. (2008b) *Sociologie des émeutes*, Paris: Payot.

Lagrange, H. (2009) 'The French riots and urban segregation' in D. Waddington, F. Jobard, M. King (eds) *Rioting in the UK and France. A Comparative analysis*, Cullompton, UK: Willan: 107–23.

Lapeyronnie, D. (2006) 'Révolte primitive dans les banlieues françaises: Essai sur les émeutes de l'automne 2005', *Déviance et société*, 30: 431–48.

Le Bars, S. (2015) 'Baltimore est une ville pauvre dans un Etat riche', *Le Monde*, 16 May: 7.

Le Bon, G. (1895/1947) *The Crowd: A Study of the Popular Mind*, London: Ernest Benn.

Le Devin, C. (2016) 'Les services antiterroristes en panne de réorganisation', *Libération*, 10 January: 9.

Legewie, J. & Fagan, J. (2016) *Group Threat, Police Officer Diversity and the Deadly Use of Police Force*, New York: Columbia Law School, Paper n° 14–512.

Lenoir, R. (1996) 'Le sociologue et les magistrats: Entretiens sur la mise en détention provisoire', *Genèses*, 22: 130–45.

Lentz, S.A., Chaires, R.H. (2007) 'The invention of Peel's principles: A study of Policing "text-book" history', *Journal of Criminal Justice*, 37: 67–79.

Lesnes, C. (2011)'Occupy Wall Street, occupy the media', *Le Monde*, 20 October.

Lim, L. (2014) 'Hong Kong People!' *International New York Times*, 30 September.

Limbergen, K., van Walgrave, L. (1989) 'The societal and psycho-sociological background of football hooliganism', *Current Psychology*, 8: 4–14.

Loader, I., Walker, N. (2007) *Civilizing Security*, Cambridge, UK: Cambridge University Press.

Lofland, J. (1985) *Protest: Studies in Collective Behavior and Social Movements*, New Brunswick, NJ: Transaction.

Macchiavelli, N. (1515/1908) *The Prince*, New York: J.M. Dent.

Manin, B. (2008) 'The emergency paradigm and the new terrorism: What if the end of terrorism was not in sight?' in S. Baume, B. Fontana (eds) *The Uses of the Separation of Powers*, Paris: Michel Houdiard: 135–171 transl in La Vie des idées, 15 December 2015: 1–35. http://www.laviedesidees.fr/Le-paradigme-de-l-exception.html.

Manning, P. (1996) 'Dramaturgy, politics and the axial media event', *Sociology Quaterly*, 37: 261–278.

Manning, P. (1997) *Police Work: The Social Organization of Policing*, Cambridge, MA: MIT Press.

Manning, P. (2010) *Democratic Policing in a Changing World*, Boulder, CO: Paradigm.

Mari, L. (2011)'San Giovanni sotto choc Alemanno: Il governo ci aiuti Ora colpire quelgli animali', *La Republica*, 17 October: 3.

Marsh, P. (1977) 'Football hooliganism: Fact or fiction?' *British Journal of Law and Society*, 4: 256–59.

Marx, G. (1970) 'Civil disorder and the agents of social control', *Journal of Social Issues*, 26: 19–57.

Marx, G. (1974) 'Thoughts on a neglected category of social movement participant: The agent provocateur and the informant', *American Journal of Sociology*, 80: 402–442.

Massey, D. (1994) *Space, Place and Gender*, Minneapolis, MN: University of Minnesota Press.

Mathias, P. (2016) 'Internet peut-il créer un espace public mondial?', *Le Monde*, 24 July: 26.

Mauger, G. (2006) *L'émeute de novembre 2005*, Lyon: Editions du croquant.

McAdam, D., Tarrrow, S., Tilly, C. (2001) *Dynamics of Contention*, Cambridge: Cambridge University Press.

McPhail, C. (2006) 'The crowd and collective behaviour', *Symbolic Interaction*, 29, 4, 433–464.

McPhail, C., Schweingruber, D., McCarthy, J. (1998) 'Policing protest in the United States: 1960–1995', in D. Della Porta, H. Reiner (eds) *Policing Protest: The Control of Mass Demonstrations in Western Democracies*, Minneapolis: University of Minnesotta Press:49–69.

Metropolitan Police Service (2012) '4 days in August: Strategic review into the disorder of August 2011'. *Final Report*, London: Metropolitan Police Service.

Ministry of Justice (2012) 'Statistical bulletin of the public disorder 6th to 9th August 2011', www.justice.gov.uk/publications/statistics-and-data/criminal-justice/public-disorder-august-11.htm. Access 22 April 2014.

Mohammed, M. and Mucchielli, L. (2006) 'La police dans "les quartiers sensibles": un profond malaise', *Mouvements*, 44: 58–66.

Monkkonen, E. (1981) *Police in Urban America, 1860–1920*, Cambridge: Cambridge University Press: 49–69.

Moore, B. (1978) *Injustice: The Social Bases of Obedience and Revolt*, White Plains, NY: M.E. Sharpe.

Morrell, G., Scott, S., McNeish, D., Webster, S. (2011) *The August Riots in England: Understanding the Involvement of Young People*, London: National Center for Social Research. Prepared for the Cabinet Office.

Mouffe, C. (2016) *L'illusion du consensus*, Paris: Albin-Michel.

Mouhanna, C. (2012) *La police contre les citoyens*, Paris: Champ Social.

Muir, W.K. (1977) *Police: Streetcorner Politicians*, Chicago: Chicago University Press.

National Advisory Commission on Civil Disorder (Kerner Commission) (1968) *Final Report*, Washington, DC: US Government Printing Office.

National Commission on Causes of Prevention of Violence (Eisenhower Commission) (1969) *To Establish Justice, to Ensure Domestic Tranquility: Final Report*, Washington, DC: US Government Printing Office.

Newburn, T. (2015) 'The 2011 English riots in recent historical perspective', *British Journal of Criminology*, 55(1): 375–392.

Newburn, T. (2016a) 'Reflections on why riots don't happen', *Theoretical Criminology*, 20, 2: 125–144.

Newburn, T. (2016b) 'The 2011 England riots in European context: A framework for understanding the 'life cycle' of riots', *European Journal of Criminology*, 13, 5: 540–555.

Oberschall, A. (1973) *Social Conflict and Social Movement*, Englewood Cliffs, NJ: Prentice Hall.

O'Connor, D. (2011) 'Evidence before the Home Affairs Committee', 29 November. www.publications.parliament.uk/pa/cm201012/cmselect/cmhaff/uc1456-viii/uc145601. HTM Access 24 April 2014.

Ogien, A., Laugier, S. (2014) *Le principe de démocratie: Enquête sur les nouvelles formes du politique*, Paris: La Découverte.

Olzak, S., Shanahan, S., McEneaney, E.H. (1996) 'Poverty, segregation, and race riots: 1960 to 1993', *American Socioogical Review*, 61: 590–613.

Oncü, A. (2014) 'Turkish capitalist modernity and the Gezi revolt', *Journal of Historical Sociology*, 272: 151–76.

Paolini, A. (2011) 'Alemanno: Attacata una sfilata pacifica', *La Republica*, 16 October: 1.

Park, H. and Lee, J. (2016) 'Looking for accountability in police-involved deaths of blacks', *International New York Time*, 27 July.

Park, R. (1904) *The Crowd and the Public*, Chicago: University of Chicago Press.

Paris, G. (2015) 'Etats-Unis: un blessé grave à Ferguson', *Le Monde*, 11 August: 4.

Pascual, J. (2016a) 'Les policiers dans la rue contre la "haine"', *Le Monde*, 19 May: 7.

Pascual, J. (2016b) 'L'Etat face à la flambée des violences', *Le Monde*, 20 May: 7.

Pascual, J. (2016c) 'Derrière les casseurs, toute une galaxie', *Le Monde*, 16 May: 8.

Pérouse, J.F. (2013) 'Le parc Gezi: dessous d'une transformation très politique', *Métropolitiques*, 24 June. http://www.metropolitiques.eu/Le-parc-Gezi-dessous-d-une.html.

Pfaff, W. (2005) 'The French riots: Will they change anything?' *The New York Review of Books*, 15 December: 88–9.

Pinckney, D. (2015) 'In Ferguson', *The New York Review of Books*, 8 January: 6–8.

President's Task Force on 21st Century Policing (2015) *Report*, Washington, DC: US Government Printing Office.

Rapoport, D. (2006) 'The four waves of modern terrorism' in D. Rapoport (ed.) *Terrorism: Critical Concepts in Political Science*, vol. 4, London: Routledge: 3–30.

Reiner, R. (2015) 'Revisiting the classics: Three seminal founders of the study of policing: Michael Banton, Jerome Skolnick and Egon Bittner', *Policing and Society*, 3: 308-27.

Reiter, H. & Fillieule, O. (2006) 'Formalizing the informal: The EU approach to transnational protest policing' in D. Della Porta, A. Peterson and H. Reiter (eds) *The Policing of Transnational Protest*, Aldershot: Ashgate: 145–74.

Riots, Communities and Victims Panel (2011) *5 Days in August: An Interim Report on the 2011 Riots*, London: Riots, Communities and Victims Panel.

Rivayrand, S. (2006) 'L'action de la police nationale dans la lutte contre les violences urbaines', *Regards sur l'actualité*, 319: 56–7.

Roché, S. (2006) *Le frisson de l'émeute*, Paris: Le Seuil.

Roché, S. (2012) 'Police science: Science of the police or science for the police? Conceptual clarification and taxonomy for comparing police systems', Cepol Conference, Lyon, unpubl.

Rosanvallon, P. (2015) 'Constitutionnaliser l'état d'urgence', *Le Monde*, section Cultures et idées, 5 December: 4.

Rothman, D. (1980) *Conscience and Convenience: The Asylum and Its Alternatives in Progressive America*, Boston: Little & Brown.

Rousseau, D. (2016) 'En délibérant, on devient citoyen', *Libération*, 8 July.

Rousset, M. (2015) "Les mille visages des indignés", *Le Monde*, section Cultures et idées, 21 February, 1: 4–5.

Rowe, M. ed. (2007) *Policing after MacPherson*, Cullompton, UK: Willan.

Roy, O. (2005) 'The Nature of the French Riots', *Riots in France*, 18 November, http://riots-france.ssrc.org/Roy HTM. Access 24 April 2014.

Rudé, G. (1964) *The Crowd in History: A Study of Popular Disturbances in France and England, 1730-1848*, New York: John Wiley.

Sampson, R. (2009) 'Disparity and diversity in the contemporary city: Social (dis)order revisited', *British Journal of Sociology*, 60: 1–31.

Sampson, R.J., Raudenbush, S.W. (1999) 'Systemic social observation of public spaces: A new look at disorder in urban neighborhoods', *American. Journal of Sociology*, 105: 603–51.

Sampson, R.J., Raudenbush, S.W. (2004) 'Seeing disorder: Neighborhood stigma and the social construction of broken windows', *Social Psychology Quaterly*, 67: 319–42.

Sassen, S. (2006) *Territory-Authority-Rights*, Princeton: Princeton University Press.

Sassen, S. (2010) 'The city: Its return as a lens for social theory', *Theory, Culture and Society*, 1: 3–10.

Savitch, H.V. (2008) *Cities in a Time of Terror*, Armonk, NY: M.E. Sharpe.

Scarman, L. (1985) *The Brixton Disorders 10th–12th April, 1981*, London: HMSO.

Schmitt, C. (1922/1988) *Théologie Politique*, Paris: Gallimard.

Schneider, C. (2014) *Police Power and Race Riots: Urban Unrest in Paris and New York*, Philadelphia: University of Pennsylvania Press.

Schneider, E. (1999) *Vampires, Dragons, and Egyptian Kings: Youth Gangs in Postwar New York*, Princeton, NJ: Princeton University Press.

Schwartz, M. (2011)'Pre-Occupied', *The New Yorker*, 28 November: 28–35.

Sciolino, E. (2005) 'A new reason for riots: Polygamy', *International Herald Tribune*, 18 November.

Scott, J.C. (1985) *Weapons of the Weak. Everyday Form of Peasant Resistance*, New Haven, CT: Yale University Press.

Sennett, R. (1970) *The Uses of Disorder: Personal Identity and City Life*, New York: Norton.

Sennett, R. (2009) 'Urban disorder today', *British Journal of Sociology*, 60: 57–8.

Shane, S. (2015) 'Riots add another scar to city battered by neglect', *International New York Times*, 30 April.

Sherman, L.W. (1995) 'Hot spots of crime and criminal careers of places', in J. Eck, D. Weisburg (eds) *Crime and Place: Crime Prevention Studies*, Monsey, NY: Criminal Justice Press: 35–52.

Sindall, R. (1990) *Street Violence in the Nineteenth Century: Media Panic or Real Danger*, Leicester: Leicester University Press.

Singh, D., Marcus, S., Rabbatts, H., Sherlock, M. (2012) After the riots: The final report of the Riots Communities and Victims Panel. London: Riots Communities and Victims Panel. http://webarchive.nationalarchives.gov.uk/20121003195935/http://riotspanel. independent.gov.uk/wp-content/uploads/2012/03/Riots-Panel-Final-Report1.pdf. Access August 2, 2014.

Skocpol, T. (1979) *States and Social Revolution: A Comparative Analysis of France, Russia and China*, Cambridge, UK: Cambridge University Press.

Skogan, W. (1990) *Disorder and Decline: Crime and the Spiral of Decay in American Cities*, Berkeley: University California Press.

Skolnick, J. (2011) *Justice Without Trial*, 4th ed. New Orleans: Quid Pro Quo.

Smith, J. (2014) 'Black Town, White Power', *International New York Times*, August 19.

Spierenburg, P. (2009) 'Violence: Reflections about a Word' in S. Body-Gendrot, P. Spierenburg (eds) *Violence in Europe: Historical and Contemporary Perspectives*, New York: Springer: 27–40.

Stark, R. (1972) *Police Riots: Collective Violence and Law Enforcement*, Belmont, CA: Wadsworth.

Stewart, J. (2000) *The Nature of British Local Government*, London: Macmillan.

Stott, C. (2016) 'Revisiting the Classics: Policing coercion and liberty: A review of P.A.J. Waddington's Liberty and Order (1994) and Policing Citizens (1999)', *Policing and Society*, 26(1): 114–19.

Stott, C. and Reicher, S. (1998) 'Crowd action as intergroup process: Introducing the police perspective', *European Journal of Social Psychology*, 28, 509–29.

Stroobants, J.P. (2016) 'Le tueur du Musée juif en lien avec les commandos de Paris et de Bruxelles?', *Le Monde*, 26 May: 12.

Sultan, C. (2010) 'Un projet éducatif ne marche pas par l'humiliation', *Libération*, 24 August: 8.

Tarrow, S. (1989) *Democracy and Disorder, Protest and Politics in Italy, 1965–1975*, Oxford, UK: Clarendon.

Tatlow, D.K. (2014) 'Reclaiming an intrinsic part of home', *International New York Times*, 10 October: 2.

Taylor, I. (1982) 'On the sports violence question: Soccer hooliganism revisited' in J. Hargreaves (ed.) *Sport, Culture and Ideology*, London: Routledge/Kegan Paul: 152–96.

Taylor, R.B. (2001) *Breaking Away from Broken Windows*, New York: Westview.

Tiberj, V., Michon, L. (2013) 'Two-tier pluralism in "colour-blind" France', *West European Politics*, 36(3): 580–96.

Tilly, C. (2003) *The Politics of Collective Violence*, Cambridge, UK: Cambridge University Press.

Tocqueville, A. (1856/1952). *L'Ancien Régime et la Révolution*, Paris: Gallimard.

Tomsen, S. (1997) 'A "top night": Social protest, masculinity and the culture of drinking violence', *British Journal of Criminology*, 37(1): 90–102.

Tonry, M. (2015) 'Is cross-national and comparative research on the criminal justice system useful?' *European Journal of Criminology*, 12, 4: 505–516.

Travers, T. (2013) 'Cities and conflict resolution' in J. Stiglitz, M. Kaldor (eds) *The Quest for Security*, New York: Columbia University Press: 276–87.

Tsoukala, A. (2009) *Football Hooliganism in Europe: Security and Civil Liberties in the Balance*, Basingstoke, UK: Palgrave Macmillan.

Turkish Medical Association (2013) 'Kimyasal Gösteri Kontrol Ajanlaryalo Temas Edenlerin Sag"hk Sorunlari De"gerlendirme Raporu (Report on Health Problems of People Contacted with Chemical Riot Control Instruments)', Ankara.

Tyler, T. (1990) *Why People Obey the Law*, New Haven, CT: Yale University Press.

US Department of Justice (2015) *Report Regarding the Criminal Investigation into the Shooting Death of Michael Brown by Ferguson, Missouri Police Officer Darren Wilson*, Washington, DC: US Government Printing Office, 4 March.

US Department of Justice Civil Rights Division (2015) *Investigation of the Ferguson Police Department*, Washington, DC: US Government Printing Office, 4 March.

Veg, S. (2014) 'Un mouvement étudiant à la fois légaliste et utopiste' *Le Monde*, 4 October: 17.

Vega, T., Williams, T., Edkilm, E. (2014) 'Emotions flare in Missouri amid police statements', *International New York Times*, 14 August.

Vincent, E. (2015) 'Les rendez-vous manqués du renseignement', *Le Monde*, 5 January.

Waddington, D. (2007) *Policing Public Disorder: Theory and Practice*, Cullompton, UK: Willan.

Waddington, D. (2013) 'A "kinder" blue: Analyzing the police management of the Sheffield anti-"Lib Dem" protest of March 2011', *Policing and Society*, 23: 46–64.

Waddington, D., Jobard, F., King, M. (eds) (2009) *Rioting in the UK and France*, Cullompton, UK: Willan.

Waddington, D., Jones, K., Critcher, C. (1989) *Flashpoints: Studies in Public Disorder*, London: Routledge.

Waddington, P.J. (1991) *The Strong Arm of the Law: Armed and Public Order Policing*, Oxford, UK: Clarendon.

Waddington, P.J., Wright, M. (2008) 'Police use of force, firearms and riot-control' in T. Newburn (ed.) *Handbook of Policing*, Cullompton, UK: Willan. 2nd ed: 465–92.

Weenink, D. (2014) 'Frenzied attacks', *British Journal of Sociology*, 65: 421–33.

Weil, P. (2015) *Le sens de la République*, Paris: Grasset.

Whitman, J. (2003) *Harsh Justice*, New York: Oxford University Press.

Wilkinson, D., Fagan, J. (2001) 'A theory of violent events' in R. Meier, L. Kennedy, V. Sacco (eds) *The Process and Structure of Crime*, New Brunswick, NJ: Transaction: 165–195.

Williams, M. (2016) 'Global policing and the nation-state' in B. Bradford, B. Jauregui, I. Loader, J. Steinberg (eds), *The Sage Handbook of Global Policing*, London: Sage: 179–92.

Wilson, J.Q., Kelling, G. (1982) 'The police and neighbourhood safety: Broken windows', *Atlantic Monthly*, 249: 29–38.

Wilson, M. (2016) 'How an elite New York police unit rehearses for a terrorist attack', *International New York Times*, July 31.

Wilson, W.J. (1987) *The Truly Disadvantaged*, Chicago: University of Chicago Press.

Wines, M. (2014) 'A racial divide remains over views of justice', *International New York Times*, 26 November: 1.

Winlow, S, Hall, S., Treadwell, J., Briggs, D. (2015) *Riots and Political Protest: Notes from the Post-Political Present*, Oxford: Routledge.

Wong, E., Buckley, C. (2014) 'For Beijing, standoff is proving to be a tough call', *International New York Times*, 30 September: 1, 4.

Wong, E., Wong, A. (2014) 'Protest hone sense of Hong Kong pride', *International New York Times*, 8 October.

Young, I. (1990) *Justice and the Politics of Difference*, Princeton, NJ: Princeton University Press.

Zald, M., McCarthy, J. (eds) (1979) *The Dynamics of Social Movement*, Cambridge: Winthrop Publisher.

Zedner, L. (2009) *Security*, Oxford: Routledge.

Zeroula, F. (2014) 'Les organisations propalestiniennes cherchent à faire front commun à Paris', *Le Monde*, 29 July.

Žižek, S. (2006) *The Universal Exception*, London: Continuum.

Zunino, C. (2011) 'Cinque ore d'inferno, la follia black block devasta la capitale', *La Repubblica*, 16 October: 2.

# INDEX

For Product Safety Concerns and Information please contact our EU
representative  GPSR@taylorandfrancis.com
Taylor & Francis Verlag GmbH, Kaufingerstraße 24, 80331 München, Germany

www.ingramcontent.com/pod-product-compliance
Lightning Source LLC
Chambersburg PA
CBHW070711280326
41926CB00089B/3909